TREATING
BORDERLINE STATES
IN MARRIAGE

THE LIBRARY OF OBJECT RELATIONS

A Series of Books Edited By
David E. Scharff and Jill Savege Scharff

Object relations theories of human interaction and development provide an expanding, increasingly useful body of theory for the understanding of individual development and pathology, for generating theories of human interaction, and for offering new avenues of treatment. They apply across the realms of human experience from the internal world of the individual to the human community, and from the clinical situation to everyday life. They inform clinical technique in every format from individual psychoanalysis and psychotherapy, through group-therapy, to couple and family therapy.

The Library of Object Relations aims to introduce works that approach psychodynamic theory and therapy from an object relations point of view. It includes works from established and new writers who employ diverse aspects of British, American, and international object relations theory in helping individuals, families, couples, and groups. It features books that stress integration of psychoanalytic approaches with marital, family, and group therapy, as well as those centered on individual psychotherapy and psychoanalysis.

TREATING BORDERLINE STATES IN MARRIAGE

DEALING WITH OPPOSITIONALISM, RUTHLESS AGGRESSION, AND SEVERE RESISTANCE

Charles C. McCormack, MSW, BCD

JASON ARONSON INC.
Northvale, New Jersey
London

Production Editor: Elaine Lindenblatt

This book was set in 11 pt. New Baskerville by Alabama Book Composition of Deatsville, AL and printed and bound by Book-mart Press, Inc. of North Bergen, NJ.

Library of Congress Cataloging-in-Publication Data

McCormack, Charles C.
    Treating borderline states in marriage : dealing with oppositionalism, ruthless aggression, and severe resistance / by Charles C. McCormack.
        p.   cm.
    Includes bibliographical references and index.
    ISBN 0–7657–0190–1
    1. Marital psychotherapy.   2. Borderline personality disorder.   I. Title.
RC488.5.M392   2000
616.89'156–dc21

                                                                    99-052079

Printed in the United States of America on acid-free paper. For information and catalog write to Jason Aronson Inc., 230 Livingston Street, Northvale, NJ 07647-1731. Or visit our website: www.aronson.com

For Chandler, Keeley, and Caitlin
the loves of my life

and

Madeleine Turgeon McCormack
(1918–1997)
who in the grace with which
she lived her life and death
taught all who knew her
the importance of living well

What I am trying to say is hard to tell and hard to understand . . .
unless, unless . . .
you have been yourself at the edge of the Deep Canyon and have come
back unharmed.
Maybe it all depends on something within yourself—
whether you are trying to see the Watersnake or the sacred Cornflower,
whether you go out to meet death or to Seek Life.

Shaman: The Paintings of Susan Seddon Boulet (1989)

Contents

Prologue

In October 1974, after eschewing a short-lived career in business, I entered a masters program in psychology and volunteered at Sheppard and Enoch Pratt Hospital in Baltimore to gain firsthand experience in working with psychologically troubled individuals. Now, in the winter of 1999, I am still on the grounds of Sheppard-Pratt, having come full circle, renting an office in the building in which I was first employed. In essence, I have lived most of my adult years on these grounds.

In October 1982, after much consideration about whether or not I wanted to treat chronically ill patients, I decided to work on B-2, a psychoanalytically oriented long-term inpatient unit. Although my previous years of exposure to treating individuals suffering from major psychopathology had deepened me substantially, the changes I was about to undergo paled the others in comparison. My basic assumptions about how to treat people clinically, largely influenced by training in structural and strategic family therapy, were to be thrown open to extensive review.

To understand the extent of my metamorphosis, the reader

should know that at the time of this transition I was in the middle of a three-and-a-half-year in-vivo training program in structural and strategic family therapy. I read the literature extensively and was well versed in paradoxical and directive interventions. I believed in their promise of empowerment of the therapist and their resulting effectiveness. Isn't it a wonderful idea, that if the patients' behavior can be changed, the psyche (if there is any such thing) will follow. How much simpler than going through all the complexity and ethereal notions that seemed to be so much a part of insight-oriented therapy.

However, to my chagrin, I discovered that these approaches, at least in relation to the treatment of major psychopathology, led to short-term gain or none at all, often followed by marked regression. I began to feel that I was doing more harm than good. In the midst of this personal struggle, the trainer, frustrated with the family I was presenting, informed me, "These are not good training cases." I was puzzled. There seemed to be some lack of integrity, if this were the case. How could a renowned treatment approach not apply to major psychopathology? It was in the treatment of seriously ill patients, struggling with life-and-death issues, that I needed help. B-2 received referrals from around the world, treating the most ill of the ill.

Upon my arrival on B-2, I was soon participating in numerous team meetings and countless hallway and nursing-station discussions. In contrast to structural and strategic orientations, the emphasis was on the pursuit of understanding rather than on doing. Within six to nine months, my need to "do something" frustrated, I was going crazy. "Process, process, process, and more process. Let's do something!" was how I felt. I seriously considered leaving. However, despite my discomfort, something kept me there: partly stubborn persistence, but even more, fascination with the question, "Why do some people who fall into the abyss manage to climb out, while others do not?" I sensed that somewhere in this madness lay the answer. Although I was not familiar with the psychoanalytic language of the staff, I sensed that these seasoned professionals knew far more than I about something that I wanted to know, although I could not define what that was. Ironically, I learned years later, it turned out to be the capacity to value "not-knowing," which stood in such contrast to the active "knowing" of the directive approaches.

I began extensive reading of the psychoanalytic literature in an attempt to come to better understand my team members, the patients, and my relationship to them. Simultaneously, I observed that the Service Chief, Dr. Maria Klement, seemed to remain calm no matter how tumultuous or crisis-ridden the situation. Though the urge to do something was quaking within me, she rarely directed staff decisions. All she seemed to do was quietly and thoughtfully ask questions that sooner or later led to deepening discussions. At times the staff seemed in danger of being torn apart by internal conflicts, the lines of division often demarcated by professional orientation. The firm-limit setters, often the nursing staff who had to deal with the patients on a daily basis, fought mightily with the psychiatrists, who, more removed from the situation, seemed to pursue ephemeral discussions without regard to any limit setting at all. The social workers, advocating for family concerns and often required to explain treatment decisions to the family, might fight with either group. Occupational, movement, art, and vocational therapists had their own concerns.

Gradually, I realized that parallels emerged between the conflicts within the staff and those within the patient and between the patient and the family. Dr. Klement was using the conflicts within the treatment team and its various countertransference reactions toward the patient and the family as a parallel transference, that is, to better experience and think through the patient's intrapsychic and interpersonal conflicts. Dr. Klement and the structure of frequent team meetings (not unlike therapy sessions) provided a forum that "held" the staff in the midst of sometimes highly intense conflicts and impeded staff attempts to abort the painful experience of uncertainty through acting out, often manifested in the impulse "to do." Once an environment was created in which each team member could express his or her point of view, the fragmentation and splitting of the staff was gradually processed and converted to integration. This process could take weeks, sometimes months. However, as the staff's conflicts subsided, the patient's often did as well. It seemed apparent that, as the treatment team internalized the patient's conflicts and then healed itself, it was better able to help the patient learn from his or her own experience.

By the end of my second year on the unit, I realized that many patients who had previously been labeled hopeless cases, were markedly improving. Because the treatment focus was on understanding rather than on behavior or symptom alleviation, the genesis of the symptoms was slowly revealed. As the staff could better identify with the seeming craziness of the patients' psychological situation, the staff became increasingly able to help the patients understand and manage their own experience. This is not to say that all the patients benefited, but many did. Seemingly hopeless cases could begin to build or rebuild their lives.

In 1988, the dismantling of long-term inpatient services by the effects of managed care was just beginning. In response, I wrote an article (McCormack 1989) on the treatment of personality-disordered marriages. My intent was to capture some of what I had learned and apply it to outpatient therapy, where the need would be growing. This book is an extension of that article and that desire. In many ways, it is the story of my own journey of failures and successes. The former taught me what I know; the latter nourished me along the way. Both continue to happen.

Acknowledgments

Writing has long been acknowledged a lonely process: the writer caught in the unremitting spotlight of the blank page. It also has been compared to a birthing process, and, as the midwife helps the mother deliver the baby, so my family of friends has helped me birth this child. But in the final analysis, at least for me, writing is just damn hard work, which has only deepened my respect for those who write for a living. As I interacted with others about the writing, relationships evolved in a way that could not otherwise have occurred. I owe much to this family of friends.

Ron Zuskin, who was with me through the years of labor and the birth itself, devoted his time, intellect, wisdom, and outrageous humor. When I despaired, he laughed. Unwavering in his enthusiasm, his insights permeate the book. Ron also authored the last chapter.

David Scharff, M.D., had the creative apperception (I sometimes thought it delusional) that this little-known, largely experientially trained clinician could write a worthwhile book when he heard several of my papers. His staunch faith in me propelled me into the fumbling and stumbling creative and developmental process of trying to discover what it was I was trying to say—and then saying it.

Roger Lewin, M.D., walked with me, as we spoke of life, family, and work. He kept saying, "Just write it." His comments on my writing were always brief and spoke to the heart of the matter, inevitably triggering significant changes.

Leonard Press provided me with the lived experience of attunement and responsiveness that have come to permeate my work and this book.

When you spend seven years writing a book, many people play a part. There is Gerry Gue-DeMarco, MSW, who held my hand in the beginning, before the arrival of her own child whose hand displaced mine. There is Jane Giovanazi, OTR, who, red pen happily in hand, reviewed the writing in the last year. An experienced occupational therapist but unversed in object relations theory, she provided eyes and mind not jaded by repeated readings of the material. She also increased gender awareness.

My supervisees provided helpful comments. Pat Alfin, MSW, brought me to the attention of the Washington School of Psychiatry and Bob Winer, M.D., edited some of these chapters when they were in the form of talks. My son, Chandler McCormack, designed the figures, and my close friend Tom Beauchamp took the author's photograph. There are my daughters, Keeley and Caitlin, who provided generous support and encouragement. I am grateful for the financial assistance provided by Sheppard and Enoch Pratt Hospital.

Finally, there are the individuals who have entrusted me with their care and their stories. If you should read this book, I hope you find it representative and respectful of our work together.

I

The Therapist

1

The Therapist's Resistance
to Understanding

When personality-disordered individuals are considered by clinicians, there is a tendency to fall into a "we" and "they" mentality, as if the plight of these individuals were alien from our own. This tendency is somewhat natural given the structure of language; however, it also suggests the therapist's resistance to identifying with personality-disordered patients. Since as human beings we all share broad developmental needs and are more alike than different, we must wonder at our readiness to distance ourselves and to perceive personality-disordered functioning as so foreign from our own. Therapists who might take issue with me could argue that personality disorder represents a fixation in development, so that the ways these individuals perceive and relate is divergent. Though in part true, this is not a compelling argument in that development is not a once-and-for-all achievement but a dynamically oscillating process between more differentiated and mature ego states and more undifferentiated and infantile ones (Bion 1962a, Ogden 1989, Stern 1985).

The reality is that we are all more alike than different. We are all vulnerable to regression and primitive functioning. Indeed, it is this very vulnerability that allows personality-disordered patients to get under the skin of the therapist. The evidence for this is entailed in our own experience, apparent in the lives we live, at least from time to time, behind closed doors. Who of us is not ashamed of ways they have misbehaved in an argument? Alternatively, who feels they have never over- or underreacted in irrational, "all-or-nothing" ways with children, mate, siblings, friends, or parents? Given an alignment between stressful circumstances and personal vulnerabilities, we are all capable of regression to more primitive ways of perceiving and reacting. What differentiates normal/neurotic from borderline functioning is that while normal/neurotics may visit borderline states, personality-disordered individuals dwell there.

Since most, if not all, of us have the capacity to function at least fleetingly in what could be described as borderline ways, why is it that we tend so readily toward a "we" and "they" instead of an "us" kind of mentality? I think the answer is that we do not want to acknowledge or remember such painful, disquieting, and unsettling mental/emotional states. We resist identification. Unfortunately, the disavowal of these traits within us constitutes a dis-integrity within ourselves, occasioning the use of splitting and denial that is both self-rejecting and rejecting of the patient, fostering disintegration, rather than integration, and limiting compassion for our patients and ourselves.

My concern is that the primary resistance in the treatment of personality disorder lies not with the patient but in the therapist's defense against understanding. Until this resistance is acknowledged the therapist's capacity to be useful to such patients is limited. The therapist, to defend against the emotional onslaught entailed in identifying with the patient's tumultuous feelings, may be driven to relate concretely, in a content-bound, solution-focused way, or with "dead certainty." As a result, the therapist may superimpose upon the patient a "solution" (i.e., a simple, concrete answer to complex human dilemmas) that is not only beyond the patient's capacity but preempts or disrupts the patient's internal process that is so necessary to the genuine resolution of his intrapsychic conflicts and deficiencies in development. When the "solution" does not work, it is replaced with another and then another in an endless process of solution after solution without resolution. Such an approach bolsters the therapist's false sense of mastery and helps him maintain his psychic equilibrium through distance and the illusion of professional certainty or knowing. Such knowing stands in welcome contrast to the chaotic pull of the patient's feelings and defends the therapist from the disquieting experience entailed in personally identifying with them, the only way to truly know them.

Tom, for example, had a history of being unable to maintain an erection with anyone for whom he cared. This affected his sexual relationship with his wife. A directive therapist may instruct the couple to set aside time from busy schedules with work and children. Unfortunately, such interventions are often only temporarily useful, if at all. If the therapist continues with such an approach to no avail, the spouses come to feel that they have failed in therapy and that their situation is hopeless. Alternatively, the therapist may label them as resistant to treatment. The spouses' early history of relationships may go unexplored, and the therapist may not discover that Tom had experienced numerous losses of primary others in infancy and early childhood that resulted in his unconsciously equating desire and intimacy with loss. Nor would the directive therapist have discovered that Peggy had lived an isolated childhood and failed to internalize a primary other as a soothing presence. Consequently, she was unable to tolerate aloneness or separateness and required the concrete experience of sex on a nightly basis to calm herself and to feel connected. Peggy's voracious need in relationship to Tom's disabling fear exacerbated the condition of each, leading to a total breakdown of the sexual relationship. It was only in bringing to consciousness the emotional meaning of the sexual relationship to each that Tom and Peggy were able to gradually establish a mutually satisfying sexual relationship.

In the absence of personal insight, the patient, in pursuit of miraculous solutions and out of an inadequately developed sense of self, attempts to conform to the "expert" therapist's artificial understanding and shaman pope prescriptions, in the hope of being magically made whole. While a chimera of progress may be created, the patient remains unable to process or metabolize his experience, for genuine development has not occurred. Repeatedly, the patient genuflects to the therapist's assumptions, continuing the practice of a lifetime, attempting to mold himself to external expectations without developing true self-relations.

Unfortunately, personality-disordered patients are all too willing to validate the therapist's assumptions, thereby avoiding the travail of development, right up to the point where they unmistakably invalidate them. Unable to maintain his externally derived and internally bankrupt self-economy, the patient ultimately fails. The patient's *false self* organization (Winnicott 1960a), molded around the therapist's all-knowingness rather than internally derived, stands in competition with the patient's inchoate and struggling-to-emerge *true self*, and begins to collapse. At this point, the patient's ongoing sense of internal emptiness and lack of personal meaning erodes and eventually undermines the illusion of progress.

Typically, the patient's growing despair spurs the therapist on to greater activity, much like the Dutch boy frantically shoring up the dike in order to dam up the looming flood of intolerable feelings. Eventually, both patient and therapist reach exhaustion, each faced by an overriding sense of impotence, threading its way like the trickle that becomes a torrent through the thickest walls of their activity. The patient's idealization of the therapist is then replaced with devaluation, for the therapist has promised much but delivered little; he has not fixed the patient. The therapist, in continuing defense against the realization of impotence (ironically the ultimate identification with the patient), arrives in exhaustion at the defensive perception that the patient is untreatable: "It's the patient, not me!" This is relief without resolution, and then only superficially for the therapist, who, on some level, suspects his self-deception.

With personality-disordered patients, the therapist is called upon to contain chaotic and sometimes horrific mental contents, including psychotic anxieties of disintegration and annihilation of the self. To the extent the therapist is attuned to the patient's experience, she is re-exposed to these intensely unsettling sensory/mental/emotional psychic states that are at least fleeting moments of every childhood. Since primitive states find their origin in fragments of infantile experience shared by all children, whose survival at such times is totally in doubt, these states represent a core threat to the sense of self. Inevitably, the patient's anxieties stimulate the incompletely resolved chaotic aspects of the therapist's own life experiences, which linger as traces in the therapist's unconscious, and resonate with the patient's fear of collapse.

The instinctive wish to flee, often via a disavowal of and counteridentification with the patient, is compelling. If the therapist acts upon this wish, the treatment relationship becomes iatrogenic, re-creating the patient's earliest relationship to a primary caregiver in which misidentification and rejection were first experienced. In this circumstance, the patient is literally and concretely mirrored in the eyes of the therapist as an "it is" rather than as a person who "can be." Consequently, the patient comes to feel invisible to self and therapist, as she felt invisible to her primary others, relegated to a twilight existence of psychological isolation that fosters alienation and an inherent sense of badness. The therapeutic relationship, instead of being transformative, becomes another reenactment of timeworn past relationships, this time given professional confirmation.

Treating personality-disordered individuals entails being revisited by the most repellent feeling states of childhood. Particularly as children, but perhaps also as adults, we have all experienced moments of feeling persecuted, deprived, abandoned, unloved, and even hated. These mental states are evident in pronounced feelings of hopelessness, helplessness, boredom, anger, resentment, dread, rage, fear, panic, dissolution, and so on. Given such experiences, there would be something perverse in the therapist's wanting to identify with or re-experience such ego states. However, for therapists, the issue is not of wanting to but of being willing to tolerate such experiences toward a therapeutic end.

Personality-disordered individuals are infamous for their refractoriness to treatment efforts and for their ability to get under the skin of the therapist. They present tragic and seemingly insoluble cases of human pathos. While normal/neurotic individuals are able to tolerate their fear and pain, personality-disordered individuals often engage in ruthless personal attacks upon their sense of self and that of their therapist, mate, or children, when their fear or pain is not readily ameliorated. They reactively act out in self- and other destructive ways in order to evacuate their intolerable feelings, often shaking the therapist and those close to them to the core.

It is necessary that the underlying dynamics and motivations of such acting out be brought to awareness, and that therapy not add to the patient's burden by re-creating relationship experiences of the past. To this end, it is of value for the therapist to become well versed in understanding the psychodynamics and modes of organization of personality-disordered conditions. It is also important that the therapist resensitize him- or herself to those parts of self-experience, the potentially personality-disordered self within, that allow identification and genuine relating to the quandary of the personality-disordered patient. It is only through identification that the therapist can empathize with, understand, and help the patient by entering into accepting relationship to him (attuned responsiveness), thereby affording him the opportunity to enter more accepting relationship to the disavowed aspects of himself and to others.

2

The Trauma of Treating
a Borderline Couple

Mark and Carol Ann, a middle-aged couple, have been married for seventeen years. Mark is a successful and handsome executive, extremely devoted, spending much time and money on Carol Ann's psychiatric treatment. He is well mannered and charming, though curiously he has no close friends. Carol Ann is an attractive woman who suffers from alcoholism, major depression, psychomotor agitation, insomnia, and self-mutilative and suicidal behavior. She is hospitalized on a long-term inpatient unit. The couple could not identify the precipitating event for the hospitalization or for those that preceded it. From their point of view, such occurrences were like spontaneous ignitions, arising without rhyme or reason, and in no way related to their own lives: almost magical.

Carol Ann is a voluptuous woman, sexually attractive in a sultry way, with an immediate erotic impact. However, the eroticism of her presence is immediately dispelled as soon as she begins to speak. She turns to Mark and spits a diatribe of words, beginning with: "You piece of worthless shit! You pompous bastard! You're lower than whale shit at the bottom of the ocean! Worthless wimp! Spineless dork!"

Carol Ann's outwardly directed rage is palpable, a living presence of its own. Immediately, her sexual aura, so present only a moment ago, is dissipated. As she continues her tirade, the atmosphere in the room seems suffused with her rage. I feel powerfully possessed by fear, nausea, and revulsion. Distance from her suddenly becomes all that matters. Confusion mounts, and thought becomes impossible, in spite of desperate efforts to *think, think, think: What can I do?* Fragments of questions flit, in bits and pieces, through the paralyzed blankness of my mind, only occasionally coalescing into complete thoughts, such as, *Who in the world would tolerate, much less want, a relationship with this woman? How can my reactions to her change so suddenly? How can I be inundated with such unattractive feelings of my own?* The wish to avoid her is stunning in its completeness, creating a drive to leap out of my skin. Remaining in the room, much less in therapeutic connection, feels impossible. Prognostic hopes quickly erode. All this transpires within the first three endless minutes of the "interview."

In the compelling push to *think, think,* I ask myself, *How can she be so awful toward her husband when he appears so loyal and devoted to her? How can she be so bitter in this apparently mismatched marriage in which she seems the only beneficiary?* Yet Carol Ann is without fear, unbending and unashamed. In fact, she is totally blaming and accusatory, spilling over with conviction born of righteous anger. *Is she psychotic or does she know secrets that remain a mystery about her husband?* The answer is not apparent. She rants and rages ad nauseam, but her complaints are not specific or graspable. They are more like fragmentation grenades that explode upon the scene. Nonetheless, through the ink cloud of her invectives at least one theme becomes discernable: She is incensed by her husband's martyred look on the one hand and what she perceives with absolute certitude as his sadistic unwillingness to meet her needs on the other. She feels trapped, damned if she does and damned if she doesn't. She feels betrayed and deprived. Swallowed up by her unfocused fury, she further martyrs her husband and presents herself in the worst

possible light. Although feeling the victim, she appears the victimizer.

The supercharged atmosphere, the absence of specific complaints, and the effort to discern themes all combine to overwhelm
my capacity to think thoughts and to feel feelings. The session and
I are in shambles. Nothing makes sense. I think, *Mark seems to do
everything right. He is patient under Carol Ann's onslaught and does not
respond in kind. Occasionally he tries to soothe her but is unable to appease
her in any way. Understandably, aside from a few frail attempts he soon
becomes completely passive, bowed under the weight of her accusations.*

The thought, *this poor man* does not invite me to intervene. I am
afraid to intervene. I realize I am concerned with my own survival,
anxiously thinking, *What will happen if I become the target of Carol Ann's
displeasure and she turns her wrath upon me?* Fear, uncertainty, and
doubt roil through my mind, eroding the boundaries between myself and the couple. Without warning, I suddenly wonder whether I
am dangerous to the couple—*Is couples therapy too intrusive or too
traumatizing for Carol Ann?*—and then abruptly question, *Are they
dangerous to me? Will I be criticized for upsetting the patient? Will she
engage in suicidal behavior during or after the session? If she does, am I
responsible? Will she escalate to the point of physically assaulting her
husband or me? Is Carol Ann's illness simply too threatening for me and
beyond my capacity to handle? Might a different therapist handle this
situation much better?* Mark's timidity, not Carol Ann's power, rockets
into consciousness.

Suddenly, I feel disgust for Mark. *He doesn't defend himself and
must have been putting up with this for years. Rather than standing up to
her, he is a whipping boy, leaving me to manage her and to make sense of this
situation as if he has no investment of his own.*

Carol Ann's sadistic attacks upon Mark are most specific in the
disparaging comments she makes concerning their lack of a sexual
relationship. She attacks his impotence, as if it stood (or did not
stand) in isolation from their relationship. *You can't even get it up!
What kind of man are you? Why couldn't I be married to a real man!*
Instantaneously, a pressing panic to get away from this woman fills
me again. Yet I feel paralyzed, movement and speech are impossible,

and I feel shriveled with fear in my chair. Detumescent, I have taken in and embodied the couple's impotence.

As the session continues, despite, or perhaps because of, the overwhelming nature of these myriad pressures, the sense of crisis this couple engenders slowly abates. Despite the threatening behavior, nothing has happened. With this realization, some perspective is gained, and Carol Ann's harangues, rather than foreshadowing violence, gradually become understood as an ever-repeating song. The lyrics change, but the melody remains the same. Serendipitously, I discover that as I attend to the melody rather than to the lyrics, the complexity and overwhelming nature of the situation are simplified. Unexpectedly, there is space and time to feel and to think. It is only now, upon its recovery, that I realize how much I had lost touch with myself. The sensation is that of a drowning man who becomes hope-filled as he discovers a glint of light promising the water's surface.

In this space for thinking and feeling, my wonder about Mark's tolerance of Carol Ann's abusive treatment of him begins to stir. *Are her complaints simply evidence of her madness, or do they represent knowledge of him achievable only in the privacy of their relationship? How am I to understand the fact that, despite the animosity in their relationship, they have stayed together by both their accounts for seventeen miserable years? I wonder how they would answer this question.* Neither Mark nor Carol Ann is clear about what attracted them to each other, nor are they clear about what keeps them together. Yet together they remain.

Nothing changes. From the first session onward, the couple argues endlessly, each session marked by Carol Ann's escalating accusations and aggressive affects of varying hues of envy, jealousy, greed, hate, sadism, and despair, while Mark sinks into growing apathy and indifference. Highly personal assaults rule the relationship. As Mark endures in silence and without curiosity, I realize that his investment in sorting through anything is as limited as Carol Ann's. He is prepared to maintain the relationship in its current form. Carol Ann continues to be inflamed, ignited in part by her inability to reach him. Logical thinking having been abandoned some time ago, images abound. At times, I see Carol Ann as she might see herself, as a witch burning at the stake of her self-abhorrence, all the while defiantly spitting out her hatred in an attempt to put out the flames that engulf her.

Each session endlessly repeats old themes, the victimizer finding her victim by whom she herself feels victimized. Eventually, Mark and Carol Ann no longer appear as two separate individuals but as opposite poles of a single psychic entity, a human projective accelerator that only amplifies the incoherent accusations of each. Each holds the other as the cause of all that was and is wrong in life. I can identify with this, for when I am with them they are irrefutably all that is wrong in mine.

Though charged with energy, the sessions, like the marriage, feel sterile, a recycling process of fission (breaking into parts) and fusion (merging of parts) that consumes and releases great energy but results in stasis rather than change. The fragmenting aspect of their cycle of interaction occurs as Carol Ann's angry accusations reach critical mass. As Mark remains unmoved, she collapses in a state of exhaustion, hopelessness, helplessness, and depression. After this meltdown occurs, in which they are joined in the immutability of their situation, the end of one cycle and the beginning of the next are marked. The therapy, like the marriage, becomes another timeworn, ever-repeating, corrosive dance to the same old song.

Out of all this only one thing is clear: neither Mark nor Carol Ann seems able to be with the other, nor are they able to "be" apart. They feel that their destructive and schismatic union is essential to their existence.

Treating borderline marriages is daunting. These couples are infamous for their oppositionalism, ruthless aggression, ability to get under the skin of the therapist, and refractoriness to treatment efforts. In addition, via their reliance on primitive defenses, they also attack the therapist's capacity to think and feel. Consequently, they cannot be treated from a distance. Indeed, the therapist comes to feel personally involved and often personally attacked. Feelings of confusion and of being overwhelmed are prominent. She may soon conclude that the relationship is untreatable.

The pessimism toward working therapeutically with personality-disordered couples is changing. Over the last five decades, the psychoanalytic object relations study of preoedipal conditions, including borderline and psychotic states, along with advances in self psychology and developmental theory, have resulted in a deepening understanding of personality-disordered ways of perceiving and relating.

A more collaboratively oriented treatment approach has evolved, where the therapist–patient relationship is emphasized over the previous view of the therapist working upon the patient. The ascension of the mother–infant relationship as a metaphor for marriage and the treatment relationship, the understanding of such concepts as the *good-enough mother* (Winnicott 1960a) and the *holding environment* (Winnicott 1960b), and the recognition of the importance of the therapist's personally felt responses (countertransference) that arise in relationship with the couple add to our understanding of and capacity to treat such patients. With these insights, rather than being simply alienating, the behavior of personality disordered individuals takes on meaning and a poignant and recognizable psycho-logic of its own.

The mutual ground of borderline relationships is located in the unrelenting effort of each spouse to master unresolved traumas of the past and resultant developmental deficits. The word *trauma* is not necessarily meant to imply a specific event or repressed memory: It refers more frequently to the cumulative intolerable frustration of the need for empathic attachment. A single traumatic event can be generative, deepening relationship to self and other, or degenerative, resulting in a breakdown or fixation in the development of the self. What makes trauma degenerative is not only the event itself, but the nature of the relationships that permitted the traumatic event to occur in it *and* allowed the significance or impact of the event upon the victim to go unrecognized, unacknowledged, and without amends. As a result, the totality of the traumatic experience, including the relationships in which it occurred, remains embedded in indigestible form in the pathological world of self and object relationships. A distortion in the development of the self, which is personality disorder, results, manifested in (1) an internal world of pathological relationships, (2) identity diffusion, (3) an idiosyncratic relationship to reality, and (4) primitive defenses.

In that the traumatic event(s) and the relationships in which they occurred have been internalized in undigested form, the personality-disordered individual is impelled to repeatedly regurgitate the trauma perceptually and experientially in an attempt to defend against it. Splitting, denial, and primitive projective-identificatory processes are used to this end. The result is the creation of polarized and complementary two-role relationships in which each spouse perceives him- or herself in the role of protagonist to the other as antagonist: child to parent, victim to victimizer, neglected to neglector, and so on. At this point, the problem is no longer felt to be within the individual, but outside the individual, located in the other, where it can be controlled. In this way, each spouse uses the other as a repository for one or the other pole of the polarized and conflicting internal part-self and part-object relationships. This process has a singular but powerful reinforcement: As the internal world of each spouse takes over the external reality of the marriage, a decrease in the experience of intrapsychic conflict results.

With this overview, it is apparent that the motivation of personality-disordered relationships is the pursuit of survival, not fulfillment. For the spouses the issue is not "How can I make the most of this relationship?" but "How is this relationship keeping me alive or killing me off?" In this persecutory form of relationship, the survival instinct runs amok, as the ultimate aim of each spouse is the attainment of defensive omnipotence. Each pursues relationship along the axis of dominance and submission, rather than of affiliation and separateness. The aim is not for genuine attachment, an experience unknown to either spouse, but to hold the other in one's power, or at least not give him the chance to inflict pain. The illusion of omnipotence offers the promise of never having the exquisitely felt precariousness of self-organization threatened again.

The personality-disordered marriage is thus a defensive compromise involving the simultaneous desire of each partner for merger and for murder. Each spouse carries the infantile symbiotic wish that the other will magically meet all his needs, without recognition that the wish is of another time, place, and relationship and can never be fulfilled. Such wishes are expressed in words, such as "If you loved me, you would know what I need," or "If you loved me, you would do what I want." Conversely, there is the desire to get rid of the other as a repository for all that is wrong in one's own life. This is evident when traits in the other are denied within oneself and when the other is treated with contempt and aggression. Personality-disordered individuals thus seek human relationship without identification, connection without vulnerability. Ironically, the yearned-for sense of security eludes them as they defensively deny aspects of internal world and external reality, living in divided relationship to self and other. The result is that neither spouse is able to "be with" the other, nor are they able to "be" apart. Both feel that their destructive and schismatic union is essential to their existence.

As Mark and Carol Ann's story unfolds in the next chapter, it will become clearer how their sadomasochistic relationship was a carryover from their childhoods, eventually turning the marriage itself into a time capsule of early experiences of relationship that are continued into the present.

II

The Borderline Couple

3

The Borderline Level of Organization

Personality-disordered individuals suffer from a disorder of the self, the general aspects of which are outlined in Kernberg's (1967, 1975) description of the borderline level of organization.[1] Self-difficulty includes four elements that, like the Four Horsemen of the Apocalypse, are devastating in their impact. These are (1) an internal world of pathological self and object relationships, (2) identity diffusion, (3) an idiosyncratic relationship to reality, and (4) primitive defenses. Together these elements interfere with learning from experience. As development is thwarted, differentiation is impeded, and confusion persists both within the self and between self and other.

THE INTERNAL WORLD OF PATHOLOGICAL OBJECT RELATIONSHIPS

The internal world of pathological object relationships is a dynamic presence that structures the experience-near perceptions, sensa-

---

1. The use of the term *borderline* throughout the book, unless otherwise noted, refers to Kernberg's notion of the borderline level of organization and personality disorders in general.

tions, feelings, images, and cognitions of adulthood through the vector of repressed childhood relationship experiences. Perhaps, when childhood was relatively harmonious—optimally gratifying and frustrating—the unconscious can be taken for granted. Given a good enough hold in childhood, the need to repress is minimized and the maternal object is internalized as a repository of not-clearly-remembered, yet known "good enough"-ness. Subsequently, in health, the unconscious functions more or less in concordance with consciousness.

However, to the degree our early and ongoing family relationships were less than adequate, the unconscious becomes the repository of powerful and unresolved pathological relationships. These are internalized in the form of the governing sensations, thoughts, feelings, and perceptions that were encountered in the early perilous pursuit of object relationship. In this circumstance, the need for defense and discharge, fostered by needs going unmet, takes priority over development, influencing our lives in ways often at odds with conscious wish. To the extent the internal world remains unconscious, past is undifferentiated from present and the unconscious makes itself known in the day-to-day climate of our lives and relationships. To our bewilderment, we become our own worst enemy. Indeed, we contain our enemy, the exciting and need-rejecting object, swallowed whole and taken to heart.

Mark

Mark, of Mark and Carol Ann, was an only child, the offspring of physically and emotionally abusive alcoholic parents. He managed his early life by absorption in school and church activities. These served as safe havens from the neglects and assaults of his family life, and as fragile tributaries to his sense of self. In school, he performed well academically and in extracurricular activities. Although never establishing close friendships, he was respected and affirmed for his academic excellence and school involvement. In church he was an altar boy and volunteered his time whenever possible, driven by the dual need to escape his home and for affirmation. As Mark later stated, "The little I remember of home is of a dark and unhappy place. I'd rather be at school or church. I was smart and did well, and the teachers and priests liked me. I worked hard, because I liked that." In contrast to the chaos and violence of Mark's home, school and church were oases of structure and stability.

Mark thus lived in two worlds: the public world of his institutional relationships to school and church, where he could earn self-affirmations, and the nightmarish world of his family, marked by parental indifference alternating with seeming hatred of him. In Mark's words, "My parents drank a lot. They would be angry with me, and I didn't know why. They yelled and hit me and threw me in my room. Sometimes they forgot to feed me. But this wasn't so bad. I know they loved me. I probably did make mistakes that I just didn't understand at the time." In these words, Mark both describes his early family situation and his defense against it. He preserves the image necessary to the survival of the child—that his parents love him—while defensively internalizing the badness of the situation: "I probably did make mistakes that I just didn't understand at the time."

His subsequent confusion over who is the real Mark, the one persecuted by his parents or the one praised by authority figures in the external world, was evident in a rare acknowledgment: "I could never figure out who I was, this good person or this bad person. I always worried that I was the bad person even if people saw me as good. I felt they just didn't know me." Mark's distress was soon undone, as he immediately followed this statement with a disavowal: "I don't worry about these things anymore." Despite his disavowal, we see the reason behind Mark's absence of close relationships: his fear that to know him is to despise him. Carol Ann is living proof.

Mark's internal world was comprised of the persecutory and sadistic relationships of his family life, in which he felt bad and thereby judged himself as bad. He used his public life to defend against his feeling of badness. In adulthood, Mark re-created this division between public and private. In the public arena, he was perceived as a hardworking, active member of the business community, a church leader, and a devoted husband. However, behind the closed doors of his marriage, Mark maintained the barbaric world of his childhood. Here, Carol Ann, like his parents, drank continuously; was ruthless and unpredictably hostile, contemptuous, and belittling; and held Mark responsible for her own unhappy fate. Mark described his experience in relationship to Carol Ann in much the same way he described his childhood experience: "No matter what I do, I can't seem to make things better."

Mark was defensively unable to recognize the similarity between his present and his past. He feared his internal world and, for the most part, avoided consideration of it. He lived only in awareness of his relationship to the external world, where "right living" was praised, earning him the esteem of all those around. However, in relationship to those closest to him, "right living" never saved him, either from his parents' sadism or from Carol Ann's loathing. As Mark's family of origin was the evil side of his childhood, so his marriage was the depraved side of his adulthood.

Mark's internal world of self and object relationships, defensively unidentified and unresolved, governed his experience of self and other. The lack of differentiation between his internal self and object representations was evident in his ongoing conflict about his own goodness and in his avoidance of close relationships. For him, closeness is associated not with security but with danger. Thereby, the threat of closeness only sounds alerts in the war room of his psyche.

We now begin to discern the genesis of Mark's psychological dependence upon Carol Ann as a primitive selfobject. By using Carol Ann as the external representation of his internal endangering objects, Mark could interpersonalize his intrapsychic conflict and stave off his underlying depression, thereby maintaining his psychic equilibrium. For him, Carol Ann's hostility and unbridled aggression accounted for any distress he experienced. In his unconscious, Carol Ann and his parents were indistinguishable, and through her he could reenact his unresolved internal conflicts in relationship to them. On the one hand, he could attempt to convert Carol Ann's view of him, to have her affirm his goodness, thereby, in unconscious fantasy, magically undoing the original trauma. On the other hand, he could blame the badness he felt on Carol Ann's abusive behavior, thereby denying that the darkness that preyed upon him was inside of him, a perception that would have been refutable in a good relationship. Instead of experiencing self-hatred from his internal rejecting objects in the form of "I hate me," he experienced the rejecting object as outside of himself in the form of "Carol Ann hates me and this is only because she is sick." Once, in a rare moment of anger and candor, Mark sternly told Carol Ann, "If it weren't for you, I would be happy." Moreover, he asserted, "I married her for better or for worse and I keep hoping she'll get better." In these statements, Mark attributed the entirety of his personal and relational difficulties to Carol Ann.

Mark's marriage to Carol Ann served multiple functions: it was a repository for his depression, a container for his inherent sense of badness, the justification of the emptiness of his own life, and a support to his preferred self-image as a saint in martyred relationship to a sinner. It also allowed him to disavow his internal self-rejecting objects. In service of these defensive needs, Mark was dependent on Carol Ann. As long as he remained in undifferentiated relationship to her, his internal world of persecutory relationships could be transposed to the marriage. The virulence of his intrapsychic conflict was apparent in the deeply toxic nature of their interpersonal conflict.

Via Mark's reliance upon primitive defenses, his adult life was shaped, almost in its entirety, along the lines and divisions of his childhood. His unconscious internal world of pathological object relationships hid in plain sight yet lurked outside of his awareness.

Carol Ann

Carol Ann was also the product of alcoholic parents. Her father abandoned the family when she was 3 and her mother was verbally and physically abusive. Carol Ann reported that her mother was divorced three times and had a series of live-in boyfriends, some of whom sexually abused her. When she complained to her mother, she was accused of enticing the men, making up stories to spoil her mother's relationships, and driving her father away. Delineated by her mother as selfish, envious, and vicious, Carol Ann came to experience herself as the victimizer rather than the victim.

In her marriage, Carol Ann recreated the sadistic, humiliating, and volatile relationship to her mother and to the father figures in her life. From the very beginning of treatment, she imbued the atmosphere of the consulting room with her ill-contained rage, sadism, and contempt. She generated feelings of terror, dread, nausea, and revulsion in the therapist, along with the pressing urge to escape, and collapsed the space in which to process and make sense of experience. In this way, she communicated to the therapist the terrifyingly perverse world of her childhood as well as that of Mark, who was so tolerant of it.

Carol Ann's relationship to her abusive internal objects was continued in her abusive, castrating, and belittling treatment of Mark. She berated him as a "worthless wimp" and "a spineless dork," perhaps ascribing to him her self-experience in relationship to her mother who attacked and neglected her, to her father who abandoned her and left her unprotected, and to the other father figures in her life who sexually abused her. Paradoxically, while she victimized Mark, she had all the feeling of being the victim. Here she was in identification with the aggressors, her internal rejecting objects, attacking Mark as she herself had been attacked, perceiving him as the victimizer rather than the victim, as she had been perceived by her mother.

In childhood, Carol Ann developed a sense of innate badness against which she could only rage impotently. Unlike Mark, she did not do well in school and had no extracurricular activities and few peer relationships. Consequently, her opportunities to internalize good feelings were limited, and she was left with little to counterbalance her internal persecutory objects and self-hatred.

Into this psychological situation, Mark appeared as her savior from the cycle of violence and degradation. His need for affirmation suited him for the role of the idealized good object and the dreamed-of source of her salvation. Predictably, Mark was unable to live up to Carol Ann's idealized expectations of him as the knight in shining armor for he did not have the magical ability to rid her of self-hatred. Consequently, Carol Ann, wedded to the hope of magical salvation, perceived Mark not as a human being with limited human capacities, but as abandoning and sadistically withholding. She felt betrayal on par with that visited upon her by her parents in childhood. In a later session, she exclaimed, "He likes to act so good and so nice, but he's really a bastard." Because Mark failed to relieve her of her self-hatred, her perception of him changed from that of a perfectly idealized good object to a perfectly devalued bad object, worthy of all of her scorn and contempt.

Although Carol Ann was attempting to nail down a good sense of self in relationship with Mark, she was unable to do so. Her infantile and dependent magical expectations obstructed her capacity to take a realistic look at herself. With a relative absence of internal good objects, her self-hatred ruled supreme and was defended against by converting the "I hate me" of the intrapsychic to the "You hate me," of the interpersonal. In this way, Mark was recruited as an external representation of her internal rejecting and betraying objects. At one point she stated, "He's just like my mother and those bastards. He's never there when I need him."

As Mark had chosen Carol Ann, so she had chosen him, and a match they were. Early in their relationship Mark had yearned to be idealized by Carol Ann, to shore up his sense of self and the illusion of his perfect goodness, and Carol Ann had needed an idealized object with whom she could introjectively identify to counter her self-hatred. Both her and Mark's magical expectations were inevitably disappointed and their hoped-for sense of faultless goodness was soon replaced by the certainty of the other's perfect badness.

When their hopes were disillusioned by reality, disillusionment became de-illusionment and cynicism (Maltas 1992). Carol Ann, in identification with the aggressor(s), instead of remaining silently hurt and victimized as she had in childhood, attacked Mark on all fronts, abusing him as she had been abused, and blaming him as she had been blamed. At one point, she exclaimed, "I'll be damned if

I'll ever let anyone take advantage of me again." Acutely attuned to betrayal and simultaneously fearful of her "badness," she did not realize how she consistently projected onto Mark and then subsequently attacked him in the defensive effort to manage her sense of badness and to ensure that she was never taken advantage of again. All the while, this dynamic supported Mark's unconscious need for Carol Ann to be his persecutory object. Each became the persecutory object of the other. In such ways, the seeds of the dream and the nightmare are sown and reaped in the same garden.

Mark served at least one other important defensive function for Carol Ann: He was an object with whom she could act out and control her own crippled sexuality. Through his passive and emotionally aloof behavior, Mark defensively repressed his need for love and attachment, which were associated with the intolerable pain of persecution and rejection in childhood. Simultaneously, he repressed his aggression, since it threatened his saintly self-image and risked evoking overwhelming retaliation. His libidinal and aggressive drives were thus fixated at a pregenital level of development. Sexually he offered no threat to Carol Ann.

Mark's psychological situation was in complementary relationship to that of Carol Ann. Her wishes for and fears of attachment were intensely sexualized because of her childhood exposure to a sexually charged atmosphere and subsequent sexual abuse. Mark's passivity and emotional aloofness, fully symbolized in his impotence, allowed Carol Ann to safely control the passions of the relationship and recurrently master the sexual traumas of her childhood. With Mark, she was assured that sexual passions would not be acted upon. In the session, in appearance and in body language, she could be sexually inviting. Yet, suddenly and without warning, she could dispel this aura and rip from Mark (or the therapist) any semblance of erotic feelings. This was illustrated in the first session when she shouted, "You can't even get it up! What kind of man are you? Why couldn't I be married to a real man?" In this way, she took her vengeance upon the abusive men in her life, now represented by Mark, whom she delighted in emasculating.

In their respectively perverse ways, both Mark and Carol Ann continue to try to master the traumatic relationships of childhood through their attempts to master each other. Now, after seventeen years of marriage, Carol Ann is simply a bitter and angry woman who holds Mark responsible for her fate and for inevitable further atrocities. For his part, Mark lives cloaked in passivity and aloofness, forever focused on his wife's life, phobically uninterested in any consideration of how he contributes to and maintains the nightmare of his own life.

IDENTITY DIFFUSION

Identity diffusion refers to two dimensions of the sense of self. The first dimension pertains to the difficulty in maintaining a continuous and coherent sense of self in relationship to others across time and changing circumstances (Kernberg 1967, 1975), that is, confusion between self and other. The second dimension refers to the lack of integration among the various facets of the self, leading to the fear of fragmentation, the feeling of falling apart from within (Erikson 1968). It is as if the different threads of the self never cohered, or were precariously formed, or were broken by trauma, so that the fabric is tattered, disintegrated, or un-integrated, rather than a whole cloth. Confusion and anxiety abound, sometimes defended against by arbitrary, brittle, all-or-nothing delineations of self and other.

In early development, self-experience originates in and is inextricably linked to relationship with others. The experience of "me" and the experience of "you," begin as largely indistinguishable. Only later, in good-enough development, do "me" and "you" become relatively differentiated. Consequently, when development has been impeded, a confusing sense of entanglement within the self and between the self and other abounds.

Where there is not an established sense of "me" and of "you," there can be little sense of "we," for my feelings may be both difficult to distinguish and confused with your feelings, and vice versa. "What is what?," "Who is who?," and "What belongs to whom?" become insoluble questions. There is little ability to wonder, "Is this your problem or mine?" or, more complexly, "What part of this is your problem and what part is mine?" This leads to the convoluted and labyrinthine experience of personality-disordered marriages.

Identity diffusion was evidenced in numerous ways in the case of Mark and Carol Ann. Neither was able to clearly identify his or her own thoughts, feelings, or perceptions; to elaborate upon them; or to differentiate them from the other's. There was almost a complete lack of separation between self and other, conveyed in the marked sense of inextricable entanglement. There was no clear definition of what the problem was, or of what they would want progress to look like. Neither was able to clarify what kept them together or what kept them apart. Instead, they conveyed a quality of never-ending, rambling complaints, explicit and implicit, without thought of solution, much less resolution. The therapist, overidentifying with the chaotic situation and his own wish to be out of it, had the impression the relationship could end at any moment. In fact, this stably unstable organization of relationship was familiar and familial, predating the marriage, without variation in form, color, or depth, and felt by each spouse as the only alternative to no organization at all and total isolation.

The severity of identity diffusion was manifested in the erosion of the therapist's own sense of bounded identity. The force of the couple's overwhelming chaos and aggression eroded the therapist's sense of self as he felt threatened and encountered increasing difficulty in differentiating himself from the spouses' tumult. He felt nonspecific feelings of fear, nausea, and revulsion so intensely that his only ambition was to flee the room. His ability to process experience severely impaired, he was dimly aware that he had lost the capacity to think. He felt like jumping out of his skin and was afraid to say anything.

The therapist had entered the couple's all-or-nothing, part-self and part-object form of relatedness that shifted radically from one moment to the next. At one moment, he was in counteridentification to Carol Ann's aggression and in identification with Mark's timidity, feeling fearful and impotent. The next moment, he identified with Carol Ann's disgust with Mark, perceiving Mark as "a wimp" who refused to stand up for himself. At another time, the therapist felt disgust for himself as he recognized his fear of Carol Ann. He failed to make the connection that Carol Ann's disgust with Mark may also have been related to her feelings of self-disgust for having been repeatedly sexually abused. The therapist was betwixt and between, confused, and captured in the vortex of the couple's interaction, unable to differentiate who was responsible for what. He therefore internalized the badness of the situation, questioning whether therapy might be too much for the couple or treatment of the couple too much for him. It was only as he recovered a separate sense of self that he realized how much he had lost himself.

IDIOSYNCRATIC RELATIONSHIP TO REALITY

The borderline's relationship to reality is characterized by intact reality testing (though this may be episodically lost), accompanied by idiosyncratic interpretations of events.

> Kerri was convinced that her therapist was going to hospitalize her and interpreted this possibility as evidence of his hatred and wish to be rid of her. When, instead, he continued to treat her as an outpatient, she perceived him as grossly uncaring and negligent, his hatred evident in his willingness to risk her death. The therapist's response did not matter. Whatever he did was perceived through the matrix of her internal world of pathological self and object relationships in which her therapist would inevitably be cast in the role of a self-hating, rejecting object.

Such idiosyncratic, transferentially imbued interpretations of reality are extremely resistant to modification through cognitive understanding alone, embedded as they are in the internal world of pathological self and object relationships.

Another patient, Caitlin, a 38-year-old single female with a long history of suicidal behavior and psychiatric hospitalizations, conveyed an image of her father as an exceptionally warm and caring man. Yet, in a peculiarly flat tone, she would describe episodes of child abuse by her mother during which her father sat calmly by, reading the newspaper. She also recounted present-day interactions in which she would tell him of her distress, to which he would respond by telling her of some concrete problem of his own, like finding a scratch on his car. Here is illustrated the personality-disordered individual's capacity for an objective description of reality in conjunction with an idiosyncratic interpretation of that reality. Caitlin's father's unempathic response to her distress did not alter her idealization of him.

In the case of Mark and Carol Ann, an idiosyncratic relationship to reality was evidenced in each blaming the other for the entirety of his or her own unhappiness. Mark never claimed ownership for any part of the problem, instead presenting himself as a martyr, regardless of the fact that his adult life paralleled that of his childhood, and that he never considered divorce no matter how horribly he was treated. Carol Ann did not look at her own behavior, instead remaining completely focused on her delineation of Mark, invariably defining him as the victimizer and herself as the victim, without recognizing the abusive nature of her own behavior or her inability to be specific concerning her charges against him.

The unrelenting and total certainty with which each of the spouses interpreted reality impaired the therapist's own relationship to reality. He became entangled and confused, unable to clarify for himself who was actually thinking, feeling, or doing what to whom. His paralyzing uncertainty stood in marked contrast to the spouses' supreme certainty. He grew increasingly uncertain in the face of the unremittingly certain, but contradictory, knowledge of the spouses. He absorbed all self-blame that the spouses did not experience.

The therapist's attempts to clarify reality stood in juxtaposition to the couple's lack of curiosity in identifying, much less thinking about, specific problems in their marriage. "Knowing" everything, they conveyed a total absence of interest in understanding anything. Theirs was a perfect knowing. Since each spouse related to the other as an internal representation, both felt they understood the other completely. Accordingly, there was no sense of surprise or of curiosity. The therapist alone was curious, and his curiosity quickly eroded in the face of the impossibility of distinguishing fact from fantasy, accusation from truth. He became exhausted and stuck, unable to go forward and unable to go backward, mired without any sense of purpose or direction.

PRIMITIVE DEFENSES

Primitive defenses are the human organism's earliest psychological survival mechanism, designed to keep the endangered away from the endangering (Ogden 1986). They are based upon splitting and denial and invariably strive for omnipotent invulnerability. As one patient said, "As long as I don't feel anything, I can put up with everything." Primitive defenses distort reality, internal and external, in the vain attempt to protect the self from the possibility of injury. Unfortunately, this interferes with the ability to learn from experience, impedes development, and inhibits the pursuit of fulfillment.

In healthy development, defenses are dynamic and evolving. Each defense has its own developmental line from simple fight-or-flight forms, without range or subtlety, to complex forms allowing for the intricate modulation of self-experience across time and changing circumstances. The infant is reliant upon her primary caregivers to bring her into manageable and secure relationship with reality. Through good-enough holding, the primary caregiver modulates the infant's exposure to reality and helps regulate the infant's self-state (Bollas 1987, Stern 1985, Winnicott 1956). For example, the good-enough caregiver is attuned to the child's needs for holding, food, and toileting. When the child is distressed, the caregiver modulates the child's anxiety through holding, rocking, and a soothing voice. Via such intersubjectively attuned acts, the caregiver augments the child's developmental capacities, lending his or her own in the service of the child and making them available for internalization by the child. Just as the mother bird partially digests food to help metabolize it for her young, so too the human caregiver helps the infant metabolize aspects of reality so that they do not overwhelm the infant's fragile psyche. When this occurs, the infant's primitive defenses gradually mature, becoming increasingly reality oriented. If the primary caregiver fails in this holding and containing function, the infant becomes overwhelmed by reality (impingement) and the need to react (Winnicott 1956, 1958a).

Impingement may come from outside, as in an act of abuse or smothering overprotection, or from inside, through the deprivation of instinctual needs, such as for food, warmth, or attachment. The determining feature of impingement is that the infant is impelled to react, suffering a discontinuity in the thread of the self. When the thread of the self is broken too often or too long, it becomes difficult to recover (Winnicott 1956), resulting in impairment in the sense of self. To counter anxiety and to escape what has been experienced as an inescapably harsh reality, the child relies upon the rudimentary psychological defenses of splitting and denial to evacuate the intolerable experience from consciousness. Although necessary to survival, this devotion of energy to defense distorts the child's relationship to reality and hinders development.

Splitting and denial are evident in Mark and Carol Ann's relationship to each other. Each holds the other responsible for all that is wrong in his or her own life; neither claims responsibility for any of the problems in their relationship. While Carol Ann discharges her rage and frustration in the form of shaming, blaming, and attacking interactions, Mark flees into near-total aloofness and withdrawal, cloaked in apathy and indifference. Both look to the therapist to remedy the situation—a magical hope, in that both split off and deny their own contribution to it, thereby aborting the capacity to observe, reflect upon, and learn from their own experience.

CONCLUSION

With their reliance upon primitive ways of organizing and perceiving, personality-disordered individuals remain obstinately opposed, with righteous indignation, to what the therapist brings to their attention. They react not only as if the therapist's comments are mistaken, but meant to add insult to injury. Their deficits in development are apparent in their chronic inability to self-observe and self-reflect. Instead, they relate in reactive fashion as if in a persecutory world, attacking or withdrawing, blaming and shaming, and using words not for communication but as projectiles. The personality-disordered individual's vulnerability to narcissistic injury is pervasive, felt at every turn that accompanies human relationship. Unresolved resentments accumulate, destroying any good feelings that may have existed. The spouses assume perpetually defensive positions, as opposed to open and communicative ones. Ruthless aggression, rather than genuine concern and compassion, thus comes to rule the day.

4

The Borderline Marriage and the
Role of Projective Identification

To better understand the personality-disordered marriage, it is helpful to have a general understanding of the intrapsychic dynamics of each spouse. To this end, the borderline and schizoid marriage provides a basic framework from which to consider all personality-disordered marriages. We shall first consider the underpinnings of both the borderline and the schizoid personalities and then examine the role of projective identification in the borderline relationship.

THE BORDERLINE SPOUSE

The core of the borderline difficulty lies in the fundamental incapacity to self-soothe, resulting from the lack of assimilation in early childhood of an object capable of helping the child manage anxiety (Adler 1980, Giovacchini 1981). This developmental shortfall leads to the individual's remaining dependent on others in external reality for the regulation of self-experience. The child, and later the adult, is caught in the throes of a never-ending rapprochement crisis, oscillating between the alternating fears of engulfment and abandonment (Masterson 1981). The individual suffered abandonment anxiety when the caregiver retaliated in the face of the child's exploratory movement away that threatened separation and loss. The caregiver withdrew either physically or emotionally, or became aggressive and pulled the child back when the child attempted to separate. This can occur literally or figuratively, but the effects on the child are similar. The child's return to the caregiver is not determined by need for support and refueling, but is motivated by the caregiver's conflicts around separation and loss. The child's return to the caregiver is an act of submission and compliance in order to avert being abandoned. Alternately, the caregiver can push the child away when the child's need for refueling is in competitive relationship to the caregiver's needs. In either event, instead of the caregiver supporting the child's development and remaining a reliable presence upon whom the child can count, the caregiver co-opts the child in the service of his own needs. The child's development of separation and individuation (Mahler 1968, Mahler et al. 1975) is abridged.

The child is in a catch-22 situation. If she submits to the caregiver and abridges the drive for separation, she is threatened with engulfment. However, if the child continues to separate, she is threatened with the loss of the caregiver, upon whom she is completely dependent, and, again, with the loss of the self. This paradox is internalized by the child, who subsequently suffers abandonment anxiety in the face of individuating thoughts, feelings, and behaviors, and engulfment anxiety in the experience of closeness, arising either from the child's need for the other or the other's need for the child. These issues result in poor self and object differentiation, the inability to recognize and integrate polarized and complementary experiences, and all-or-nothing part-self and part-object relatedness. Derivative difficulties include chaotic relationships; the incapacity to be alone or safely with another; unstable mood; impulsive and unpredictable behavior; and chronic feelings of insecurity, worthlessness, and emptiness. The borderline's relationships become marked by hostility and contempt for the self and for the other, alternating with unremitting neediness (McCormack 1989).

THE SCHIZOID SPOUSE

The core of the schizoid difficulty is an overwhelming fear of the need for attachment, which is experienced as endangering (Guntrip 1961, 1962). For the schizoid individual, the pursuit of early dependency needs resulted in the encountering of rejection and humiliation. Parent–child interactions were centered upon the needs of the parent, while the needs of the child were disregarded. One patient recalls: "I felt like a picture on the wall, just a thing. Every once in a while, my parents would take me down to show me off or entertain their friends. They would have me dance on the top of the kitchen table. Then they would put me away again and I was ignored. Getting their attention sometimes felt good, but I couldn't get it when I wanted it, only when they wanted it. If I made a fuss, I was put in my room. I felt that something was wrong with what I wanted and with me. I learned that my room was a safer place. I kept to myself. It's only in thinking about it over the course of the last year that I realize how I must have been feeling."

The schizoid's anxiety derives from (1) the expectation of the rejection of his needs, along with (2) the anticipation of resultant hurt and humiliation, in conjunction with (3) the mounting aggression that results from the anticipation of rejection or neglect and the rising tension of unmet needs clamoring for attention. The child experiences his needs as potentially destructive to both self and other, for, as they become aggressively charged, they threaten the idealization of the parents upon whom the child is dependent. To cope, the child enters into a relationship antagonistic to his needs, for they, rather than the rejecting other, become perceived as the *source* of his pain and frustration. The child denies his needs as a means of controlling them and his underlying aggressive feelings, thus protecting the relationship. Subsequently, the later adult develops relationships in which he is never fully involved (Guntrip 1962); he always has one foot in and one foot out of every relationship, including the marriage and the therapy.

In the pursuit of absolute self-control, the schizoid denies the world of fantasy, dream, and spontaneity, which threatens him with the uncontrolled welling up of intolerable thoughts and feelings. Instead, he constricts himself to the logical and the concrete, without feeling, like Mr. Spock of *Star Trek* fame. In effect, the schizoid empties himself of feeling, which leads to an impoverished sense of self and an exoskeletal form of relatedness designed to keep others out and himself in.

Unable to give or accept freely in relationships, the schizoid individual exhibits little desire for social involvement and has few if any friends, including family members. Emotionally truncated, he is uncomfortable and inept in social situations, rarely appears distressed by isolation, and usually engages in solitary interests. He is narcissistically vulnerable, while lacking empathy for the feelings of others. He hates to make mistakes and feels severely humiliated if a shortcoming is exposed. His lack of empathy, manifested in callous and insensitive behavior, derives from his anger toward others and his fear of his need for them, as well as from the inability to identify his own feelings and, consequently, the feelings of others.

As a result, the schizoid is extremely frustrating to anyone who would aspire to engage in a relationship with him. He avoids defining who he is or what he thinks or feels. Moreover, there is a seemingly unbridgeable chasm between his thoughts and his feelings, as he, in antagonistic relationship to his feelings, is cognitively oriented to the extreme. Emotions, when they do emerge, are highly charged, usually in the form of narcissistic injury and rage.

In terms of the borderline and schizoid marriage, we may say that as the borderline spouse is unable to be alone, so the schizoid spouse is unable to be with others. To understand the interlocking nature of this type of relationship, it is necessary to understand the role of projective identification.

PROJECTIVE AND INTROJECTIVE IDENTIFICATION

Simply put, primitive projective identification is the psychological process whereby the projector attributes split-off and denied aspects of his or her self (internal self or object representations) to another. In complementary fashion, introjective identification is the psychological process whereby aspects of another are taken in as part of oneself: introjective identification is projective identification going the other way (Sandler and Perlow 1987).

Interpersonally, projective and introjective identification work hand in hand. As the projector attributes disavowed aspects of self to other, so the other, to be affected by that which is projected, must introject (take in) the projection. If the target of the projection does not identify with that which is projected, then the projection remains a psychological process of the projector with limited impact upon the projectee. In essence, the projector, through her behavior, sends an "invitation" to the other, who may or may not accept the offer to serve as a repository for the projection. For example, if I have a poor body image, I can disavow my concern and instead become concerned with your appearance. Subsequently, I can treat you in a way conducive to your feeling ugly. If you possess a secure body image, you will remain relatively unaffected by my behavior (differentiated) and will recognize that something is wrong with me, rather than you. However, if you are concerned with your appearance, you may be vulnerable to my projection, for within you is the fertile ground in which my projection may take root, namely your own insecurities. You will *feel* unattractive as your anxieties are stimulated. I can then observe your management of your discomfort, identify with your struggle, and even benefit from your efforts to resolve it.

Interpersonally, this process can apply to any area of insecurity that lies within both the projector and the projectee. The projector will attempt to master his anxiety by splitting and disavowal, and by projecting it onto the other, where it can be controlled. In turn, the introjector will take in the projection, as it resonates with already present insecurities. A projection is always *onto* an object (animate or inanimate); whether or not it gets *into* that object is largely determined by the intensity of the projection and the recipient's level of differentiation.

The concept of projective identification clarifies how, in relationship, each partner may become a repository for disavowed aspects of the other, and of why opposites attract. It also highlights the importance of the development of separation, individuation, and differentiation to healthy relationship. When the spouses remain relatively undifferentiated, misinterpretation and misrecognition abound. In fact, spouses may intuitively sense the responsiveness of the other's reverberation to their projective invitations and consciously interpret this as attunement, love, and the feeling of being whole or one in their coupling.

THE FUNCTIONS OF PRIMITIVE PROJECTIVE IDENTIFICATION

Primitive projective identification serves a variety of functions (Joseph 1984, 1985):

> **To relieve anxiety and pain.** This aim is manifested in the commonly noted experience that "misery loves company." Misery also makes company via projective identificatory processes.
>
> **To avoid the experience of separateness or loss.** Projective processes may be used to undermine the esteem of another, so that the other will be less likely to feel confident enough to leave the relationship. Alternatively, they can be used to maintain a past relationship in the present. For example, a patient accused me of consisting of nothing more than "springs, nuts, and bolts." Her description of me paralleled that of her father, who had just died. In re-creating her experience of him in me, she defended against loss.
>
> **To place the intolerable aspects of internal self and object representations into another, where they may be dominated**

or controlled. A spouse may project denied dependency needs onto the mate, who then carries the needfulness in the relationship. The needs of the mate may then be dominated and controlled, either by repudiation or by offering unending and eventually resented efforts at cure. The use of projection to control and dominate aspects of oneself in the other is particularly evident in childhood sexual abuse. For example, the abuser may hold the child responsible for the abuse and punish the child for being evil: "You put the Devil into me."

To damage or destroy the object. One spouse filled with self-hatred may perceive the other as unloving or unfaithful, when this is not the case. The projecting spouse may then attempt to damage or destroy the "unfaithful" mate by monitoring his or her every movement and destroying autonomy.

To get into an object in order to take over its capacities and make them one's own. This is illustrated when one spouse, envious of the social graces of the other, publicly humiliates the other to diminish the other's social capacity or, at least in his or her own mind, to feel raised up by lowering the other.

As a "direct communication" (Casement 1985, Winnicott 1971), **to imbue the other with one's own feelings.** A patient, Beverly, had been promiscuous without curiosity or wish to change. She seemed intent on relating to self and other as strictly sexual objects. As she was about to enter another such relationship, I could not stand my feeling of emptiness and helplessness as I observed her denigrating herself in this way. Abandoning interpretation, I firmly but quietly said, "You've been misbehaving for a long time now, and you need to stop." After a pause, she burst out crying and then laughed in delight. After a while I remarked, "I have the fantasy that no one has cared enough about you to tell you this." She responded, "No, it was worse than that: No one cared enough to notice." Through unending reports of her perverse sexual encounters, she filled me with her sense of emptiness and helplessness that she herself did not notice. She had not felt recognized or loved in childhood and accordingly was unable to recognize and love herself in adulthood. Projection is also used to fill others with our own reactions to them. For example, the husband who is enraged with the wife treats the wife in such a way that she feels a similar rage toward him. When this is effective, his own rage is ameliorated.

To communicate something about the projector. Regardless of motivation, projective identificatory processes always communicate something about the projector. The projection tells something of what projectors find intolerable or missing within themselves: a particular pain or anxiety, a fear of separation or loss, a fury over real or imagined damage, a sense of deficiency, a need to feel understood, or the need to wound the other as the projector feels wounded.

THE INTERLOCKING NATURE OF THE BORDERLINE AND SCHIZOID MARRIAGE

The borderline and schizoid marriage is a polarized and complementary part-object relationship typified by each spouse failing to relate either to self or other as a whole person. The primary motivations for the relationship are the pursuit of survival and the need to use the other to fill deficiencies in the sense of self (McCormack 1989). Via the use of primitive projective identificatory processes the spouses re-create and reconfirm their respective internal worlds of self and object relationships in the external reality of the marriage. Each spouse then attempts to control the other, thereby hoping to master in the external world of the marriage that which they were unable to control in childhood. If nothing else, the marriage maintains the continuity of the familiar and the familial, the stability (even if stably unstable) of ego-relatedness, along with the relative certainty that this provides.

THE BORDERLINE'S ATTRACTION TO THE SCHIZOID[1]

A prominent attraction of the borderline wife toward her schizoid husband is his investment in maintaining a stable and predictable existence that stands in welcome contrast to the borderline's emotional anarchy and alternating fears of engulfment and abandonment. Later, given her proclivity to feel engulfed, she will perceive her mate as engulfing, even when he may only be expressing his wishes. Alternately, given her vulnerability to abandonment anxiety, she may feel abandoned whenever her partner is not responsive to her needs. She thus experiences the normal oscillations in relationship between togetherness and separateness as alternately engulfing or abandoning.

From the borderline's point of view, caring is the willingness to sacrifice her own needs and wishes to those of her mate, but with the unspoken expectation that he will sacrifice his for her. Of course, when she feels strongly about something her needs must predominate. This is an engulfing and an abandoning experience if ever there was one. In essence, she expects her husband to live by her lights and to sense and fill her every need. Inevitably, her expectations are disappointed, and she feels engulfed by his needs, victimized or used, or abandoned and betrayed. She becomes hostile and attacking or depressed and withdrawn.

The borderline herself is thus alternately engulfing and rejecting, although she sees herself exclusively in the role of victim. Of course, this view fits hand-in-glove with her schizoid husband's experience of his needs as lethal. His inclination is to withdraw into the fortress of aloofness and apathy at the first sign that his needs are burdensome. Narcissistically injured, he feels guilty of engulfment, while from an external point of view he appears abandoning. He feels guilty of a crime he may not have committed. For this

---

1. For ease of communication, I shall refer to the borderline patient as female and the schizoid patient as male. The dynamics described hold true regardless of the gender and diagnosis configuration.

reason, he is a ready receptacle for his wife's engulfing and rejecting projections, while she retains the role of victim.

Vignette: the Borderline as Engulfing and Rejecting

Sally had been hospitalized following a suicide attempt by overdose and self-mutilative behavior. About six months into treatment, the focus in couples therapy shifted from survival issues to Sally's frequent assertion that Rob, her husband, did not value her. She supported her belief by pointing to his aloofness, indifference, and shallowness, and she was contemptuous of his lack of introspection and lack of feelings. Rob did indeed present as an empty vessel, marooned in logic and reason, uninformed by feelings.

I worked with Rob to help him identify and express his feelings and it seemed that some small progress was made. This was evident in relatively rare and awkward moments in the session when Rob would struggle to convey his feelings. Such moments were heartening. Yet, a pattern became apparent in which Rob would suddenly shut down and withdraw into his shell. Subsequently, he was unable to shed any light upon the cause of his radical shift, and without benefit of his assistance I was left puzzled and strangely shut out.

I reasoned that in the midst of his struggle to express himself he must experience a threat to his sense of self that, although outside of his awareness, triggered his withdrawal. I knew that the source could be intrapsychic and/or interpersonal. With this in mind, I began to attend more closely to Sally's behavior whenever Rob became more vulnerable and expressive within the sessions. I noticed that Sally did not seem put off by these sudden disruptions in Rob's efforts. Indeed, I became aware that she subtly conveyed an air of boredom, as if the whole process was a waste of time. This puzzled me, given her frequently avowed desire that Rob become more feeling. As I continued to observe, I also discovered that Rob's withdrawals seemed timed with slight shifts in Sally's behavior. She would raise an eyebrow, as if silently editorializing about what he was saying; shift impatiently in her seat, as if she were bored; or make a barely audible noise, somewhat like a chuckle, as if she were laughing at a joke at his expense.

Previously, I had been unaware of these behaviors. Now, more attuned and identified with Rob, I found them irritating and discombobulating, particularly in the context of his fledgling and vulnerable attempts to understand and express himself. Now, Rob's humiliation was evident to me, and I felt angry toward Sally and her fleeting but powerfully undermining behaviors. Feeling very protective of Rob, I confronted Sally, first to get her to stop the behavior and then to understand it. Sally, looking befuddled, instantly apologized and claimed, perhaps honestly, that she was unaware of doing anything. When I explored my feeling that her behavior conveyed impatience and the sense that Rob's efforts were silly, moronic, or unimportant, she acknowledged that she was impatient and found Rob's effort tiresome at best. Given Rob's narcissistic vulnerability, he had been immediately aware of what I had missed, and he had withdrawn.

What was striking to me was how unconsciously this interpersonal dynamic was carried out. Though Rob had responded to it immediately, he had not known what he was responding to, and Sally had conveyed her attitude without conscious awareness. The interpersonal interaction had also escaped my notice, perhaps due in part to my lack of attunement to Rob's exquisite narcissistic vulnerability and in part to my overidentification with his seeming insensitivity to those around him. In addition, the spouses' collusive unconscious interaction formed a joint communication by impact (Phillips 1988), which can collapse the space for awareness.

As I mulled over the couple's interaction, I was amazed at how instantaneously Rob had succumbed to his fear of humiliation and of his needs being burdensome. For reasons outside of his own awareness he would become confused and withdraw. In further exploration of this dynamic it became apparent that in these ways, for years, Sally had in effect unconsciously rejected and isolated Rob, while to all appearances and in terms of his own experience, Rob seemed to be unavailable to her. As Rob's self-observing capacities developed, he would catch himself withdrawing and recognize his fear that his needs were invalid and burdensome.

THE SCHIZOID'S ATTRACTION TO THE BORDERLINE

The schizoid husband initially perceives his wife's needfulness as evidence of her capacity to love and relate, two areas in which he is sorely deficient. She provides a much-needed experience of ego-relatedness that protects him from total isolation and resultant psychotic breakdown. In addition, she meets his need for relationship without his having to acknowledge his need for it. Whenever he feels needy, he can elicit her abandonment anxiety by withdrawing. The wife suddenly feels needy and pursues contact with him.

Conversely, whenever the schizoid husband feels threatened by closeness he can alienate his wife by resorting to nitpicky criticisms and demands that trigger her feelings of worthlessness and fears of engulfment, leading to the distancing entailed in rage or depression. In this way, he treats her the way he was treated when feeling needful.

The schizoid husband's initial attraction to the borderline mate is undermined as he begins to recognize an old dynamic, that is, like he was by his parents, he is treated as a commodity by his wife. This is evident if he should express a need that is incongruent with her own. At such times, she may pull away out of fear of engulfment, or criticize him. She thereby confirms his fear that his needs, and thus he himself, are burdensome.

This dynamic was apparent in the relationship of Rob and Sally. Although Sally had complained about Rob's lack of feelings for years, her material wishes had been well met: Her wish to quit her job, to start her own business, to buy a quality riding horse, to purchase paintings, and to buy a new home had all been supported and financed by Rob. In contrast, his wish to maintain a contribution to retirement savings and his request that Sally not purchase major items without discussion had not been respected. To the contrary, Sally had treated these requests as niggling concerns or interpreted them as Rob's attempts to control her. In addition, she later acknowledged her spending to be an effective way of venting anger toward him as well as an attempt to nurture herself, a substitute for real relationship.

As treatment progressed, Sally connected her oppositionalism to Rob's needs to the feeling that he was either attempting to control her or to deprive her, in other words, as engulfing or abandoning. In response, she rejected his needs. Gradually, Sally saw that in misrecognizing and misinterpreting Rob's needs she was treating him as her mother had treated her. She further realized that her father had always given her whatever material objects she had wanted. She had equated such largesse with love and had unconsciously expected the same from Rob.

Interactively the spouses enter polarized and complementary part-self and part-object relationship in which each spouse relates to disavowed aspects of internal self or object representations in the other. Neither relates to the other as a whole person with separate and important needs of his or her own. As the unconscious of each partner is "peopled" by polarized and conflicting pathological part-self and part-object relationships, so each enters into divided and conflicted relationship to his or her mate. Interpersonal conflict displaces intrapsychic conflict. As each partner becomes a repository for the disavowed aspects of the other, the proclivities of each become amplified. The borderline becomes more feelingful in response to the schizoid's defensive counteridentification with feelings, as the schizoid becomes more reliant on the cognitive and the logical in response to the borderline's chaotic feelings and behavior. This situation worsens as each partner increasingly attempts to dominate and control the other.

THE SCHIZOID AS COUNTERPUNCHER

The schizoid's use of projective identificatory processes is not easily identified. He will debate ad nauseam the charge of being nitpicky and, despite everyone's best efforts, will remain impervious to the charge of being angry, insensitive, or uncaring (McCormack 1989). To use a boxing analogy, the borderline spouse is a puncher, whereas the schizoid spouse is a counterpuncher. Fights often appear to be instigated by the borderline spouse, centered on the charge that the husband is uncaring. In fact, her charge makes sense, for the schizoid's style of effecting a projection is to be found not in what he does, but in what he does not do. Although the process is subtle, the effects are not.

Imagine, for example, going to the movies. You may not enjoy what the borderline projectionist is putting on the screen, but at least there is action and the illusion of life. However, with the schizoid projectionist nothing at all appears on the screen. You sequence from impatience to boredom, to frustration, to anger, and then to hostility.

Just as the borderline treats her others as she herself had been treated in childhood, so the schizoid treats his others as he had been treated. Accordingly, he effects his projective identifications through lack of responsiveness, withdrawal, withholding, apparent indifference, and treating the needs of his mate as burdensome and excessive. Thus he projects his terrible isolation, emptiness, and rage.

Vignette: What's the Point of Feelings?

Debbie and Fred had recently attended the funeral of Fred's mother. Debbie had disliked her mother-in-law, and Fred's relationship with her had been a dysfunctional one. His mother's acknowledged favorite, Fred had been used as her confidant, and she complained endlessly about his father, her children, and her fate in life. Fred learned to listen attentively while never placing demands on her. When he made the mistake of expressing a need, his mother, by look or deed, would equate him with all the other demanding people in her life, thereby threatening Fred with the loss of his special relationship to her.

Fred's father was an emotionally constipated, distant, and aloof man who spoke little, spending his leisure time in front of the television set. Accordingly, Fred had no experience of relationship that included his needs. Thoroughly repressed, Fred did not remember many childhood events. However, his sister told Debbie that he had had a history of temper tantrums. Once he refused to eat after his brother took a bite from his pancake, until his mother cooked more. Another time he refused to get down off the roof of the family car, upon which he had roosted when his mother insisted that he allow passengers to exit from his door. Yet another time, he chased his sister with a fireplace poker, smashing the door to her bedroom when she locked it against him.

Fred's temper tantrums ceased as he immersed himself in a world of fantasy. In adolescence, he spent hours each day obsessively gathering baseball statistics, graphing the rise and fall of players while standing apart from the fray of human interaction. When asked about peer relationships, he responded, "I'm sure I had some," as if he were speculating upon the life of another.

During the session to be described, Debbie reported that to her surprise she had wept at her mother-in-law's funeral, while to her dismay Fred remained dry-eyed and unmoved. Debbie wondered, "If I die will Fred cry for me?" She probed his feelings but found only cold logic. Fred responded as if her feelings represented a curious flaw within her. He dispassionately acknowledged being unmoved at his mother's funeral and puzzled by Debbie's concern. He reasoned, "There is no point in having feelings about my mother's death. Feelings bring pain, and they don't change anything. What's the point; it won't bring her back."

As Debbie, Fred, and I discussed this situation, I was aware of feeling frustrated in my efforts to connect with Fred. Gradually I noticed, to my own annoyance, that under Fred's circular reasoning, I was beginning to feel that something was wrong with me. As Fred maintained the mathematical certainty of his logic, uncontaminated by feelings, I asked myself, "Why is it so important to me to connect with Fred?" An answer did not come readily to mind. All that I knew was that I was allied with Debbie's exasperation with him and felt increasingly isolated from him. An image came to mind of Debbie and me being treated like insects in a petri dish, studied by Fred, the coolly objective scientist, looking down upon us. Only later did I realize that this also may have been how Fred felt in relationship to Debbie and me.

It is not clear how Debbie came to cry on behalf of Fred, expressing his loss for him. Perhaps Fred projected his feelings via his total repudiation of any human response to the loss of his mother. However, what I did come to recognize, through my countertransference, was that my futile efforts to connect with Fred paralleled his own efforts to connect with his mother, first in life and then in death. In a flat tone, Fred described his conversations with his mother as longwinded monologues. He felt "captive," "helpless," and "frustrated," further noting that his mother had had no interest in what he might be thinking. Similarly, in Debbie's and my attempts to connect with Fred, we felt helpless, devalued, worthless, and frustrated—feelings very similar to those Fred had been warding off for years.

I shared with Fred my observations. He thought they were interesting, but nothing more, and continued to respond in coldly logical fashion, only amplifying my exasperation. Now I wondered angrily, "What's the point?" I then recalled that this was the same question Fred had asked about feeling the loss of his mother. In that instant, I realized that I had come to appreciate Fred's experience of his relationship with his mother, which had lasted for decades while mine with him lasted only a few minutes a week.

Time passed and little changed. I came to believe that Fred's investment in therapy was offered only as a means of mollifying Debbie and maintaining his relatedness to her. In this way, he defended against the experience of total isolation while continuing to use Debbie as a repository for his feelings, which could then be controlled or destroyed.

When I hesitantly offered this interpretation, Fred, to my surprise, came alive and wholeheartedly agreed. During the next several months, this issue was explored in greater depth. At that point, Fred opted to end his involvement in treatment, stating resolutely that he had no wish to change. "I have constructed my life so that it is endurable. Change promises pain and threatens every-thing that I have constructed."

I can only speculate that Fred had been so wounded in childhood that his basic pessimism could not be overcome without the guarantee of the perfect gratification of his needs. In addition, his fatalistic attitude was reminiscent of his mother's *and* was a tie to her that he was unwilling or unable to forego. Therapy provided a necessary clarification for Fred and Debbie. Debbie now had the wherewithal to make a more fully informed decision concerning the direction of her own life, as Fred had made for his.

Vignette: Presence through Absence

Kris was a gregarious woman, while her husband, Ron, was shy and reticent. Whenever he endeavored to express his feelings, Kris would make sarcastic comments or jokes. When I questioned her behavior, she would apologize, noting that humorous thoughts that had nothing to do with Ron or what he was talking about would spontaneously come to mind. However, as her behavior continued, I was unconvinced by her disavowals and saw her as destructive and sadistic. Finally, unable to tolerate the situation anymore, I angrily asked her to remain silent when Ron was speaking. In the midst of my ill-disguised tantrum, I realized that I was acting and feeling as if the problem were between Kris and me, rather than between Kris and Ron. I recognized that I was countertransferentially acting out my feelings, rather than using them to better understand and work with the couple.

With newfound perspective, I observed that Ron, in contrast to my own feelings of involvement and outrage, appeared indifferent and unaffected, as if he were an observer instead of a participant. It was then that I realized I was fighting a battle rightly his and that, via withdrawal and apparent indifference, he had left the emotional field while I was hard at work. As I pondered my reaction, I recognized that I had perceived Ron's ostensible shyness and reticence as indications of sensitivity and vulnerability that had summoned from within me the image of him as a little boy who needed my protection. I had succumbed to playing his champion, and all I had accomplished was to support the status quo of the relationship, including Kris's belittling view of him.

As I analyzed my internal images of Ron and Kris, I reminded myself that the spouses probably served equally important functions for one another, and thus each held equal power in the relationship. Kris's power was clear, evident in her sociability and in the sarcastic wit with which she skewered and undermined Ron. Ron's power was less evident, found not so much in what he did but in what he did not do. His power was not in what was present, but in what was absent: his anger. He created a vacuum of relationship that I had been unconsciously filling. I had become Ron's champion, supporting him in the role of victim, and, I suspect, secretly delighting him whenever I confronted Kris. In addition, I reasoned that my angry overinvolvement might be extracting his anger and personal feelings of involvement, thereby relieving him of them and maintaining his psychic equilibrium (as well as my own). Action for me had been far easier than feeling.

I then remembered that Ron had reported that his parents often fought about him, to the extent that his concerns were lost and he felt of no importance at all. This experience was being re-created in the session. As I fought with Kris, what Ron was feeling was lost. With these hypotheses in mind, I radically altered the nature of my involvement in the sessions. Now when Kris interrupted, rather than centering my attention on her, I would work with Ron to elaborate his experience in that moment. Immediately, I felt a new connection with Ron, as I ignored Kris's interruptions and remained focused on him. Gradually, he began to identify his own anger over Kris's interruptions. His underlying rage was dramatically illustrated during a session when Kris gently prodded him with her foot while he was speaking. He reactively kicked her in the leg with force. With this behavior, Ron revealed his rage, which he only recognized and acknowledged once he had acted it out. From this moment on there was a qualitative shift in the relationship. Ron and I continued to work on the identification and expression of his feelings, including his rage at Kris's belittling treatment of him. Subsequently, he confronted Kris's behavior, using words instead of actions.

THE COLLUSIVE NATURE OF THE COUPLE'S PRIMITIVE PROJECTIVE IDENTIFICATORY PROCESSES

To this point, the spouses' projective identificatory processes have been discussed primarily from the point of view of one spouse or the other. What I would like to focus on at this point is the vortex of the spouses' interaction, created unconsciously and without effort by them, which so easily catches the therapist in its grip and from which the therapist must break free. The interpersonal expression of the couple's projective identificatory processes is akin to an artist's brush strokes. Part of their enormous power resides in the fact that up close, as in the interpersonal interactions in the consulting room, the painting appears as an unintelligible commingling of daubs and smears of color. However, with the gaining of perspective, presumably achieved via analysis, each stroke is seen in context, creating a form and substance that convey a particular emotional charge. Once this wider perspective is gained, it is possible to appreciate the genius behind the individual brush strokes upon which the painting as a whole is reliant, and to identify the central projections around which the overall picture is organized.

The following vignette illuminates the interlocking nature of the spouses' projections, which constitutes both the principle resistance to treatment and the vehicle by which growth may be renewed. In addition, it illustrates that it is by attending to the discordances, incongruities, dis-integrities, irregularities, cracks, and fissures of the spouses' perceptions, in conjunction with countertransference reactions, that the therapist may break free of the the couple's projections and grasp their internal world of self and object relationships.

Vignette: Projective Identification as a
Defense against Development

Jared, suffering from borderline personality disorder with narcissistic features, recurrent major depression, and chronic suicidality, had been hospitalized at an inpatient psychiatric unit for six months. An angry, complaining man, often visibly bloated with rage, he felt victimized by the stupidity of one and all around him. His wife, Ceil, a veterinarian, was highly intellectualized and devoid of emotion, with no history of psychiatric treatment. She seemed asexual as she sat rigidly, back straight, with close-cropped hair, practical shoes, slacks, and a buttoned-to-the-neck blouse.

During the three months preceding hospitalization, Jared had been bed-bound with depression while Ceil worked full-time, nursing him in the evening and on weekends. This pattern of relatedness was characteristic of their relationship. In the hospital, as his depression began to lift, Jared repeatedly denounced Ceil's "clinical treatment" of him and her lack of emotion. He pushed her to acknowledge that she had psychological problems of her own.

Ceil met Jared's perceptions with cool intellect, as if sitting with an unreasonable and ranting child. She invariably denied his claim, asserting in a measured tone that, as far as she knew, she was fine, and that she stayed and took care of him because she had married "until death do us part." Although increasingly frustrated, Jared persisted, pointing out that his problems were apparent during their extended courtship and that she had married him anyway. Ceil's denial of this allegation gradually crumbled as Jared established the weight of his case, incident upon incident. She then pedantically asserted that she had been "blinded by love" and that she must have assumed that Jared would get better and not worse. Such arguments, focused on Ceil's lack of feeling, often comprised the content of their sessions. Although little progress was made in terms of this issue, Jared's mental state gradually stabilized sufficiently to allow his discharge.

Three months after discharge, they attended a session following a visit to Ceil's family in the Southwest. To my amazement, Ceil not only began the session but also expressed a poignant forlornness tinged with memories of unrequited yearning and feelings of desolation in relationship to her parents, particularly her father. She mused about her role as the firstborn and female, how she had assisted her overwhelmed mother in the care of her five younger siblings. She felt that her own needs had been forsaken. As she reminisced, she spoke of her father's sadistic teasing and often painful pinching, done in the guise of play. She then recounted her favorite memory of her father. For the only time in her life, he had taken her, without her siblings, to an ice cream parlor. They had eaten in silence, and she had reveled in the feeling of specialness. Then, during their walk home, the wind blew her favorite hat from her head into the mud. As she began to cry, her father angrily balled the hat into a wad and threw it away, sternly admonishing, "Don't be silly; it's just a hat." Ceil immediately stopped crying, and they continued home in silence.

The pathos of Ceil's storytelling was compelling, bringing to life a childhood memory in the session. I was feeling privileged to be part of the experience, caught up in the threads of Ceil's story, when Jared, who had been out of my mind's eye, suddenly began yelling at Ceil. Startled and confused, I felt forcibly jerked out of a dreamlike state into the harsh light of reality. I strained to orient myself. I could think of nothing in the content of the session that accounted for Jared's onslaught. His words carried little information; "Bitch, selfish bitch" would summarize them. I could only imagine that Jared was upset over Ceil's using the session to talk about herself. Yet, his tantrum appeared completely nonsensical in view of his long-held desire that she talk more about herself. I wondered, "Had she said or done something that I missed?"

Although I was confused, Jared and Ceil acted as though they were not. Ceil apologized to Jared, and he settled down. No explanation of what happened was given. While they seemed to be smoothly dancing over familiar ground, I was stumbling over my feet. I wondered at the great distance I had traveled from the poignant enchantment of Ceil's storytelling to the emptiness of the current interaction. However, beyond these observations I could not travel, and so I asked the couple to guide me out of my confusion, noting that they seemed to understand what had happened, but I did not.

Upon my self-disclosure, Jared and Ceil appeared confused; it was apparent that neither had given thought to what had happened. For them, there had been only action and reaction, and both were grateful that things were stable once again. Ceil recalled that during Jared's outburst she had suddenly felt guilt and emptiness. She felt she had selfishly taken time for herself without regard for Jared. Jared revealed his own confusion, noting that Ceil's feelings had suddenly become unaccountably frightening to him, that he had feared that "things would get out of control." Struggling to express himself, Jared used the chalkboard to draw a breastlike figure, a circle with a point in the center. He noted that when first married he might have drawn two circles, representing Ceil and himself as separate people. However, now the two had merged into one, and he felt swallowed up and dependent upon her. He realized that during Ceil's storytelling he had become fearful that she would leave him and that he would be unable to survive without her. He had then visualized putting a shotgun into his mouth.

This interaction could be analyzed in countless ways. There was a reversal of roles evident in Ceil's heartrending expression of feelings while Jared and I listened. Now, she was the sensitive one and the focus was on her. Perhaps Ceil's forlorn and forsaken feelings resonated with Jared's own childhood, in which he and his brothers were intimidated and abused physically and psychologically by their father. Perhaps Ceil's feelings flooded him and threatened his precarious capacity for containment. Conceivably, it was difficult for him to identify introjectively with her stability at a time when she was suddenly emotional.

However, one thing was certain: Ceil was relating from a developmentally more advanced capacity for human relatedness. I believe this evoked Jared's realization of her separateness and threatened him with the fear of being left that he described in his chalkboard drawing. His terror that he would be unable to survive without her was conveyed with the image of his putting a shotgun in his mouth. From this perspective, his words "Bitch, selfish bitch" become self-evidently understandable.

Given this interaction, we can now surmise that the supposed obstacle to the relationship from Jared's point of view, Ceil's lack of feeling, was in fact a much-hated but much-needed aspect of Ceil that preserved her rocklike stability and prevented her from becoming autonomous, both of which helped Jared maintain his psychic equilibrium. Ceil's capacity to feel her feelings threatened Jared with separation and individuation, a developmental leap—hers and his—for which he was not ready and which thereby threatened that "things could get out of control."

Jared's fear of separation and abandonment may have been exacerbated by the fact that, while Ceil talked, he had not been in my thoughts or the center of attention. Via his angry denouncements, he reclaimed control of Ceil's attention and mine.

The session also re-created Ceil's family situation with herself in the role of surrogate mother: in the face of Jared's anger, she instantaneously felt that a focus on her own feelings was selfish and immediately forsook her relationship to her feelings with a concern for his.

It is also noteworthy that the session replicated Ceil's interaction with her father at the ice cream parlor. Her father had given Ceil much longed-for attention, but later, after her hat had fallen into the mud and she had become upset, he had wadded up the hat and thrown it away. In attacking Ceil's distress with his own, he extractively introjected it (Bollas 1987),[2] robbing her of her feelings. She had immediately stopped crying. Similarly, as Ceil was again expressing feelings of sadness and loss, Jared angrily attacked her, essentially wadding her feelings up and throwing them away,

---

2. Whereas primitive projective identification is the putting of an aspect of one's self into the other, and introjective identification is identifying one's self with an aspect of the other, extractive introjection is taking an aspect of the other out of or away from the other into the self. By robbing the other of this experience, the extractor maintains her own psychic equilibrium, which was threatened by the feelings of the other.

extractively introjecting them with the intensity of his anger. Then, as now, Ceil was emptied of her feelings, and Jared's and her own psychic equilibrium were restored.

The remarkable aspect of the marital session was that both spouses behaved as if business as usual were occurring, when in fact a rich subtext was driving their interaction. Both ignored the irrationality of their interaction, within which were hidden the early anxieties, developmental conflicts, and deficits of each.

THE COUPLE AS A PROJECTIVE ENTITY

Projective processes permeate all levels of relatedness, ranging from short sequences of interaction to protracted scenarios that are so ingrained in the marriage that they take on the quality of immutable reality. Because of the encompassing nature of these marital structures, the fact that they are the creation of the couple, rather than an immutable reality, can easily be forgotten. When this occurs, the therapist loses curiosity and the creative capacity to imagine the couple as a potential. Instead, she unwittingly becomes a contributing member to the couple's concrete construction, focusing on what is rather than on what can be, on what has been made, rather than on what might yet be made.

Vignette: External Presentation as the Inverse of Private Reality

Jenna glided down the hallway to my office like a float in a Macy's Thanksgiving Day parade. Short in stature and wide of beam, she had bedecked her rotund body with a print dress of swirling colors. Her jovial, rosy-cheeked face peered from beneath a huge wide-brimmed hat garishly strewn with brightly colored flowers. Brett, a tall weed, body by Nautilus, draped in a dark Brooks Brothers suit that underscored the paleness of his skin, was cadaverous in comparison and appeared to be towed in Jenna's wake. His slicked-back hair highlighted a prominent forehead, conveying an aura of intelligence, power, and control.

Brett was the comptroller of a major corporation. His treatment history consisted of a single short course of individual therapy for depression that was treated with medication. He was the archetype of a "number cruncher" in mind and soul. The product of a West Virginia coal mining family that his father deserted when Brett was ten, Brett was the man of the house, working after school and later attending college at night, helping to support his mother and sisters. He spoke matter-of-factly of his early years: "It was just something that needed to be done and I did it."

Jenna's treatment history was extensive. She suffered from bipolar disorder with borderline features and had been hospitalized nineteen times in twenty years. She was the only child of parents who divorced when she was 4. She moved with her mother to the maternal grandparents' house and lost touch with her father. Her grandfather sexually molested her over a number of years. When she spoke of this, her voice rang with rage and anguish. She loved her grandfather, who was the source of the affection and attention she so craved.

After several years of therapy, Jenna insisted on divorcing her sober and unromantic husband. She explained that through years of treatment, she had unsuccessfully attempted to enliven their relationship. Now that her children were adults, she felt there was nothing for her in the marriage.

I was alarmed, wondering if she were becoming hypomanic, and was privately opposed to a divorce, given her years of disability. Brett had at least provided her with a stable, albeit staid, environment. I thought, "How can she do better than Brett?" and feared she would end up as a street person or on the back ward of a state hospital.

Part of my concern derived from Brett's lack of concern. In a typically monotone voice, he expressed brief and passionless opposition to Jenna's wishes to separate, thus underscoring Jenna's primary complaint. Fueled by Brett's lack of concern, Jenna remained adamant. I reluctantly referred the couple for divorce mediation. They separated and ended couples treatment.

Six months later I encountered Brett at a fast food restaurant. He had aged. He was hunched over, unshaven, and disheveled, and he shuffled when he walked. He appeared depressed, mumbling an embarrassed hello before moving away. I was disturbed by this encounter, imagining him reclusively living within the dark and shuttered confines of his home.

On the other hand, Jenna's individual therapist reported that she had been hospitalized at a state hospital, but only for a few weeks. She had then lived in a group home and subsequently moved to an apartment. Eighteen months later, Jenna continued to maintain her apartment. Brett had contacted her and they were dating.

Brett and Jenna presented as a mismatched couple. Brett was highly functional in the business world, while Jenna was chronically disabled. Each dressed his or her part. However, in their marriage they were in inverse relationship. Jenna was Brett's mainstay, meeting his unspoken needs for ego-relatedness while he provided materially for Jenna and their children. Needful of a more affectionate relationship, Jenna left him after the children left the nest. Perhaps exposing the children to separation any earlier would have been too similar to her father's desertion of her. She stayed in the relationship, but at the cost of her emotional needs and developing competencies.

For his part, Brett had maintained his role as the man of the house who worked constantly and provided materially but was not in relationship to his dependency needs and was rejecting of Jenna's. It was only with Jenna's courage to separate that the underlying organization of the relationship was revealed.

CONCLUSION

We have explored how, through projective and introjective processes, each spouse comes to play a supporting role in the internal-world drama of the other while concurrently starring in his or her own. Each spouse continuously recapitulates both problem and solution, but without resolution. In addition, the costs of excessive reliance on primitive projective identificatory processes were noted. Introjects exist as foreign bodies within the personality, bringing with them the characteristics of the internalized object, infringing upon and diminishing the area of one's self. Conversely, projections empty into the outer world affect and ideation, which comprise the self (Meissner 1987, Sandler 1987). Identifying and working through the projective and introjective processes operating within the relationship is an essential component of treatment, which, if not addressed, will inhibit the possibilities of further growth for each spouse and for the relationship.

5

The Borderline Marriage as a
Primitive Self-Object Relationship

Marriage constitutes far more and far less than a present-day relationship. Each person's way of perceiving and relating derives from a complexly formed biopsychosocial matrix shaped in the forge of childhood relationships. Unfortunately, when the vicissitudes and vagaries of relationship have been severe, the drive for attachment becomes encumbered, and the individual, instead of developing toward independence, becomes caught in the web of unmet infantile needs. Emotionally immature, he or she remains relatively undifferentiated, continuing to have difficulty in distinguishing self from other, past from present, and internal world from external reality. With the difficulty in differentiating the "ghosts in the nursery" (Fraiberg et al. 1975) from contemporary relationships, the personality-disordered marriage becomes an intergenerationally woven paradigm of pathological self and object relationships.

Healthy development entails the optimal meeting and frustrating of dependency needs that supports a manageable process of separation, individuation, and differentiation; resultant autonomy; and the ensuing ability to live in relationship to reality. However, when prematurely exposed to external reality, the infant or young child is overwhelmed and experiences reality as the Great Terrorist, a terrifying, harsh, and desolate landscape, populated only by the uncaring nothingness of things.

In that the world of the infant is an egocentric one, the child sees himself mirrored in the eyes of his caregivers and how he feels in relationship to them. From these early experiences in relationship, the child internalizes a self-representation (self image), an object representation (object image), and the affective links between the two (self and object relationship). For example, in relationship to an adoring caregiver, the child basks in the gleam of his eye and experiences self in all its magnificence. Conversely, in relationship to a rejecting or depleted caregiver, the child experiences himself as burdensome or hateful. The child internalizes this experience, forming a disturbed and disturbing internal world that is peopled like a gothic fantasy with persecutory self and object relationships that threaten to envelop the self. Subsequently, as internal world comes to be projected into external reality, coloring events with idiosyncratic and perverse meanings, so is perceived reality re-internalized, confirming the perception. Inside and outside enter into circular and self-reinforcing relationship.

At the borderline level of organization, each partner, engaged in this self-reinforcing perceptual process, locates his or her sense of self in the mate and feels either loveable or hateful as mirrored by the mate. Both are oblivious to the fact that what they are perceiving and experiencing is often their own projection. Nonetheless, each projectively maintains the locus of self-experience in the other and holds the other responsible for the way he or she feels. When feeling secure, one perceives the other as loving. When feeling insecure, one perceives the other as engulfing or rejecting. Typically, in personality-disordered relationships, the latter scenario predominates and the spouse is perceived as a defective selfobject and held responsible for failing to maintain the subject's sense of self. A highly tumultuous, narcissistically vulnerable relationship ensues, in which each spouse is in hostile dependent relationship to the other.

Stolorow and colleagues (1987) note that "the term selfobject does not refer to things in the environment or to people, but to a dimension of experiencing an object (Kohut 1984, p. 49), which is required for maintaining, restoring, or consolidating the organization of self-experience" (pp. 16–17).

Self-object usage has a developmental line ranging from the primitive to the mature. Personality-disordered spouses use their mates in a self-regulatory fashion that is felt to be vital to existence. It is the spouse's incapacity to self-soothe that drives the enmeshed, codependent character of their relationships.

These are primary object relationships (Balint 1968), an example of which includes the relationship between man and water or air. In such relationships, the object, such as air, may be taken for granted and even abused or misused (polluted), but nonetheless its absence is felt as life threatening. Consequently, upon the risk of loss of air (the object), great energy will be expended to bring about its return.

Similarly, personality-disordered spouses may abuse each other until there is a threat of the loss of the other, at which time great energy is expended to resuscitate the relationship. This is one reason abusive relationships can be long lasting. Each spouse operates with the conviction that a toxic relationship is better than no relationship at all.

THE THERAPIST'S USE OF SELF

Sometimes we fool ourselves into thinking we know the meaning of the words "separation," "individuation," and "differentiation." However, such knowledge is repeatedly discovered, lost, and discovered anew in different ways. We may be able to recite the definition and to intellectually understand the process, but these are different understandings than those derived from the psyche-soma, which is known in one's bones, or gut, or whatever other physical locale in which the raw knowledge of it is embedded. In less differentiated relationships separateness is terrifying, threatening to throw the rotation of one's internal world off its axis. The lived experience is of the threat of fragmentation resulting from being spun out into space, the infinite void, all alone. The memories of the profound losses of infancy and childhood are sensory, inscribed in the body. In adulthood, such feelings may emerge like tidal waves or in the figurative experience of the ground falling out from under one's feet. Stunning in their sudden appearance and devastating impact, they are remembered somatically in headaches, wrenching stomach pains, constipation, diarrhea, night terrors, and awakening in the middle of the night, as one husband did, finding his hands in pain from having been clenched for hours in sleep.

In training programs and in supervision we are told to "take your thinking up a notch" as an injunction to become more conceptually oriented. Conceptualization is important. It helps organize experience so that it may be reflected upon. However, whatever the couple—be it mother and infant, therapist and patient, the marital couple, or the internal couple of self-relationship—the relationship is always of psyche and soma. Indeed, it is the capacity to sense and feel, sometimes foreclosed by excessive reliance on cognition, that is the fertile soil from which future trial identifications and empathy may emerge in direct relationship to the couple, providing experience-near sensory data from which subsequent perceptions and concepts arise. Consequently, to fully appreciate and understand the personality-disordered individual's terror of the process of separation, individuation, and differentiation, one must also "take your thinking down a notch," so that the more elemental sensations, thoughts, and feelings may be identified as they arise in relationship with the couple. It is this capacity of the therapist to identify, sensed by the patient, that counters the patient's feeling of aloneness. Therapy then becomes an ongoing process of taking our thinking down a notch to identify with the patient and then taking it up a notch to make sense of what was experienced. In this alternating process, the therapist ties the data of his lived experience in relationship with the couple to his conceptualizations of them, providing them with the lived experience of the difference between separateness and abandonment. This is the therapist's use of self.

Even so-called normal relationships suffer a version of the terror of separation. In couples therapy, separation is always an issue in that for a successful outcome the relationship must be modified in its configuration. Even necessary endings, including separation and divorce, elicit separation anxieties that entail the rending of the past; the disruption of the future; and, perhaps most painfully, the ending of the marital dream, at least with a particular person. The potential permanence of the loss is unbearable. The profound impact of the possibility of love's ending is inescapable. Such instability drives the almost universal wish, if not action, of recently separated individuals to become immediately involved in another relationship, striving to compensate for the loss of the other and to divert themselves from the terrible anxiety of their own aloneness.

Vignette: Primitive Self-Object Functioning in Relationship

Sean and Lindsey had been together for thirteen years, the last four marked by an absence of sexual activity. Two years previous to this therapy Lindsey had bought her own house but continued living with Sean until her parents, who had financed the house, decided to visit. Lindsey's unstated expectation when buying the house was that Sean would move in with her, but he refused. In an effort to clarify their relationship, Lindsey and Sean decided on a trial separation, which was now of eighteen months' duration. However, each regularly initiated contact with the other, by telephone and in person, and they often slept together, although without sexual interaction. In this preoedipal manner they remained entangled, unable to separate and unable to be together.

At the initial interview, Sean stated a wish to sort out their relationship. For him this meant either to "be friends" or to end the relationship. He wished to be friends. When asked why he had not simply stated this to Lindsey and gone on about his life, he explained that he did not want to hurt her. He attributed his breaches of their separation agreement to his concern for her well-being, which drove him to call her from time to time to assure himself that she was okay. He further expressed liking the feeling of knowing that he was always in her mind, and commented that the only time he felt an intense longing for her was when she was dating others.

As Sean spoke, Lindsey oscillated between moments of panic and periods of fury, particularly in response to his declaration that he wanted a friendship and not a romance. She accused him of sending mixed messages and adamantly claimed that she could not imagine existing without a romantic relationship with him, as if he were responsible for the rawness of her need. Distraught and agitated, she paced with her arms wrapped around herself, alternately wailing in despair and screaming with rage. At other times she would sit, flashing Sean looks that could kill, and then, frustrated by his responses, override them, declaring her confidence in his love of her and assuring him that she understood that he himself might not recognize it.

In this brief interaction, we obtain important information about Sean and Lindsey's self-object functioning. Sean, although denying the wish for a romantic relationship, is as unable to separate as Lindsey is. He speaks of his need to know that he is always in her mind, a situation that was threatened by the separateness entailed in her dating. He also reports seeking contact with her when he becomes worried about her well-being. However, these contacts, unsolicited by Lindsey, seem prompted more by his experience of her growing separateness (he called her when she hadn't called him) and the resultant erosion of his sense of self in the face of the loss of his selfobject. His sense of self was contingent upon his relationship to Lindsey. He needed to know that she was there for him and always kept him in her mind. In this light, Sean's calls to Lindsey were not so much to reassure himself of her well-being, but to re-establish his own.

For Lindsey's part, she felt that her existence was contingent upon Sean's being in her life in a romantic way; although for years she had settled for less she could not imagine giving up the hope of a romantic relationship with him. To stave off nihilative anxiety (the threat of non-being), she denied the data of her own experience:

the platonic relationship of the last four years. She refused to let reality get in the way of what she wished to believe. Lindsey's fear is so compelling that she insists that Sean is mistaken about his lack of romantic feelings for her and that with her help he can discover the truth, thus reassuring herself.

If we understand the personality-disordered individual's terror of separateness, we begin to appreciate the power of the panicked effort to hold on to the mate to defend against separateness while simultaneously holding the mate responsible as a deficient self-object. The personality-disordered individual wishes to avoid simultaneously the terror of separation and the realization that much of his dissatisfaction is internally derived and cannot be resolved by another.

It is natural for living creatures to want to flee painful experience. Who among us elects to feel pain, terror, fragmentation, and disorganization? Unfortunately, there are no shortcuts. Substituting one relationship for another is not the answer. Indeed, every shortcut attempted, every effort to sustain image-inary (Lacan 1964, 1977) relationship, results only in the need to retrace our steps if we are to evolve rather than revolve, move on rather than repeat.

This is not to say that shortcuts do not have their purpose. Temporary diversions may be needed to make the journey bearable, but they do make it longer. Ultimately, it is only in facing our fears and managing to locate the other in ourselves, ourselves in the other, and both in reality, that we have the opportunity to lay claim to genuine relationship to self and other. This entails mourning our losses and realizing that the terror and catastrophic thinking associated with them stem from unresolved childhood anxieties that arose in relationship to another time, place, and person.

Although having all the feel of being real, these catastrophic reactions do not have to be real. As we live with our anxieties and discover our self, we come to understand that we are no longer 6 weeks of age—or 6 months, or 6 years—but adults who can draw upon considerable resources that were not available in childhood. We are no longer totally dependent, even though we may feel that way. As we gradually assimilate the losses and ameliorate the terror, we come to recognize our own substance and value: "I am-ness." We realize that our losses do not have to destroy us, and that there is a future beyond them, if we are willing to pursue it. This is by no means merely a cognitive process, but a cognitive-affective one including psyche and soma.

In recognizing our lack of omnipotence, our self-deceptions, our finiteness and limits, and the importance of the ability to think our thoughts and to feel our feelings, we feel more truly alive. We discover that life does not go as we originally envisioned or scripted it in our minds. Instead, it shapes us as we shape it, and we realize that the future is both created and discovered.

As we learn to manage these feelings, we come to recognize that we have choices aside from the all-or-nothing, ambivalence-aborting choices to end a relationship or to stay in it no matter what. There are the more complex considerations of confronting one's self as mirrored in the relationship and the equal challenge of recognizing the other as he or she is, rather than as we wish him or her to be.

We may choose to remain and grow in the relationship, recognizing the potential for change in ourselves and in the other, for being a "couple of beings" in progressive evolution, with the opportunity to have our "beingness" periodically validated. Or we may choose to end the relationship if we recognize a terrible stuckness that only re-creates the anxieties of past relationships and keeps us unfulfilled. The wisdom derived from the recognition of our limitations and those of the other allows us to cease struggling to win a battle that cannot be won. This recognition involves the awareness that the two individuals who comprise the relationship have developmental needs that are too different and so are destructive to each other, ensuring a disservice to both.

To the extent that there is a reintegration of the denied aspects of the self, both partners are free to continue the relationship or to move on, less reliant on ancient time-tested and time-failed solutions. Rather than re-solution after re-solution (concrete answers to complex problems) there is a moving toward *resolution*, perhaps never fully completed in the never-ending process of going-on-becoming.

6

Development as Diachronic and Synchronic

When we consider that personality disorder is a disorder of the self, characterized both by internal conflicts and deficits in development, we begin to understand the importance of the therapist's being able to relate across various levels of development and modes of organization in order to treat personality-disordered individuals and their relationships. An understanding of development also informs the therapist of what developmental milestones the therapist needs to help the spouses traverse, in order to function in more normal/neurotic ways.

Most of us have the illusion of a single self or unity of experience. However, it is more likely that we are comprised of various parts or facets that arise from relatively distinct modes of organization and ways of perceiving (Ogden 1989, Stern 1985, Sutherland 1989). In general, health is evident in the relative integration of these different modes of organization and resultant whole-object capacity for relationship, whereas illness is manifested in an ongoing lack of integration and resultant part-object relationship.

Traditionally, development has been viewed diachronically,

with progress and regress represented in movement up or down the rungs of a single developmental ladder (Figure 6–1). In this way of thinking, one organization of experience inaugurates and is superseded by the next. However, it appears likely that development is also synchronic (Ogden 1989, Stern 1985), each mode present in at least fledgling form from near the beginning of life and continuing throughout, each both defining and negating the others. Graphi-

Figure 6–1. Development as Diachronic

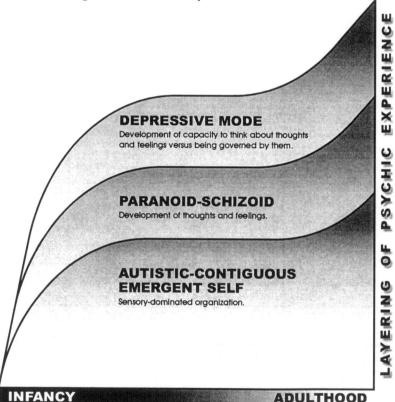

DEPRESSIVE MODE
Development of capacity to think about thoughts and feelings versus being governed by them.

PARANOID-SCHIZOID
Development of thoughts and feelings.

AUTISTIC-CONTIGUOUS EMERGENT SELF
Sensory-dominated organization.

LAYERING OF PSYCHIC EXPERIENCE

INFANCY   ADULTHOOD

cally, development as both diachronic and synchronic may be imagined as three intertwining strands, spiraling upward (Figure 6–2).

From a diachronic point of view, development proceeds from sensory experience (the autistic-contiguous mode); to the emergence of thoughts and feelings (the paranoid-schizoid mode); to the capacity to think thoughts and feel feelings, self-observation and self-reflection, and the ability to learn from experience (the depressive mode). From the synchronic point of view, development is not a once-and-for-all achievement but an ongoing interrelating of the

Figure 6–2. Development as Synchronic

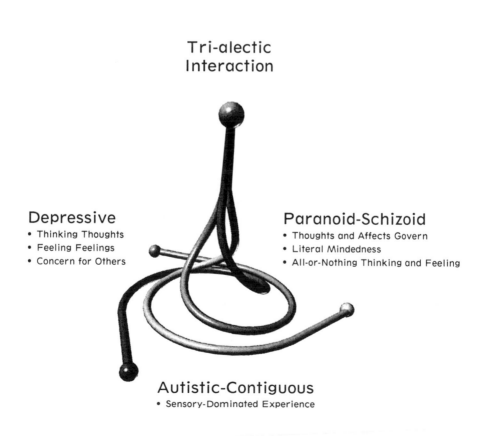

Tri-alectic
Interaction

Depressive
• Thinking Thoughts
• Feeling Feelings
• Concern for Others

Paranoid-Schizoid
• Thoughts and Affects Govern
• Literal Mindedness
• All-or-Nothing Thinking and Feeling

Autistic-Contiguous
• Sensory-Dominated Experience

different modes of experience throughout life, leading to a continual process of formation and reformation of the sense of self.

To better understand this process we might imagine the three modes of organization as different instruments in a three-piece jazz combo: the piano (keyboard), drums (percussion), and bass (strings). Each of these instruments has a developmental line of its own representing diachronic development from simple to complex. For example, in rudimentary form the keyboard could be on the level of a three-octave child's piano with little range, all the way to a multi-thousand-dollar electronic keyboard with myriad capacities. When we place each of these instruments together in the three-piece jazz combo, each enters dialectic interaction with the others, the sound of each defining, augmenting, and negating the sound of the others. For instance, at a particular moment in time, one instrument may play solo. The music then takes different shapes as the other instruments are brought into play. The jazz combo is capable of tremendous complexity and fluidity, moving at will from one organization of sound to another as well as weaving the distinct sounds together in an infinite number of ways. A breadth and depth of music is thus created, far beyond the possibility of any single instrument.

This triadic interplay is illustrated in Figure 6–3, each corner of the triangle representing a single mode of organization and the encircled area within representing the mutually enriching interchange among the modes. Illness is indicated when one mode chronically predominates to the relative exclusion of the others, thus limiting development and narrowing the ways of organizing and perceiving. Personality disorder is considered to reside between the autistic-contiguous and paranoid-schizoid modes with a relative absence of the depressive mode (Figure 6–4).

Some people may function highly in one area of life, such as career, playing intellectual and cognitive notes well, but be markedly unsuccessful in another, such as personal life, lacking or being out of tune with the keys that require more affective attunement: the stereotypic ruthless businessman. Conversely, other individuals may be affectively attuned and nurturing, but lack the capacity to make

**Figure 6–3. The Three Modes of Organization in
Mutually Enriching Relationship**

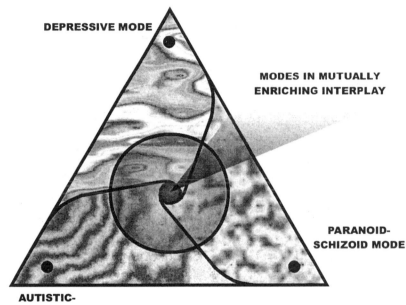

their way in areas requiring reason or logic: the stereotypic starving artist.

When one mode of organization is relied upon to the relative exclusion of the others, the capacity to maintain perspective and to learn from experience is impeded. The capacity to think becomes childlike (literal and concrete) and the individual is easily overwhelmed by the complexity of reality. This is a central reason personality-disordered individuals are infamous for their refractoriness to treatment efforts and their inability to learn from experience. Consequently, it is the task of therapy to foster the development of each mode of organization and the relationship among them so that

Figure 6–4. Collapse of Function in the Borderline Personality

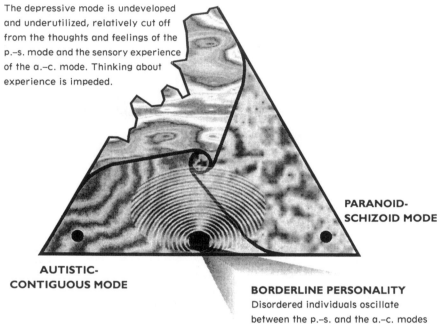

DEPRESSIVE MODE
The depressive mode is undeveloped and underutilized, relatively cut off from the thoughts and feelings of the p.–s. mode and the sensory experience of the a.–c. mode. Thinking about experience is impeded.

PARANOID-SCHIZOID MODE

AUTISTIC-CONTIGUOUS MODE

BORDERLINE PERSONALITY
Disordered individuals oscillate between the p.–s. and the a.–c. modes of organization.

the patient can learn and grow from experience rather than having to repeat the same experience time and again. To this end, the next three chapters will examine in more detail the three modes of organization, each of which involves a particular way of perceiving and relating manifested in the quality of symbolization (thinking), the leading anxiety, the primary defense, and the quality of relationship to self and other.

7

The Autistic-Contiguous Mode

Vignette: The Beautiful Woman Who "Knew" She Was Ugly

Lanz and Kayla had been married for four years. Both were in individual therapy: Kayla for panic attacks without rhyme or reason that led to emergency room visits and occasional psychiatric hospitalizations, and Lanz for schizoid personality disorder with obsessive and passive-aggressive features. For Kayla, the worst part of her panic attacks was the experience that she was losing her mind. Kayla initiated marital therapy because she wanted to have a baby but wasn't sure the marriage would last, and both she and Lanz were unhappy with their sexual relationship.

What struck me most about this couple was that Kayla, although an attractive woman, "knew" herself to be ugly. In addition, she experienced sudden rage and acute feelings of self-disgust and self-repulsion whenever she attempted sexual relations. She had been treated in individual and group therapy for survivors of incest, even though she had no recall of incestuous experiences and did not feel like that explanation fit. Her inability to fully accept this explanation was felt to be unconscious resistance on the part of her therapists. Another interesting aspect of work with this couple was the primacy of their sensory mode of relating, which served multiple complex functions, from self-organization to defense to self-expression. To begin with, they were both artists, that is, engaged in sensory-oriented occupations and means of expression.

Kayla was warm and engaging but had difficulty making sense of experience and thus was highly reactive. Lanz was reserved and held himself rigidly. Though I liked them both, I felt unable to enter into substantial relationship with either, as each seemed to skate upon the surface of human relationship.

Lanz related to Kayla as he had to his mother. Irresponsible and disorganized, he left Kayla to deal with external reality demands. She complained of feeling like a mother to him, weighted with responsibility. As with his mother, Lanz often "forgot" what he was told, and, like his mother, Kayla was often enraged with him. Paradoxically, it was at these times that Lanz was most accessible, his thoughts, feelings, and ability to express them coming together.

Lanz's artwork was incredibly obsessive. It consisted primarily of figures comprised of thousands of minuscule lines, painstakingly drawn to create the desired image. One drawing was of a red-eyed green demon so stunning in its vividness that it appeared to leap from the page. It seemed to me that anyone who could author such a work knew something about envy, jealousy, and rage. Lanz concurred and acknowledged that he often communicated his understandings in visual ways, but was unable to identify these traits within himself. He also spoke of how he could lose himself in the experience of drawing the countless lines he used to create his images. He lost all track of time and awareness of anything happening outside of this tightly regulating sensory experience.

Kayla also expressed herself in her art. In an impressionistic style, she used swirls of color to make near-formless patterns that evoked various feelings in the viewer. One such painting, of, in her words, "vagina-like shapes" that were pocked with black and red ulcers and oozing sores, revealed the intensity of her self-revulsion; other paintings expressed profound chaos and threat.

Kayla's biological father was a violent man who left the family when she was 6. She remembers the air of violence and her fear, although her mother insisted that everything was fine. I imagined that her panic attacks related to this time. I also wondered if perhaps her father had sexually abused her, given the rage and self-repulsion she experienced whenever genital touch was involved. At the same time, given Kayla's own sense that this explanation did not "feel right," I suspended coming to any position on this topic.

Early in treatment, as we explored the problems in their sexual relationship, Kayla scoffed at my use of the term "lovemaking." For her, sex was sex, a biological function equivalent to going to the bathroom. Lanz approached sex in much the same way. There was little foreplay and no romance. This was fine with Kayla, who, disgusted and repulsed with herself, was interested in "getting it over with as soon as possible." As for Lanz, he could not imagine any other quality of connection. He felt himself to be a burden and lucky that Kayla was willing to engage in sex at all. Together they created a hard-skinned, mechanized, cold, and impersonal sexual relatedness, without warmth or personal meaning. I wondered what it communicated and re-created. For Lanz it was an important aspect of his relationship to his mother. His father had left when he was 3, and his mother, overwhelmed by the fears and responsibilities of single parenthood, had had little time for emotional connection. In addition, when she returned home exhausted after work, she placed a premium on quiet and discouraged contact with Lanz. This early experience seemed to be captured, relived, and conveyed in the hard-versus-soft and cold-versus-warm essence of his sexual relationship with Kayla. He felt his needs a burden to Kayla as he had felt himself a burden to his mother. In addition, the only time he had any semblance of emotional interaction with his mother was when she became enraged at him for "forgetting" to do his chores. Again, Lanz had reconstructed a similar means of contact with his enraging irresponsibility with Kayla.

In exploring Kayla's history we discovered nothing that would account for the feelings of self-disgust and self-repulsion, or her mechanization of sexual contact. To the contrary, she remembered her mother frequently telling her that she was beautiful. I was puzzled. I wondered how, accepting Kayla's depiction of her childhood and the fact that there was no sexual abuse, the infant and child Kayla could be held lovingly in her mother's arns and look into her mother's loving eyes but not take in a beautiful reflection, if that reflection were there.

Eighteen months into treatment, I encountered Kayla as she was waiting for her individual therapist. She was holding her newborn daughter Christiana. I noticed an older woman sitting next to her. Kayla warmly returned my greeting and the woman smiled stiffly. Although she smiled, I felt strangely uncomfortable. Her smile was painted on and she seemed on edge, sitting rigidly upright, literally on the edge of the chair. She conveyed the brittle and impermeable quality of a porcelain shell. I wondered if she were Kayla's mother, but Kayla did not introduce us. As I continued on my way, I thought that perhaps they were strangers simply joined together in admiring Christiana. Nonetheless, my sense of the woman stayed with me.

The next session, Kayla confirmed that the woman was her mother. After I divulged my impressions, Kayla related, for the first time, that her mother was a physically uncomfortable person and did not like to be touched. She realized, to her own surprise, that she had no memory of ever being hugged or kissed by her mother. Although she did remember initiating hugs in early adolescence, she stopped as she invariably felt her mother stiffen and pull away. Kayla blurted out, "She recoiled, as if repulsed by me." Suddenly, she realized that she was describing her experience of herself. As we spoke further, Kayla uneasily noted that she was not comfortable leaving Christiana with her mother. She explained that her mother held Christiana stiffly away from her body. Moreover, she would hurriedly leave the room whenever toileting and diapering were required.

It appeared that Kayla's self-disgust and repulsion were related to her sensory experience in the mother–infant unity and beyond. The experience of sensory rigidity and repulsed touch would surely be amplified in the holding, diapering, and genital cleaning of infancy. Such powerful sensory experiences would certainly contradict her mother's oft-spoken words of Kayla's beauty, just as Kayla's lived experience of her father's violent rages would repudiate her mother's reassurance that everything was fine.

In the ensuing months of exploration, this hypothesis was confirmed as Kayla was gradually able to experience a more stable and pleasurable sexual relationship with Lanz. In part, these gains were attributable to her growing differentiation of her self-experience in the sexual relationship from her mother's touch in the mother–infant unity. Lanz also contributed in that he made continuing progress in identifying and risking the expression of his feelings. However, much of Kayla's progress was attributable to the lived experience of core connection and attunement she encountered in the direct sensory experience of the mother–infant unity she had established with Christiana. Kayla unabashedly enjoyed holding and caring for Christiana and one day remarked, "This feels so wonderful. It makes me wonder if a sexual relationship could also be beautiful. If it can be, I want that for myself."

The way these spouses used sensory experience to manage their anxieties was further evident as the therapy evolved. For example, when their sexual relationship became a more connected love-making, Lanz would afterwards withdraw for hours, infuriating Kayla, who felt rejected. As this situation was explored it became apparent that Lanz returned to his obsessive and solitary artwork to defend himself against the feeling of agonizing separation that followed their sexual union. Learning to emotionally negotiate the experience of alternating togetherness and agonizing separateness was another developmental milestone. Their progress was also evident in Kayla's unselfconsciously beginning to use the expression "lovemaking" and an increase of playfulness in therapy sessions and in their sexual relationship. For example, Kayla humorously reported surprising Lanz with the wearing of a cowboy hat during one episode of "lovemaking."

THE SENSORY FLOOR OF EXPERIENCE

All of development emerges from a sensory base. Through sucking, touching, hearing, seeing, and smelling we orient ourselves in the world. Sensory experience provides the early sense of self and becomes both a core aspect of identity, comprising the floor of the sense of self (McDougall 1989, Ogden 1989, Stern 1985), *and* our first memories. It is to this sensory *sense* of self and other that we may unconsciously seek to return in adult relationships. It does not matter how pleasant or toxic this early sensory experience was or is; like salmon fighting their way upstream, the human animal strives to find its way home to the feel of the familiar and the familial. Quite literally, we are grounded in the familiar feel of the "hold" that early others had on us.

The importance of sensory experience to object choice is evident in the following quotes. A wife reports, "When I first met my husband it wasn't anything like love at first sight. What stood out for me was the way he smelled. It was a familiar smell, and I knew right away that he could be family." A husband remarks, "It was the sound of her voice, her smell, and the way she moved." A woman asserts, "It was the soft look in his eyes; he never glares at me." Her husband responds, "I love her gentle smile that is always there for me." The color of his wife's hair was the magnet of another husband's attraction, as the "crinkling of his eyes when he smiles and his habit of putting his hand over his face when embarrassed" was hers.

The infant's relationship to its mother exists before the concept of self or (m)other. The infant has no overarching self-organization or self-awareness. His is an emergent self—a self in process, but not yet formed. With no formal sense of self or overarching self-organization, the infant's "is-ness" is of the sensation of the moment. He does not observe or reflect upon his sensation; he *is* sensation (Stern 1985).

The importance of the infant's sensory experience is instinctively known by the good-enough mother. She spends the majority of her time regulating the infant's sensory state (Stern 1985): feeding, diapering, holding, hugging, rocking, and swaddling. On the physical plane, the mother is a "transformational object" (Bollas 1987), constantly transforming the infant's "is-ness," from one thing to another: from empty to full; from tense to relaxed; from wet to dry; from instinctually driven, primal, and raw to calm. Many individuals unconsciously spend their lives searching for a transformational object and attempt to re-create the feel of the early mother–infant relationship. Even if toxic or uncomfortable, the feel is pursued for it maintains the sensory platform of the sense of self and other that defends against the terror of non-being, nihilistic anxiety. For this reason, the infant exposed to grossly intermittent attunement and responsiveness may become the adult in love with inexorable tension and tribulation followed by unpredictable release. Further, transformational object relationships are manifested in self-relationship, that is, in how we treat ourselves and in the lives we create.

Vignette: Lateness as a Self-Organizing Experience

Donna is never on time, forever creating interpersonal conflict, pressurizing herself, and feeling overwhelmed. Arriving late for her session, breathless and harried, she exclaims, "Something is always coming up to get in the way [of being on time]." Unconsciously, she re-creates the sensory experience of childhood. Her mother suffered from bipolar disorder and was given to frequent and unpredictable rages, while her father worked long hours and was away from home. Donna was always kept waiting by her parents; for example, dinner was never regularly scheduled and she was never picked up on time from school. She reports, "I'd wait from half an hour to two hours. I never knew how long it would be. I'd get anxious and tense, angry and sad. Cars would appear and I would get excited. Then they would disappear with other kids in them. It was embarrassing to be the last kid left. Then, my father or mother would arrive, but I would lose them again as each was absorbed in their concerns and not with me."

Whereas in childhood Donna was kept waiting, in adulthood

she keeps others waiting. She cannot be on time. Though emotionally costly and physically uncomfortable, her chaotic existence
provides her with a sense of continuity and organization. "I can't
help myself. I don't feel myself if I'm on time. It's like a drug. Like
I'm in a love–hate relationship with the tension of being late, of
feeling harried, of the uncertain reception that awaits me. I don't
know what I would do with myself if I were on time."

    In adulthood, sensory experience remains the platform to the
sense of self and comprises the bedrock of marital relationships. For
example, spouses may seek an evening together, from dinner to
dance to lovemaking, in which the tension and relative disconnection of a stressful work week is transformed into a fulfilling hold and
relaxation as they re-engage with one another. By the same token, as
we saw in the relationship of Lanz and Kayla, the unconscious
pursuit of early toxic or unpleasant sensory experience is the
foundation upon which the more formal psychodynamic structures
of the spouses may rest.

THE AUTISTIC-CONTIGUOUS MODE OF ORGANIZATION
AND WAY OF PERCEIVING

The designation "autistic-contiguous" first refers to the form of
defense—autistic—that is a preverbal and nonreflective sensory-
dominated mode of perception, and second to the mode of relatedness—contiguous—wherein cohesion or boundedness, the first
requirement of self-organization, arises from the juxtaposition of
skin upon another surface (Ogden 1989, Tustin 1984). Subsequently, the child, as she sorts through the relative variance and
invariance of sensory experience, comes to recognize an inside,
proximal sense of "me" (relatively invariant sensory experience)
and an outside, distal sense of "not-me" (relatively variant sensory
experience).

    The emergent self is dependent upon the early holding environ-
ment for protection from impingement (Winnicott 1958b, 1962a,
1965). It is in the state of going-on-being that the inherent organiz-

ing tendency of the self has the opportunity to sort through the relative variance and invariance of sensory experience, leading to an internally derived organization of self. Conversely, impingement is an environmental demand that prompts reactivity from the child and results in destruction of the state of going-on-being and a "discontinuity in the thread of the self," Winnicott's definition of trauma (1956, p. 303). Impingement that is too intense, too frequent, or too prolonged disturbs development (Winnicott 1957). Both abuse and neglect are impinging. The former forces the child to react to outside stimuli, while the latter causes the child to react to unmet instinctual needs. Caregiving may be plotted along a continuum from empathic parenting to abuse, neglect, and infanticide. Abuse overwhelms the child with "too much, too much," while neglect overwhelms with "too little, too little" (Shengold 1989).

We are all exposed to impingement and frustration arising from temporary misattunements in the mother–infant unity. Perhaps this is why most of us can relate to abuse and neglect. However, we often have greater difficulty fully appreciating how chronic abuse and neglect can radically affect the capacity to enter a relaxed state of going-on-being, or a secure and deepening feeling of going-on-being with another or with one's self.

Vignette: Falling into the Eyes of the Other

Tom Ericson sought me out for individual therapy. He explained that he and his wife had been in marital therapy on and off for approximately nine years of a twelve-year marriage. During his first session, he sardonically reported "great intellectual insights, but no change," thus suggesting a predominance of thinking over feeling or sensation.

Long before his marriage, Tom had discovered that he was unable to have intercourse with any woman that he loved. At the thought of intercourse with these women, he felt terror. Conversely, when he did not feel romantic love, sex was not a problem.

Tom felt that his marital problems began in earnest when his wife complained that "something was missing" when they made love. She wanted a "soulmate," to "hold hands," and for him to "look deeply into her eyes." He commented, "I can't do that. It terrifies me. It's like falling forever, and if I don't stop there will be no me."

The experience of losing oneself in the eyes of the other is of the autistic-contiguous mode. In the midst of such an experience, there is no experience of an "I" that is looking, or that it is looking into an "eye," or that it is the eye of an "other" (Stern 1985). There is just a bottomless pool, no "I," no "eye," and no "other." If the individual has a secure sense of self, this temporary loss of self is romantic and enjoyable, leading to a momentary sense of lightness and oneness or merger. However, for Tom, his very being was threatened, suggesting a deficiency in the state of going-on-being of the mother–infant unity.

Tom's difficulty is better understood in light of his childhood history. At the time of his birth, his father was suffering from a life-threatening heart condition. Tom's mother, a depressed woman, was more depressed and anxious than usual in the face of her husband's illness in conjunction with postpartum depression. It had to have been an overwhelming time for her. At 3 months of age, Tom was given into the care of his maternal grandmother, "not a particularly warm or caring person," so that his mother could devote her time to her husband. At 1 year of age, after his father's condition had stabilized, Tom was returned to the care of his mother. However, family life continued to be organized by his father's illness. Tom and his sister were admonished not to make any noise. Moreover, Tom noted a family value to the effect that "Ericsons never have any problems and are always upbeat and happy." Consequently, he felt puzzled awe when twenty-five years later his father, dying, told him, "Every day for the last twenty-five years, I've been afraid of dying. Now it's here." Never before had anyone spoken of his father's illness and the underlying fear.

Typically upbeat, Tom was ready with humorous editorial comments about his condition. However, he described with all seriousness his feeling that his marriage was in jeopardy, and that he was not sure he cared. In addition, he reported, "I feel like I'm holding myself back and that I'm not becoming who I can be."

Given Tom's symptoms and his history, it is possible to draw sensory connections between the two. Imagine Tom's psychological situation from birth to 3 months, held in the low-vitality field of a depressed mother and a gravely ill father. His mother's capacity to attend to infant Tom was impeded. In addition, his father was unable to support the mother–infant unity, threatening it instead with his own needful state and potential desertion through death. The infant Tom would have experienced this sense of anxiety and depletion, and when he looked into his mother's eyes would have seen exhaustion, anxiety, and depression in place of his own gleam and to the relative exclusion of his own reflection.

When baby Tom was 3 months old, he was given into the care of his "not particularly warm or attentive" grandmother. Tom was dropped from the mother–infant unity. His mother's eyes, the arms that held, and the voice that soothed abruptly disappeared. In the ensuing nine months, they would appear, disappear, and reappear as she visited Tom each day. The net effect was an inability to form a secure attachment, to relax into a secure hold. At 1 year of age Tom was returned to his mother, but the time of the mother–infant unity had passed. His sense of attachment was precarious and made more insecure by the ever-present, but unacknowledged, pall of death. He was admonished to be quiet so as not to disturb his father. In addition, the fact that Tom was awestruck when his father spoke of his years of fear indicated how fully Tom had internalized the family-delineated identity of "never having any problems" and of "everything always being all right." His father had put into words Tom's own long-held and unacknowledged fear.

Tom's difficulties with needfulness, being a "soul mate," and becoming one (intercourse) with women for whom he feels romantic love are now more understandable. His early sensory experience was not only of recurrent loss and instability, but of literally losing himself in the eyes of his mother. When he looked into her eyes he either didn't see himself there or saw himself as depleting and burdensome, perhaps even lethally so. Consequently, his capacity for a secure, arms-around, loving experience was contaminated. In addition, needfulness was frowned upon and the identification and spontaneous expression of feelings were felt to be dangerous. For example, the noise of children playing could be bad for his father. He felt held back because he held himself back. Consequently, he was unable to identify and pursue his own needs and unable to become (going-on-becoming) who he could be. Divorced from his own feelings, he held himself rigidly against in-depth attachment and the loss of self it forewarned.

The sensory pull of the familial and the familiar is strong. As Tom's needs came out as a result of therapy, he would experience something similar to the feeling of falling forever. He would become disorganized and panicky. On one occasion he anxiously reported, "It's crazy. I was shaving and looked at myself in the mirror. Suddenly, I was filled with needs. I wrote them down immediately so I wouldn't forget. Then I became dizzy and had to lie down. I felt angry, anxious, and nauseous, all at the same time. I didn't know what was happening to me." Was the fact that Tom had this experience in front of the mirror coincidental? Or did he look into his own eyes and see the "angry, anxious, and nauseous" look of his mother?

LEVEL OF SYMBOLIZATION
(CAPACITY TO THINK ABSTRACTLY)

The autistic-contiguous position is a presymbolic, nonreflective state of being. "Cognitions, actions, and perceptions, as such, do not exist. All experience becomes recast as patterned constellations of all the infant's basic subjective elements combined" (Stern 1985, p. 67). In that there is no organized sense of self, there is as yet no "me" to have thoughts or feelings—much less an executive function, an "I," to reflect upon them. Consequently, the autistic-contiguous mode is presymbolic. There is no "me" to have thoughts and feelings and no "I" to think about them.

One consequence is that words in this mode of organization

have no meaning, they don't symbolize anything; there is only direct experience. Meaning is in the direct experience of rhythm, tone, pitch, and body language of the speaker—in the melody, not the lyrics. The symbolic value of words comes rather late in psychic development. Even then, words only refer to an experience; they do not convey the experience directly. The way words are said renders much of their meaning. Such is the difference between the excited and panicked yelling of "Fire in the theater!" which is felt as a palpable force, versus the discussion two days later, over a cup of coffee, that there had been a "fire in the theater."

We are moved in similar ways by the varying use of colors, shapes, forms, and textures found in paintings and by the kinesthetic energies and fluidly mutating shapes and images of dancers on the stage. Aromas and textures are often most evocative. These sensory means of expression and of experiencing appeal and speak to us in ways that are both before and beyond that found in the literal meaning of words themselves.

Both Lanz and Kayla communicated their experience directly both in their artwork and in their sexual interaction. Lanz's artwork was tightly bounded and bounding and the demon he drew so malevolent and lifelike that it inspired terror, as it was so clearly motivated by envy, greed, and rage. So it was that Lanz himself felt his needs as burdensome and, as also evidenced in his artwork, tried to hold them in through obsessive sensory activity. In addition, he seemed capable of more genuine connection only in and immediately after the throes of rage-filled fights between him and Kayla that were so sensorially reminiscent of those between him and his mother. Initially, none of these things could be thought about or talked about: the only connection and communication was in direct experience.

The same was true of Kayla. Although she was able to use the words *disgust* and *repulsion*, the only way she could really convey their meaning to her was through the direct sensory experience of her artwork. This was often formless, reflecting a lack of internal structures, and when form was most apparent, it was in disease-ridden vaginalike shapes that evoked repulsion and disgust. Indeed, it was only in my direct sensory experience of her mother and my putting my experience into words that Kayla was able to identify and articulate her own experience.

THE IMPORTANCE OF LANGUAGE

Vignette: The Theater of the Body

Symbols (words, images, sign language, dance movements, and pictures) allow us to represent experience so that it can be thought about. Jennifer was unable to relate well on this level. For example, she responded, "I'm fine" when asked, "How are you?" but her body betrayed her words, which seemed more in the service of keeping me away than in communicating with me. She was in continual movement, her limbs seeming to have a life of their own. She began to lift an arm and then interrupted the movement, her arm suddenly suspended in air. She then placed her hands beneath the pillow on her lap, moving them again before they could nestle there. Each movement was interrupted by the next. If her arms settled, her legs began to move; if she lifted a foot to rest it upon a chair, it too became frozen in air, then returned to its original position. She appeared like a marionette, pulled by invisible strings held by an anxiety-ridden puppeteer. I asked, "Are you anxious?" Some time later, she responded, "No, restless." She repeatedly tried to speak, but her mind and tongue, like the other parts of her body, could not fully commit. After much difficulty, she noted, "My mind is empty," one thought being chased away by the next before any could settle in. Later she said, "I feel like I'm jumping out of my skin."

While she spoke physically, I spoke verbally, my voice slow and calm, as I empathized with her tortured state. My remarks came from how her movements moved me, how I imagined I would be feeling if I were she. I asked questions or made comments as thoughts and associations arose in my mind, without expectation that she answer. She told me that the sound of my voice tethered her to the world.

Eventually I commented, "When experience cannot be put into words, it becomes inscribed in the body (McDougall 1989). Your mind is empty, and your body is overflowing. I think that whatever you're struggling with would be better put into words and into your mind, so that we might make sense of it, rather than leave it in your body, where it only returns." For whatever reason, Jennifer was able to grasp these words and began a long and twisted journey of recounting bits and pieces of memories and images of sexual abuse. She was often filled with the terror and sensations of physical invasion. "I feel like things are inside of me." In start-and-stop fashion, much like her movements, we were gradually able to talk of her sensory experiences, rather than leaving their only channel of remembrance and communication within her body. It became apparent that her strange movements were in defense against the sensation of things being inserted in her. She invariably questioned the validity of her sensations as memories, feeling that if abused she would hate her parents for not protecting her. However, she also felt that if she did not acknowledge the abuse, she would continue to feel crazy and disgusting for having "put these sensations in my own mind."

Jennifer told the tale of abuse in sensory fashion, as a living experience, unable to formulate the thoughts or words to symbolize and think about it. Over time, as she learned to identify and put her experience into words (symbolize) she was able to think about it, which allowed her to manage her experience rather than be managed by it. Her body movements, once her only means of expression, became a relatively minor part of her treatment experience.

THE LEADING ANXIETY

The leading anxiety of the autistic-contiguous mode is of the breakdown of sensory organization, manifested in nameless or formless dread. Symptoms include the terror of disintegrating or dissolving; decaying; falling in endless, shapeless space; or losing the capacity to contain bodily fluids (Ogden 1989). When the rhythm or patterns of daily sensory-motor experience are disrupted, anxieties arise. In infancy and childhood, such disruptions may become a source of "unbearable awareness of bodily separateness [that results] in an agony of consciousness" (Tustin 1986, p. 43). Whereas for most of us impingement or neglect has been short-lived, for others it has been the cardinal reality. The resultant anxiety is comparable to that of being indefinitely immersed in the watery darkness and stillness of a sensory deprivation tank, all alone.

DEFENSES

Autistic-contiguous defenses are devoted to the self-generated continuity of sensory experience to maintain the sensory cohesion upon which the "integrity of the self rests" (Ogden 1989, p. 70). They include rhythmic rocking, head banging, thumb sucking, self-mutilation, the rituals of bulimia and anorexia, compulsive masturbation, and drug intoxication. They are manifested in unrelenting eye contact or unending chatter, telephoning the therapist to hear her voice, or driving by her office just to see it. They are evident in obsessive imaginings of symmetrical geometric designs; in ruminating upon a series of numbers; and in driving a car for hours on end, the rhythmic sound of the engine and the thrum of the tires on the highway calming and giving order to one's self (Ogden 1989). They may also be witnessed in self-mutilative behaviors. In more normative form they are evidenced in the self-touching in which we all engage endlessly, such as the stroking or scratching of our skin, and in playing the same tune over and over again in our mind.

Autistic shapes, such as pillows, teddy bears, and blankets, provide a sense of security, relaxation, warmth, and affection (Meltzer et al. 1975, Ogden 1989). Hard and angular autistic objects such as fingernails or keys pressed into the palm of the hand, provide a feeling of hardness with which the individual may "adhesively identify" (Ogden 1989, p. 37), creating the illusion of body armor to defend against the fear of intrusion or invasion.

Autistic defenses are omnipotent. They are absolutely and reliably present. They are also tyrannical, in that the patient is dependent on the perfect recreation of the sensory experience (Ogden 1989) to protect against the terror of vulnerability. About cigarette smoking one friend says, "It's hard to give up. It's like saying goodbye to twenty friends that I can call on at any time." Another friend refers to alcohol as "a warm soothing introject" upon which he can rely.

Pathological autism is a form of sensory experience that only leads back to itself. It aims at the elimination of the unknown and the unpredictable, substituting for relationship "with inevitably imperfect and not entirely predictable human beings" (Ogden 1989, p. 59). When excessively relied upon, it results in psychological deadness and a paralysis in the ability to think or feel.

Part of Lanz's way of making art performed autistic defensive functions. His obsessive use of thousands of minuscule lines to produce his art led reliably to a perfect re-creation of his sensory experience. The repetitious drawing of thousands of lines created a sensory experience that only led back upon itself, effectively encapsulating him and blocking out the rest of reality.

Similar autistic functions are what make computer games like Tetris and Solitaire so attractive. In Tetris, for example, the player becomes engaged in repetitive physical movements and perceptions. Reality becomes narrowed to the column of falling shapes that are manipulated to fit together and the tensions that absorb the individual, thus providing a tiny organizable world that is free of other people and far simpler than complex reality itself.

QUALITY OF RELATIONSHIP TO SELF AND OTHER

In the autistic-contiguous mode, there is no sense of self or other. Self and object relations, if we are to use such terms, are limited to the "mutually transforming interplay of (nascent) self and object" (Ogden 1989, p. 51). This is "not a relationship between subjects, nor between objects. Rather, it is a relationship of shape to the feeling of enclosure, of beat to the feeling of rhythm, of hardness to the feeling of edgedness. Sequences, symmetries, periodicity, skin-to-skin 'molding' are all examples of contiguities that are the ingredients out of which the beginnings of rudimentary self-experience arise" (Ogden 1989, p. 32).

Personality-disordered couples reproduce their early sensory impressions in the prevalent climate or atmosphere of the relationship. Some couples are warm and suffocating; others are cold and distant. Some elicit protective feelings; others dread, and others rage. The prevailing climate of the couple captures the atmosphere of the early object relations of each spouse. The climate is conveyed through how the spouses look (or do not look) at each other, their body postures (rigid or relaxed), voice pitch and tone (calm and soothing or tearing and attacking), the intensity or absence of their emotions, and their kinesthetic energy (trying not to disturb a single molecule of air in the room or tornadic, mindlessly compressing the space to feel and think in order not to feel or think). The climate of the couple is created not only by what is present, but also by what is absent. The latter is sometimes discovered in the therapist's asking herself, "What is wrong with this picture? What is irregular in the couple's presentation or between what the spouses seem to be feeling and what I am feeling?"

RELEVANCE TO CLINICAL WORK

Personality disorder is a disorder of the self. Consequently, treatment must, at least initially, focus on the development of the self and not on conflict resolution, which requires a relatively differentiated sense of self and other. The emergent self requires time and space for experience in order to develop. Consequently, the focus of treatment is on the creation of a holding environment that is conducive to development. Foremost, this entails providing each spouse with relative freedom from impingement, valuing being versus reacting. The therapist supports room for experience, delving more deeply into and elaborating upon the experience (internal dialogues, thoughts, feelings, sensations) of each spouse. This is accomplished by the therapist's intervening between the spouses when impingement occurs and then entering into separate dyadic interactions with each spouse to create space for the experience of each.

The recently popular three-dimensional illusion pictures help illustrate how the self emerges. These computer-generated 3-D pictures first seem to be comprised only of points and splotches of color. Knowing how to look at the picture is the key to discovering its underlying structure. The instructions advise the viewer to find a quiet place and then, rather than focusing upon the surface (manifest content) of the picture, to "look through it" without any attempt to force organization upon the picture (projection, impingement, ambition, premature interpretation, prejudgment). Upon meeting these conditions, the viewer enters a state of going-on-being-with the picture and eventually the natural organizing tendency of the self begins to take hold of the three-dimensional organization inherent in the picture itself. Just as in therapy, no one can say when this will occur; however, one thing is certain: If the viewer should attempt to force organization upon the picture, he will be locked in surface relationship to it and the three-dimensionality embedded in the picture will not emerge.

This process is analogous to the development of the self in the clinical situation. Given the state of going-on-being, the patient's self—comprised of bits, pieces, and fragments of perception—gradually coalesces into threads of experience and emergent self-organization (going-on-becoming). Under these conditions, the self emerges in a "now you see it and now you don't" manner. With each sighting of the self, the next sighting becomes easier.

When spouses are accustomed to and forever on the alert for impingement, real or imagined, it is difficult for them to relax and feel safe. Consequently, this process may take considerable time and patience. However, if the patient or therapist should attempt to force organization or to hurry things along, as in jumping from problem to solution without regard for the underlying process, the development of the self will remain impeded. When the problem is centered in being, the solution does not lie in doing.

Paradoxically, as internal experience—sensations, thoughts, and feelings—emerges into awareness the patient often feels worse. The growing awareness of unmet needs and the emerging memory of their rejection threaten psychic equilibrium. The patient may complain of "going crazy" or have dizzy spells (as in the case of Tom Ericson), which are related to the inevitable disorganization experienced in the transition from false-self organization to internally emergent self-relations.

For the therapy itself not to be impinging it is the patient who must set the pace of treatment. The therapist's failure to be empathically attuned to the spouses' pace re-creates their pathologic relationships of impingement and neglect. This occurs whenever the therapist hurries along to call progress a "cure."

The spouses' sense that the therapist is with them and, therefore, that they can be with the therapist, is founded in their experience of the therapist's empathic attunement and responsiveness. Although putting the spouses' experience into words so that it can be thought about is crucial, the therapist's empathic attunement is most often conveyed in sensory and affective connections. In fact, without these it is hard to imagine the therapist's understanding being anything more than intellectual. No matter how accurate the therapist's interpretations, if he does not feel the patient, the patient will not feel him. If the therapist relates only intellectually, the patient will feel dropped and alienated, instead of held or attached.

The power and importance of the capacity to "be with" in the autistic-contiguous mode is illustrated by an occurrence in my own life. I was walking with a friend, Roger Lewin, M.D., at a time when I was struggling with a personal loss. Looking for words to convey my feeling, I described it as one of "fundamental despair," frustrated that the words did not adequately capture or convey my experience. Roger, quiet for a time, responded, "It doesn't sound 'fun' . . . and it doesn't sound 'mental.' . . . It's just da." It was the sound "da" that resonated with my experience, encompassing my feeling of confusion and the wordlessness of my situation. The sound "da" conveyed to me Roger's empathic understanding of my experience. I felt recognized, less alone, and, consequently, less despairing. Someone understood.

ON THE DEVELOPMENT OF PERSONAL MEANING

Through sensory relationship, the infant expresses herself and the mother meets her gestures (reaching, crying, and smiling), thereby imbuing them with meaning (Winnicott 1960a). For example, the infant gives a hungry cry and suddenly finds herself nestled in her mother's arms, enjoying a good feed. In like fashion, the therapist's attunement and responsiveness help the individual transform an amorphous experience into one that can be identified and thought about. For example, the therapist comments, "You seem sad," tone and facial expression congruent with his feel for the wife's experience. The wife responds, "I guess I am." The therapist's empathic identification of the wife's experience is reflected back to the wife in the totality of his response, not just in his words. It is only by the therapist's mirroring of the wife's experience that she is able to identify it for herself.

The therapist's empathic attunement and responsiveness are transmitted across all the modes of organization (including sensory) and form the foundation of the transformational experience of therapy. Attunement requires that the therapist stand with one foot where the patient stands. Responsiveness requires that the therapist stand with the other foot in his own experiential space, sorting through his identification with the patient. The therapist shifts his weight from one foot to the other in the evolving relationship of therapy.

The following vignette, again from my personal experience, illustrates how sensory responsiveness to the patient's gestures helps the patient understand his experience. A friend asked me for a referral to a therapist. I took this responsibility seriously and after much thought settled on an esteemed senior psychiatrist, Dr.

Jerome Styrt. I knew him to be sound, reliable, and above all a human being. I phoned, prepared to speak to the omnipresent answering machine when, to my surprise, he answered in person. Discombobulated and still in "message mode," I launched immediately into a description of some of the issues with which my friend was grappling. When I paused, Dr. Styrt responded, "Charlie, I'm very sorry; I don't have time available, and I don't expect any in the near future."

I suddenly felt paralyzed in thought and feeling, and vaguely guilty. I had not made space for Dr. Styrt and had said too much about my friend before ascertaining Dr. Styrt's availability. I struggled to collect my thoughts. After an awkward silence, Dr. Styrt uttered the sound "umph." At that instant, I realized I was either breathing shallowly or not at all, and that my experience was of the wind having been knocked out of me. With Dr. Styrt's utterance of "umph," my sensory experience was given representation in sound and made recognizable. I felt understood. Dr. Styrt's attuned response recalled to mind the reason I had wished to refer my friend to him in the first place.

SOME CHARACTERISTICS OF THE ADVOCATED TREATMENT APPROACH

The advocated treatment approach is not on the level of modeling "I" statements or "teaching communication" (though these may be helpful). It is oriented toward trying to develop a secure experience of going-on-being and going-on being-with another, first in relationship to the therapist and then in the marriage.

Going-on-being is achieved in the state of meditation or reverie, a dreamy state that allows inchoate experience to cohere and become identifiable, not through the intellect proper, but by way of the innate organizing tendency of the self. The development of the capacity for going-on-being is dependent upon the secure experience of going-on-being-with another (Winnicott 1958c). Going-on-being requires a stillness in which the patient is able to attend to emergent experience. We see this when the therapist makes a comment and the patient is quiet, trying to relate the therapist's comments to his experience, to sense what feels like it fits and what does not. Or the patient may pause in the attempt to give words to what he is feeling as he enters into a mutually transforming interplay with what he is struggling to describe.

In going-on-being the capacity to flounder is vital (Winnicott 1960b). The patient needs the therapist's active support in tolerating and, later, becoming interested in the spectrum of his experience, including, but not limited to, ambiguity, oscillation, paralysis, wavering, confusion, awkwardness, uncertainty, and vulnerability. The therapist educates, cajoles, encourages, recognizes, values, and praises the spouses' capacity to flounder. The therapist may explain the importance of yet-to-be-understood experience, encourage associative thinking, examine internally censoring judgments, and challenge the idea that only complete or coherent thoughts or feelings are productive. The therapist may also encourage the patient to stay with his feeling outside of therapy by sitting quietly, going for walks, playing an instrument, or writing about his experience, rather than by engaging in distracting behaviors or marital fights. The spouses' attitude toward their experience begins to alter in the face of the therapist's unwavering interest in the not-yet-understood of their experience.

Therapist attunement often arises in a reverie that grows out of going-on-being-with the spouses. Therapeutically attuned reverie is akin to therapeutic preoccupation, echoing the maternal preoccupation (Winnicott 1956) of the good-enough mother. The therapist must translate empathic attunement into attuned responsiveness, supporting the spouses' sensing and sorting, their fumbling to recognize and stumbling to name their experience. The therapist's processing of his experience in relationship to the spouses often precedes, parallels, and supports the spouses' processing of their own experience.

This is a difficult job. The common countertransference reactions to pathologic autistic-contiguous mode experience entail amorphous and unpleasant feelings. They may include feeling tyrannized or tyrannizing, swallowed up or invaded, swallowing up and invading, physically small or large, inadequate in the ability to form a sense of relatedness, invulnerably hard or mushy soft, calloused or raw nerved, cold or warm, sharp or dull, bored or stimulated, repulsed or attracted, sleepy or alert, or over- or underprotective toward the spouse(s). Body sensations may include the twitching of limbs, stomach pain, a feeling of bloatedness; skin sensations of warmth or coldness, tingling or numbness; or skin impressions like the tightness of garments. Feelings of drowsiness or reveries of warm liquids such as embryonic fluid (Ogden 1989) may come to occupy the therapist's mind. The therapist may also enter states that evolve like bad dreams, with sleepiness, boredom, coma, a feeling in the back of the eyelids similar to the fetus's view of its watery world, or a feeling of floating or being engulfed or submerged—abruptly followed by a panicked feeling of "Help! I'm drowning," from which the therapist awakes with a start. It is only in the therapist's going-on-being-with the experience that its meaning in relationship to the spouses may be understood.

CONCLUSION

The marital therapist in general, and the therapist of personality-disordered couples in particular, must be able to recognize the importance of sensory experience as the platform of the sense of self and other upon which subsequent senses of self derive. The pursuit of the re-creation of early sensory experience is often a motivation for relationship and a defense against external reality. Sensory experience is also a form of memory and means of communication. As the therapist is able to tune into and abide with the sensory experience of the spouses, she is permitted to form attuned identifications with the spouses and is in a position to help them translate their sensations into thoughts, feelings, and ego needs, where they may be thought about.

8

The Paranoid-Schizoid Mode
of Organization and the Development
of Psychic Structure

THE DEVELOPMENT OF THE UNCONSCIOUS

With the advent of the core self and core other, the emergence of "me" and "not-me," and the recognition of the core other as a transformational and selfobject, all the elements needed to develop psychic structure are present. Fairbairn (1940, 1944, 1946, 1949, 1951, 1952) posited the first systemic theory of intrapsychic development, and his theory is recounted here because it provides a useful tool for thinking about intrapsychic and interpersonal dynamics.

THE SPLITTING OF THE EGO AND THE SPLITTING
OF THE OBJECT

In every living thing, there is a natural tendency to withdraw from the endangering. This presents a particular dilemma for the child, who, in a state of absolute dependence, has nowhere to run. He cannot physically escape or change a threatening situation and therefore is driven to use the only means at hand—psychological escape.

The child escapes through splitting and denial, relegating endangering experiences to unconsciousness, forming the dynamic unconscious. The child is unable to manage the paradox that the need-satisfying (fulfilling) and the need-frustrating (rejecting) object are one and the same. Consequently, to maintain a defensively idealized relationship to a "good" object in consciousness, he denies his perception of the need-frustrating and endangering object. In that the ego is the organ of perception, this entails a primary splitting of the ego resulting in the creation of the central ego, which houses consciousness, and of the dynamic unconscious, which becomes peopled by persecutory self and object representations and the affects that bind them together.

It is important to understand that the totality of the need-frustrating experience is relegated to the unconscious (Figure 8–1). Fairbairn (1944) coined the term *libidinal ego* to represent that

Figure 8–1. Splitting of the Ego and Splitting of the Object

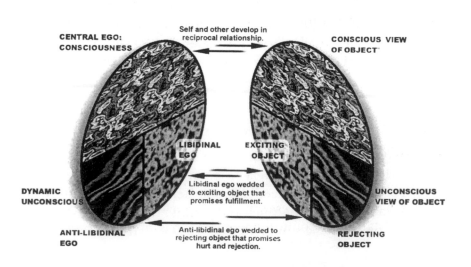

CENTRAL EGO:
CONSCIOUSNESS

Self and other develop in
reciprocal relationship.

CONSCIOUS VIEW
OF OBJECT

LIBIDINAL
EGO

EXCITING
OBJECT

Libidinal ego wedded
to exciting object that
promises fulfillment.

DYNAMIC
UNCONSCIOUS

UNCONSCIOUS
VIEW OF OBJECT

ANTI-LIBIDINAL
EGO

Anti-libidinal ego wedded to
rejecting object that promises
hurt and rejection.

REJECTING
OBJECT

aspect of the unconscious that houses the unsatisfiable longing, desperate need, and anxious arousal associated with the child's excitement for, and seeking of, vital relationship to the object (Scharff and Scharff 1992). He used the term *exciting object* to represent the need-exciting aspect of the parent, who promises to satisfy the need. The libidinal ego is affectively linked to the exciting object and only to the exciting object. The yearnings of the libidinal ego bring the child, and later adult, into harm's way. Its expectations are so idealized that they cannot be met in reality and expose the child to the possibility of rejection.

Fairbairn (1944) created the term *anti-libidinal ego* to represent that aspect of the unconscious that contains the affects of anger, rage, and sadness (Scharff and Scharff 1992), that arose in response to the child's experience of the rejection of her needs. The anti-libidinal ego is affectively wedded to the *rejecting object* and only to the rejecting object. Consequently, it expects and is exquisitely alert to the possibility of rejection or impingement, constantly scanning for malice in the slightest misattunement or in real or imagined failures in responsiveness.

The libidinal and anti-libidinal egos are in conflicting and competitive relationship, leading to intrapsychic conflict. Intrapsychic conflict inevitably arises as the needs of attachment of the libidinal ego elicit the fear and anxiety of attachment of the anti-libidinal ego. The anti-libidinal ego supports the central ego in the repression of the libidinal ego in order to protect the self from further injury and to preserve the defensive idealization of the parent in consciousness (Figure 8–2).

Vignette: Marinating in Piss

The conflict between the libidinal and anti-libidinal egos is illustrated in the session of Pamela, a young woman who, libidinal desires repressed, was as directionless in her therapy as she was in her life. Unable to discern, much less commit, to what she wanted, she was left in a decaying situation of depression and despair, against

Figure 8–2. The Internalization of Self and Object Relationships

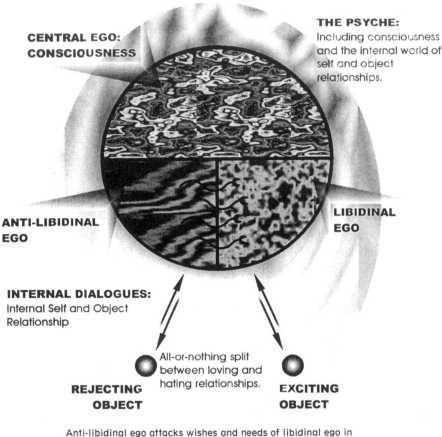

CENTRAL EGO: CONSCIOUSNESS

THE PSYCHE: Including consciousness and the internal world of self and object relationships.

ANTI-LIBIDINAL EGO

LIBIDINAL EGO

INTERNAL DIALOGUES: Internal Self and Object Relationship

All-or-nothing split between loving and hating relationships.

REJECTING OBJECT

EXCITING OBJECT

Anti-libidinal ego attacks wishes and needs of libidinal ego in that they make the psyche vulnerable to rejection, pain, and rage that threaten to break into consciousness and destroy the security maintaining perception of the object as good.

which she defended with promiscuous and clinging relationships. However, if the object of her desire came to desire her, she would become derisive, drive him out of the relationship, and then, when libidinal yearnings reemerged in his absence, try to seduce him back again.

Despite her anguish, she mocked my efforts to explore her

situation. She would respond to tentative interpretations with "I've never heard anything so stupid" or "Did you get that out of Chapter 13 of some book?" or with scornful laughter. During two years of therapy, only her reliable attendance and inevitable acting out in the face of my planned absences belied her devaluation of me. Despite her behavior, I liked her spitfire quality and empathized helplessly with her disabling conflict.

The session to be reported began when Pamela picked up a brochure that described my practice.

P: "Oh! You're in such bad shape that you need to advertise? How pathetic, it makes me lose even more respect for you." As she continued in this vein, she slowly tore the brochure into tiny pieces. She took smug satisfaction in destroying it as she said, "I'm going to throw this paper on the floor and I'm *not* going to pick it up." Head down, focused on her work of destruction, she peeked at me carefully to gauge my reaction. When I did not rise to the bait, she escalated her provocation. "There's nothing you can do about it!" She looked at me directly and defiantly, but with what to me seemed a humorously mischievous manner. After a moment of hesitation, she tossed the bits of paper into the air, they descended upon us, a sun-struck cloud of confetti as the paper captured the light from the window. I was privately delighted with the ironic symbolism, enjoying her mischievousness and her apparent liking of me despite herself. She reminded me of a daughter playfully flirting with her father. She was surprised and frustrated that I was not upset, finally commenting in a more seriously challenging vein, "I'm really tired of this shit. I've been seeing you for two years now and I'm not getting any better. I'm getting worse!"

T: "I agree."

P: "You agree?! Then how can you charge me for these sessions? I know I don't pay anyway (she had accrued a balance on her account), but still how can you charge me? I think you ought to see me for free."

T: At this time, two years into treatment, I made comments to Pamela that I would never have made before, and I do not recommend them as standard practice. Nevertheless, they demonstrate that the timing and nature of some comments arise within the spontaneity of the moment in the relationship. "I think I should increase my fee."

P   (in total surprise and confusion): "Increase your fee?! But . . . but . . . you just agreed that I was getting worse, not better. Why would you increase your fee?!"

T: "Because I have been marinating in your piss for two years and I think that's worth something."

P: "I can't believe you just said that. What kind of therapist are you?"

T: "One that's good at marinating in piss. You know what your problem is?"

P: "What?"

T: "Even though I have been marinating in your piss for two years, I still like you, and you can't stand it."

     Pamela was quiet for several minutes.

P: "How have I been pissing on you?"

T: "How have you not? Every time I make a comment or try to think about something with you, you piss all over me, embarrass me, and humiliate me. And every time I try to explore your need to do that, you simply do more of it. That's why we're not getting anywhere."

P: "I'm not going to allow you to talk to me that way. I'm leaving." She jumped up and headed for the door.

T: "I wish you would stay so we could talk it through."

P: "Are you crazy? I'm leaving and I'm never coming back."

T: "I'm sorry you don't feel able to stay and I hope you change your mind about coming back. I'd like to understand why you can't stand my liking you."

     Pamela exited, slamming the door behind her. Fifteen minutes later, as I worried that she would not return, the telephone rang. It was Pamela.

P: "I'm sorry for walking out. I was just confused. And I'm sorry for throwing the paper on your floor. I want to work with you, too, and I want to make sure you don't give my time away for next week."

T: "I'm glad you had the courage to call. I know it wasn't easy. I'll see you next week."

P: "Okay."

This interaction was a turning point in Pamela's therapy. The fact that such comments came to mind and that I felt free to say them, two years into treatment, reflected the time and relationship necessary for establishing a sufficient holding environment and building a treatment alliance vital to such a communication. In my identifying and articulating her wish for relationship, evident in her reliable attendance and acting out in the face of my absences, and her fear of relationship, evident in her acting in ways designed to be rejecting and rejected, Pamela felt both recognized and understood. As her libidinal and anti-libidinal elements were brought to awareness, without the feared rejection by the object (the therapist), she was able to decrease her reliance on primitive defenses. She painstakingly developed a capacity for self-observation and reflection.

UNCONSCIOUS RESISTANCE

The intensity of the devotion of the libidinal and anti-libidinal egos to their respective objects is more often than not critically underestimated in the treatment of personality-disordered individuals. The more pervasive the experience of abuse or neglect in childhood, the wider the schism between conscious and unconscious and the more dedicated the libidinal and anti-libidinal egos to their respective objects.

In that the libidinal and anti-libidinal egos are formed in early childhood, they are the repositories of intense infantile-dependent wishes and fears that have not had the benefit of maturing in relationship to reality. Consequently, the libidinal ego is in voracious and desperate pursuit of a fantastically idealized exciting object that promises a magical-miracle world of perfect oneness in which every wish is instantaneously met. The extremely idealized nature of these strivings results in inevitable disappointment felt on the level of narcissistic injury, and results in the hurt and rage of the anti-libidinal ego. The anti-libidinal ego of personality-disordered individuals is formed in the direct experience of abuse and neglect. Accordingly, it is always in relationship to a hostile, sadistically depriving or powerfully invasive object.

One might think that given these problems individuals would be willing to forego the pursuits of the libidinal and anti-libidinal egos in favor of normalcy. However, this is not at all the case: The far less omnipotent, idealized, and intense offerings of "normalcy" present both a loss and a threat. For the libidinal ego, the recognition of realistic limits and the stability they provide only promises the loss of the possibility of the yearned-for fantastical merger with the exciting object and threatens the individual with what is felt as intolerable exposure to separateness and an unbearable reality. For the anti-libidinal ego, the idea that others can be caring or nurturing, as well as hurtful, is the most dangerous of ideas, given the predatory world of rejecting objects. Finally, returning to the autistic-contiguous mode of sensory-dominated experience, we cannot underestimate the malignant pull of toxic sensory experience, which has become equated with all that is familiar and familial and forms the platform of the sense of self.

Given these polarized motivations toward attachment, as the spouses express their consciously held wish for relationship the therapist must keep in mind the unconscious conflicting motivations of the libidinal and anti-libidinal egos, which, until uncovered and resolved, will continue to obstruct the couple's conscious aims.

Vignette: Voraciousness

A couple's therapist, with whom they were dissatisfied, referred Gail and Lee. Gail, the spokesperson, reported that they had had many therapists, most of whom were incompetent. She was deprecating of therapy and therapists in general, telling stories in which she, as a health professional, was far more able than the social workers with whom she worked. She carped about their discomfort when dealing with aggressive families. A social worker myself, I experienced Gail's stories like an opening salvo against any competence I might have. I was struck with the immediacy with which she introduced her persecutory world of self and object relationships into the treatment setting, with herself in the role of vanquisher of incompetent and pitifully weak objects.

After this ominous beginning, Gail described how she and Lee came from abusive backgrounds. She reported that Lee's father and uncle had sexually abused him and that he suffered from dissociative disorder and had a history of psychiatric hospitalizations. I marveled how she spoke for him as if he were not there or incompetent to speak for himself. Gail felt that Lee exaggerated the abuse and used it to rationalize his behavior. In total control of the session, Gail went on to describe her own family, which she characterized as verbally and emotionally abusive, stating that family members were often humiliated and brought to tears by her domineering father. She then ended the story extolling the family members' great love for one another. When I expressed puzzlement over this incongruous ending, she arrogantly responded, "You have the cultural bias of most therapists. If everything is not touchy-feely you think it's bad. You'll need to get over yours if you're to work with us." Gail thus foreclosed any exploration of loving and hating interactions in her family life and what they might mean to her. Somehow, she had reconfigured abuse and humiliation into love.

Gail's presenting concern was that the relationship had been going well for four months when, without warning, Lee sought hospitalization for suicidal impulses. To her dismay and outrage, Gail was barred from the inpatient unit and discovered that Lee's therapist would not speak to her. Moreover, Lee would not return her telephone calls. Gail met with Lee and the inpatient social worker to discuss these issues, but abruptly left the meeting when "the social worker was condescending" toward her. Gail stated that she needed Lee to apologize for being hospitalized without any warning to her. What's more, she needed Lee to tell her why the inpatient unit, Lee's therapist, and Lee himself had treated her as persona non grata. Finally, she demanded reassurance that his unexplained behavior would not happen again.

By the second session, Gail had vented enough to allow Lee to gather and express his thoughts. He explained that Gail had thought they had been getting along better in the months preceding his hospitalization because he had kept his thoughts and feelings to himself. He declared to Gail, "Whenever I tell you what I'm thinking, we fight. It's either your way or no way at all, and I get worn out and just agree with you so we'll stop fighting." Gail responded with righteous indignation, "You know you can tell me anything. Of course, I'll fight you if it's your usual bullshit. Apologize to me!" As Lee's response was not immediate, Gail filled the space with a torrent of words, essentially carrying on with herself for the rest of the session. When I gently interrupted to suggest she might leave room for Lee to comment, she told me that other therapists had told her that in the past and that she was working on it. She then criticized me for being condescending and treating her like a child. At that moment, I understood how needy she felt (libidinal ego), and that she could not stand it (anti-libidinal fear and disgust toward her own needfulness). She equated compassion with condescension, as if compassion was a talking-down-to and as if being needful was a one-down position. She found compassion disgusting (anti-libidinal attack upon the libidinal ego) as it recognized her desperate neediness, against which, in projected relationship to rejecting objects, she was compelled to defend.

As treatment proceeded, Gail took up most of the time in the sessions, although she invariably left feeling that she had not gotten her fair share of attention (voracious need and disappointed libidinal strivings for perfection). She accused me of being the problem (frustrating object) by not forcing them to get to important issues. Yet when I attempted to keep her on task or to make room for Lee's thoughts, she complained that I was insensitive to her feelings and favoring of him. In such ways, Gail expressed the libidinal ego's voracious need for one hundred percent need-satisfying object relatedness, alternating with the anti-libidinal ego's rage and feelings of persecution when such magical expectations are not met.

Throughout this process, Lee sat silently, interjecting only occasionally. I assumed that he was dissociating much of the time. His tendency to withdraw was supported by Gail's lack of interest or criticism of anything he had to say. Given the tyrannizing intensity of her strivings, I suspected that treatment was doomed to fail regardless of my efforts. Yet to allow Gail's infantile demands and expectations to run the session would accomplish nothing. Committed to hearing from Lee regardless of the consequences, I frustrated Gail's ravenous and tyrannical yearnings for immediate and complete satisfaction by becoming more insistent in creating space for Lee's experience. Predictably, Gail more than ever perceived me as a rejecting object. She gave lip service to understanding that if Lee did not speak she would never know what was on his mind. However, whenever Lee spoke she interrupted continuously, grilling him like a prosecuting attorney and thereby collapsing any space in which he could safely express, elaborate, and explore his own perceptions.

By the tenth session, Gail was totally disenchanted with therapy and with me as a therapist. However, in the start-and-stop fashion created by her intrusiveness and my fighting it off, Lee had become increasingly assertive. He described Gail as obsessive and perfectionistic. "She constantly looks over my shoulder, repeatedly second guesses me, and is never satisfied with my efforts. She holds me responsible for every problem in our lives." He gave an example of her blaming him for their cat becoming stuck in a tree. This was more outspoken than Lee had ever been before, and Gail, furious, screamed at him that he was a liar and a manipulator, and screamed at me that I was condoning his wrongdoing by listening to him. She totally ignored any attempts to examine what part she might play in repeatedly being in situations—at work, home, and therapy—in which she felt ganged up on. When I asked why she wanted to stay with Lee or what she hoped to gain from couples therapy if she did not trust anything anyone had to say, she responded, "I'll know when he's telling the truth."

I continued to make room for Lee while trying to massage Gail's jangled nerves. However, she invariably experienced my efforts to comfort her as condescending and became increasingly aggressive and intimidating, as if my compassion only fanned the flames of her anti-libidinal rage and frustration. She verbally attacked Lee's personality and mine, calling us "weak men" (the anti-libidinal attitude toward vulnerability), and accused me of being the "typical therapist, touchy-feely crap, afraid to say what's on your mind" (anti-libidinal disgust for anything other than power and dominance). Gail ignored my observation that she seemed to rage most when I said what was on my mind. I also spoke to how I didn't know that I could be of help in that she seemed to experience any point of view divergent from her own as attacking or a lie, thereby discounting it.

During our last session, Gail was particularly vociferous as Lee stood up for his right to speak. He confronted her interruptions and challenged her mean-spirited depiction of him. He expressed his fury with her devaluing response whenever his point of view was at odds with hers. Gail, taken aback by his anger and his articulateness, expressed confusion as to why he was so upset. Her confusion seemed to entail a moment of openness to self-reflection, and I gently commented, "You seem unaware of how enraging you can be." Unfortunately, rather than opening an area for further under-standing, my attempt at connection served only to renew Gail's rage. "How can you as a therapist say such a thing?! How can you tell a patient she's enraging? What kind of therapist are you? He's done so much wrong and yet you never tell him how wrong he is, only me! You're both just trying to shut me up. My father would beat me to try to shut me up and he never could. Do you think I'll let you two pantywaists do it?" At this point, Gail stormed from the room as Lee prophesied to her in an attempt to get her to stay, "You won't return. You never do." Gail called the next day to end treatment, trium-phantly reporting, "I consulted with a former therapist, who agrees that your behavior as a therapist is atrocious, and that you don't know how terrible Lee is, and that you are obviously threatened by a strong woman."

Gail was so captured by rejecting forms of relatedness that she was unable to consider the existence of any other kind. On the one hand, she pursued with pit bull intensity the wish for perfect merger, in which she was omnipotently in charge, and yet on the other, any form of genuine relationship only spurred her fear of attachment. Faced with the disappointment of her strivings, she expressed talonic rage, both because she perceived her others as abusive and sadistically depriving and in an attempt to bring them under her control.

What did not become apparent until Gail's comment about her father, partly because she had made the exploration of her history taboo, was how extensively she had transferred her sadomasochistic relationship with her father to the marriage, to authority figures at work, and to me in the therapy, as if we were all interchangeable objects. In doing so, she felt victimized by us while simultaneously treating us in exactly the tyrannizing and abusive fashion against which she railed, re-creating the totalitarian regime of her youth in the world of her adulthood. As I had feared, my name was unceremoniously added to the heap of disreputable therapists; Gail had won another battle in her losing war.

THERAPIST NEUTRALITY VERSUS NEUTERING OF THE THERAPIST

Of course, the spouses' competing motivations have an effect upon the therapist. Often one or both spouses, in good faith, will present a compelling story that evokes the desire of the therapist to make things better. However, if the therapist should forget or minimize the power of the dual unconscious motivations—one for the possession of the need-exciting object and the other to defend against the rejecting object—what appear to be incomprehensible obstacles to the treatment effort will soon be encountered. Seemingly simplistic communication problems will elude resolution. Undeterred, the naïve therapist may excitedly promote libidinal yearnings for vital and satisfying relationship or, frustrated and disenchanted with the lack of progress, may identify with anti-libidinal feelings and become attacking or withdrawn, even implicitly or explicitly advocating separation and divorce.

In such circumstances, the therapist is countertransferentially participating in the spouses' polarized form of relatedness, paralleling in his relationship to the spouses their relationship to each other. Though treatment may continue, progress is impeded if the therapist does not recognize that he is caught in and countertransferentially acting out one or the other pole of the spouses' divided motivations. This is most often signaled in the therapist's entering a competitive, rather than exploratory, relationship to the spouse(s) or, conversely, in the therapist's carrying the motivation for the treatment effort.

Nonetheless, as messy as it is, countertransference is inevitable. Paradoxically, it is both vital to the treatment effort and can obstruct it. Fortunately, the therapist's loss of neutrality represents an opportunity as well as a dilemma. If the therapist is never under- or overinvolved, he cannot develop his own personally meaningful understanding of the couple, or treat from relationship. On the other hand, when the therapist is under- or overinvolved he invariably fans the flames of resistance of whichever ego element has gone unrecognized within each spouse.

Treatment from relationship is not an intellectual exercise. Every "cure" of the couple includes a "cure" of the therapist (Searles 1975) and involves the therapist's working with and through his countertransference. The issue is not to remain neutral, but to be aware of over- and underinvolvement and to personally experience, and therefore more fully understand, the affectively charged dynamic pushes and pulls of the couple. If the therapist is only analyzing then he is not in relationship, and if only in relationship then he is not analyzing. Both relationship and analysis are required to help the spouses think about and learn from their experience.

THE PERSONALITY-DISORDERED MARRIAGE AS A SINGLE PSYCHIC ENTITY

In the relationship, each partner projects one or the other pole of his or her unconscious world of pathological self and object relationships into the mate. Accordingly, one partner identifies with the libidinal ego's yearning for relationship to an exciting object, while the other partner becomes identified with the anti-libidinal ego's fear of relationship and expects rejection or betrayal. In that each partner possesses both egos, if one partner should shift in the direction of the other, the other will shift in the countervailing direction, thereby maintaining homeostasis in the relationship. Although change has occurred in the role of each partner, the relationship configuration itself remains the same.

Vignette: I Want to Be Closer, Don't I?

Sandy, the overresponsible oldest daughter of a highly dysfunctional family, complained bitterly of her husband Paul's couch potato ways. She yearned (libidinal ego) for his fuller participation in the family, her sadness touching. As Paul's passive-aggressive behavior (rejecting object) was explored, he recognized that he was clinging to the illusion of relationship of his childhood, in which, as the "fair-haired boy," he could do no wrong. Desiring more substantial human connection (libidinal yearnings), he became more concerned for Sandy and with the meeting of her needs.

Sandy, appreciative, happily reported Paul's greater participation, noting how surprised she was to find him doing more without having to be asked. Over the next several sessions, she continued to remark on his growing responsibility and involvement, but with decreasing enthusiasm. She wistfully commented, "I know it can't last. As soon as I trust him, he'll do something to disappoint me" (anti-libidinal ego relationship to rejecting object). As the weeks passed into months, she became agitated and less functional (anti-libidinal ego alarm in the face of dependency needs), complaining of how she felt anxious and depressed. She exclaimed, "He's driving me crazy. I know he can't be doing this for me" (view of Paul as an inevitably persecutory object).

Sandy cognitively recognized that her response was pushing Paul away in express contradiction of her stated desires. However, she felt helpless to do anything about it as her paranoia increased. She reluctantly accepted a referral for individual therapy, but soon began canceling couples therapy sessions and then stopped treatment all together.

Here we see that as Paul responded to Sandy's wish for attachment (libidinal strivings), she was beset by her own fear of attachment (anti-libidinal ego). Her accustomed role to self and other jeopardized, she repeatedly predicted (exhorted) that Paul would return to his old ways. When this didn't occur she felt she was going crazy. Unfortunately, rather than addressing these issues, she withdrew from treatment. Eventually Paul, having lost rather than gained connection to Sandy and unwilling to consider divorce because of their young children, returned to his previous state of uninvolvement. Sandy (at least in her own mind) returned to the role of the beleaguered responsible one whose own needs must be put aside (anti-libidinal ego rage and frustration).

The conflicting motivations both toward and away from relationship are well worth analyzing. Otherwise, although the couple may spend much energy in therapy, the movement they make only circles back upon itself, maintaining the stultifying balance between the wish for relationship and the fear of it.

Typically, the spouses are resistant to this effort. On the one hand, they defend against the recognition that their infantile wish of merger in relationship cannot be met, for such recognition would confront them with the intolerable awareness of separateness and loss. On the other hand, they do not want to consider that their perception of the other as a rejecting object has its roots in antiquity, the Dark Age of their childhood. Differentiating past from present would leave them open to the agony of hope and the possibility of disappointment and, even worse, as we have seen, satisfaction in the present-day relationship.

THE INHIBITION OF DESIRE

The dynamic unconscious arises as defense, providing the important survival function of keeping the self out of the possibility of harm's way, real and imagined. The anti-libidinal ego, linked by hatred to the rejecting object, is far more severe in its repression of libidinal needs than would characteristically be the object in external reality, particularly once adulthood has been achieved and object choice is available.[1] The anti-libidinal ego, functioning with the efficiency of an internal "star wars" system, shoots down libidinal strivings before they can emerge into consciousness and threaten the self with the risk of rejection. In extreme form, this leads to the aloofness of schizoid personality disorder and is the principal dynamic involved in problems related to the inhibition of desire.

Nonetheless, despite the forces and the harshness of the defenses arrayed against it, the libidinal ego continues to clamor for satisfaction. It twists and winds its way to emerge in displaced or perverse form in consciousness. Disguised, these now pathogenic yearnings are designed to meet the original need while minimizing the risk of rejection.

Vignette: I Don't Want to Feel

Larry, unwilling to enter a relationship that would involve the sharing of needs and feelings, explains: "What's the point? I'm not willing to risk feeling, unless Susan [his wife] guarantees me that she won't hurt me. I can't tell you what she would have to do to assure

---

1. Of course, there are exceptions to this rule dependent upon the external reality. At times the object in reality may be very dangerous—herein is the extreme danger to the self of further abuse if it fails to heed its own warning signals. Real danger in the environment may actually provide relief from unbearable internal tension generated by the persecuting, rejecting object, from which there is never any escape. Even in a relationship with a sadistic tormentor, there is a patterning of predictability of danger and assault that brings moments of actual relief and a clear sense that at least the danger is "out there" and not "inside me" or "all over me."

me of this; I'm not sure. But, even if I did know, I couldn't tell her, because then she could just pretend. I can survive like this, without pain, and that's okay by me." Larry's relationship to Susan as a rejecting object is clear. He defends against Susan as the rejecting object by foregoing the desire for a vital and pleasing relationship. In essence, Larry is developmentally unable to risk the normal disappointments inherent in relationship to a good-enough object in contemporary reality.

Still, his libidinal strivings for object relatedness continued to clamor for attention. This was unmistakably evident when Susan awoke one night to discover Larry masturbating himself with her hand. In this desperate fashion, he endeavored to attain the illusion of relationship while maintaining his omnipotent defense against the vulnerability that would accompany it.

Under the repressive regime of the central and anti-libidinal egos, when libidinal needs do emerge they do so with rapacious intensity. The individual, compelled by long-frustrated desires, engages in the unrelenting and often compulsive pursuit of satisfaction. This may be manifested in sexual harassment or entail the use of prostitutes. Often, there is a refusal to take "no" for an answer or unrestrained rage when the need is not met. The intense feelings of anxiety, pain, and humiliation that result from the frustrated need is exactly the experience the anti-libidinal ego dreads and, paradoxically, feels affirmed in finding. In this sense, relationship strivings for personality-disordered individuals in particular are always wish/ fears. They entail the libidinal ego's wish for fulfillment and the anti-libidinal ego's fear of rejection.

CONCLUSION

In particularly unhappy childhoods, the splitting-off of the libidinal and anti-libidinal egos is exceptionally harsh. In such circumstances, awareness of need itself can become a source of intolerable pain and frustration. Consequently, libidinal strivings are repressed by the central and anti-libidinal egos, but at the expense of the individual's relationship to self and other. The illusory sense of security provided mainly by splitting, denial, and primitive projective identificatory processes is an anxiety-ridden one, purchased at the expense of the child's (and later adult's) knowledge of her needs and the capacity to develop personally (internally) meaningful relationships. Chronic feelings of emptiness, despair, and depression result.

When libidinal needs do emerge, they take a variety of forms, disguised, displaced, and distorted like the gnarled limbs of a tree that were tied down when a tender sapling. Subsequently, otherwise normal strivings take perverse form. Men seek out prostitutes although they have willing lovers at home, and women overidentify themselves as mothers, seeking merger with their children to the exclusion of adult needs and desires. Men and women engage in the omnipotent and paradoxical pursuit of intimacy without vulnerability.

The lived experience of the pathological aspects of childhood relationships is embedded in the internal world of pathological self and object relationship templates. In cases of severe abuse or neglect, these templates become far more captivating than the less than perfectly reliable human relationships of contemporary reality. Wedded to internal objects and infantile wishes, fantasies, and fears, personality-disordered partners projectively seek, evoke, provoke, identify, and "discover" them in the present. Psychological rigidity and isolation, living of a defensive life, and a focus on survival rather than fulfillment are maintained.

The ensuing developmental arrest makes itself known in every aspect of the individual's way of being and relating, and is manifested in the level of symbolization (thinking), use of words, primary motivations, defenses, and quality of relationship to self and other. These characteristics of the paranoid-schizoid mode of organization will be examined in the following chapter.

9

Perceiving and Relating in the
Paranoid-Schizoid Mode

Personality disorder affects every aspect of the individual's way of perceiving and relating. If the encompassing effects of the disorder are not understood, the therapist may assume that his own way of perceiving and relating applies to the couple. The normal/neurotic therapist may then speak a developmentally different language, implicitly demanding that the couple relate to him, rather than he to them. The danger is that when the therapist encounters the chasm between his understanding and theirs, for which he is unable to account, he may pathologize the spouses, rather than deepening his understanding of their situation.

SELF-RELATIONS: THE CORE SELF

The paranoid-schizoid mode is "a mode of generating experience characterized by . . . a very limited capacity to experience oneself as the author and interpreter of one's thoughts and feelings" (Ogden 1989, p. 149n). In this regard it is similar to Stern's concept of the core self, which is an experiential sense of self. "A crucial term here is 'sense' as distinct from 'concept of' or 'knowledge of' or 'awareness of' self or other. The emphasis is on the palpable experiential realities of substance, action, sensation, affect, and time. Sense of self is not a cognitive construct. It is an experiential integration. This sense of a core self will be the foundation for all the more elaborate senses of the self to be added later" (Stern 1985, p. 71). Without "knowledge of," "awareness of," or "concept of" a self or other, there is little upon which to establish a secure sense of self across time, or self-observation and self-reflection. There is no "I" (a development of the depressive mode) to observe the data (perceptions) that accrues to the "me," of the paranoid-schizoid mode. Accordingly, the individual's sense of self is reactive, rather than reflective, governed by the direct experience of the moment.

Without self-awareness, the patient has little capacity for self-reflection and, thus, for self-direction. Instead, as the dreamer to the dream, the patient feels that things are always happening outside of his control. And, as with the dreamer, the patient forgets that he is not only a participant in his life, the dream, but also the author and producer of it, including the meaning of events and his reaction to them. Just as the dreamer feels lived by the dream, so the personality-disordered individual feels lived by life, in scripted relationship to self and other.

Being and relatedness in the paranoid-schizoid mode may be examined in terms of the level of symbolization, the leading anxiety and motivation, the defenses, and the quality of relatedness to self and others.

LEVEL OF SYMBOLIZATION

The paranoid-schizoid mode includes ". . . a form of symbolization in which the symbol is barely distinguishable from the symbolized ('symbolic equation,' Segal 1957)" (Ogden 1989, p. 149n).

The word "paranoid" refers to a form of defense in which thinking is used to evacuate endangering mental contents from consciousness. One version of this is found in primitive projective identification, which was discussed extensively in Chapter 4. Another version is found in the patient's relative incapacity to think. In the paranoid-schizoid mode the individual equates thoughts and feelings with reality. The spouses often say, "What's to talk about, that's how I feel. That's the way I am. That's the way it is. Can you fix it?" Unable to think about their thoughts and their feelings, the partners are limited to being lived by their perceptions. Indeed, they equate their perceptions with "the thing in itself" (Segal 1957), that is, as equivalent of absolute reality. This level of perceiving and relating is called symbolic equivalence: a primary level of symbolization marked by a lack of differentiation between the symbol and the symbolized (Segal 1957).

Symbolism proper requires the thirdness of an interpreting subject, a development of the depressive mode. The interpreting subject stands between the symbol and the thing symbolized, giving the symbol its meaning. For example, (1) a wedding ring, the symbol, represents (2) the marriage, the thing symbolized, by (3) the spouses, the interpreting subjects. In symbolism proper, the ring symbolizes the marriage to the spouses. The spouses are able to cognitively and affectively distinguish between the ring and the marriage. Thus, if the ring is lost, the spouses may feel upset, but do not respond emotionally as if the marriage itself is threatened.

In the paranoid-schizoid mode, there is no interpreting subject, an "I," to stand between the symbol and the thing symbolized. Consequently, the individual may cognitively differentiate between the ring and the marriage, but affectively they are felt as the same. Accordingly, if the ring is lost, the individual may react as if the marriage was doomed. In like manner, an individual may cognitively recognize the difference between the flag and the country it represents, but respond to the burning of the flag on a television news broadcast with an emotional intensity concomitant to the country itself being set aflame. Similarly, leaving the cap off the toothpaste or the toilet seat up may become affectively equated with an absence of love, although the mate is otherwise reliable; while handholding, flowers, sweet talk, and fine dining may be affectively equated with love, although the mate is known to be philandering.

Symbolic equivalence is evident in a patient's equating her physical imperfections with an ugly sense of self. Rose, an attractive woman, equated real and imagined small physical imperfections with her inherent sense of internal ugliness and shame. Consequently, she felt compelled to pursue plastic surgery in the conviction that uplifting her physical appearance would uplift her sense of self. As a result, she spent thousands of dollars on plastic surgery that she could ill afford. She described her horrific dilemma given the inevitable ravages of time: *"It's like trying to bail out a sinking boat with a teaspoon. I can slow the sinking, but I can't stop it. Everyone will see how ugly I am."*

Symbolic equivalence is also evident in the negative-transference reactions in therapy and in marriage when an individual responds to the therapist and/or the mate not as a symbol or representation of an internal object but as the living embodiment of the object itself. This was illustrated in many previous vignettes in which one partner equates the mate or the therapist with his own mother or father.

Thinking as a Mental Apparatus for Processing Thoughts

In good-enough development there are the inevitable satisfactions and frustrations attendant to any relationship. Normal development includes planned and unplanned failure by the mother, through which the infant discovers that he is not omnipotent but dependent upon a less than perfectly reliable other for care (Winnicott 1958b, 1967b). It is in the introduction to reality, which occurs in the area of frustration that arises between the onset of a need and its satisfaction, that thoughts and feelings, and subsequent psychic structure, develop (Bion 1962b). Theoretically, if an individual never experienced frustration, psychic structure would not develop. There would be no need of it if the infant's needs are always met before they have a chance to become recognizable, as in too-frequent feedings: The infant has no opportunity to experience hunger and thereby to identify and label it, nor to develop operational thinking that would help him satisfy the hunger. Thus, if an individual is brought up wrapped in the smothering blanket of overprotective parents, later in life he or she may have difficulty in identifying or pursuing the meeting of needs.

A similar result is incurred if a child experiences too-frequent or too-prolonged frustration of needs. Under these conditions, the awareness of need only brings intolerable frustration, in that the need is not met. Consequently, thinking, as a mental apparatus for processing thoughts and feelings, develops as a means to rid the child of his thoughts and feelings, thereby limiting awareness of his insufferable burden. In this circumstance, thinking is used to deny sensations, thoughts, feelings, and needs, not to construct pathways in reality toward gratification. This is the state of the individual in the paranoid-schizoid mode of organization.

On Words

The concept of symbolic equivalence has profound implications, not the least of which has to do with language, the primary tool of therapy. Words are symbols, referents, and "no-thing" in themselves. They allow us to identify, represent, process, and communicate mental contents, providing the opportunity to think as an alternative to acting out. However, when words lose their symbolic value, they become equated with the sensations, feelings, thoughts, and actions to which they refer. Instead of referring to the thing symbolized, they become the thing in itself. As a result, as thought and action are felt as the same, reflection is impeded. To think about something becomes dangerous, evoking as it does the thing in itself.

The power of words felt as things in themselves is recognized and defended against in the childhood chant "Sticks and stones may break my bones, but names will never hurt me." This mantra fends off words, which are felt as projectiles, affectively equivalent to sticks and stones that do break bones, the skeletal structure of the vulnerable self.

In normative form, symbolic equivalence is witnessed in the emotional reaction of a rape victim while talking about the assault or in the thought of a deceased loved one re-enveloping the mourner in the feeling of all-encompassing loss. The words and the affective memory they represent are so closely associated that the telling of the story re-evokes the experience itself. However, as the story is repeatedly told and thought about, the words become differentiated from the event itself.

Words may also take on palpable idiosyncratic meanings that can become quite confusing if the therapist is unaware of the process. After several years in treatment, Alicia referred to her father as a "touchy-feely" kind of person, a description that jangled discordantly with my internal image of him as a self-centered domineering figure. When I asked what she meant by "touchy-feely," she became impatient, clearly resenting my obtuseness. Disgruntled, she exclaimed, "Touchy-feely *means* touchy-feely!" When I persisted in my obtuseness, she angrily jumped up and shouted, "Every time my father would talk to me he would do this," and repeatedly poked herself painfully in the chest with her rigid fingers.

Alternately, patients may seize upon the therapist's use of particular words as if they were the totality of the communication. When words have an overdetermined meaning to the patient, intrapsychic conflict is suggested.

Vignette: Words Equated with Action

Richard insisted on being precisely quoted, so that his words had to stand by themselves without meaning. Richard parenthetically noted in the initial session that one concern he had was that Hope did not go to bed at the same time as he and often fell asleep on the couch. I assumed he missed her and asked him if this were the case. Angrily he responded, "I didn't say that! It's no big deal. I'm just worried about her health. She would be more comfortable in bed."

Later in the session, as Richard was reporting some of his history he noted that his father had died when he was five and that his mother had never remarried. He then stated matter-of-factly, "In recent years, I have had little to do with her. There has been little contact and I want none. I can't wait for her to die." When asked the source of these stunning feelings, he responded, "She wasn't given to praise." When I observed, "Given your hatred of her, it seems likely that something more went on than an absence of praise," he was appalled. "I never said *that* word. *That* word never came out of my mouth." After a few moments, I realized he was referring to the word "hatred." I was impressed that he could not say the word. Upon review, I commented, "I agree that the word 'hatred' did not come from you. I guess it reflected my assumption that this was how you felt since you wished your mother dead." Now, nearly apoplectic, he asserted, "I didn't say *that* either! I never said *that!*"

As I watched him strip his words of meaning, I commented, "Again, you're right. That was my interpretation of what you were saying when you said you couldn't wait for her to die." Richard appeared confused, finally unable to refute my quotation of him. Yet, he acted as if these meanings had never occurred to him and were totally unacceptable, although he could not think of any alternative meaning to them. Finally, he simply reiterated in a flat tone, "Those words never came from me." I agreed to the literal accuracy of his statement and did not push the issue. Richard, somewhat mollified, went on to describe his mother's ever-critical and emasculating attitude toward his siblings and him. "She ridiculed and belittled our every effort and success." It struck me that he in turn seemed to be highly critical and belittling of others, in particular his wife and me, but I said nothing, knowing he would feel attacked and misinterpreted by such an observation.

The concept of symbolic equivalence helps the therapist to better tolerate and explore such moments and to better understand the patient. The alternative is for the therapist to reactively engage in self-defensive maneuvers, perhaps escalating the fight-or-flight interaction and impeding deepening understanding. Of course, some patients will not allow a deepening understanding, repeatedly insisting upon "moving on" or ending treatment when meaning threatens.

Given the complexity of words and that patient and therapist are often using the same words with different meanings, it is important for the therapist to never assume understanding until that understanding has been reflected back to the patient for correction or confirmation. Indeed, this is an important function of interpretation, which allows the patient to understand what the therapist does not know (Winnicott 1963). It is in the struggle toward knowing, perhaps never fully achieved, that the therapeutic relationship becomes meaningful.

THE LEADING ANXIETY AND THE LEADING MOTIVATION

The leading anxiety of the paranoid-schizoid mode is the fear of nihilation: the loss of the self or of the other upon whom the individual is dependent. Psychologically dependent upon the object for the maintenance of a sense of self, the borderline suffers fragmenting anxiety when threatened with the loss of the other. This is manifested in the fear of falling apart or breaking into bits and pieces, which is so frightening that the individual much prefers to remain in toxic relationship than to risk the void of no relationship at all. In the face of separation or divorce, the individual experiences her self—not only her life—as falling apart.

Vignette: Disintegrative Anxiety

After discovering his wife's affair, Klaus spent several sleepless nights and agitated days. He feared closing his eyes, for when he did he experienced his mind as a black spherical chamber. Inside this chamber, hidden doors would randomly open and close, out of which tumbled his thoughts and feelings, imagined as acrobats dressed in black, leaping and spinning chaotically past each other and ricocheting off the walls of the chamber. All was chaos, without rhyme or reason, pattern or organization. Klaus's world, his organization, had suddenly fallen apart. He could no longer think, overwhelmed as he was by his tumbling and racing—fragmented and fragmenting—thoughts.

DEFENSES

Splitting is both the primary defense and means of organization of the paranoid-schizoid mode. All primitive defenses are founded upon splitting, which is the basic survival mechanism of removing the endangered from the endangering (Ogden 1986). It is used to deal with the tension of paradox, complexity, and uncertainty, and results in a reductionistic, pre-ambivalent, all-or-nothing way of perceiving and relating.

Splitting is also essential to healthy development. In that almost every event is complex, that is, comprised of positive and negative elements, a total failure in splitting results in anxiety and chronic ambivalence, which can interfere with the capacity to relax, to concentrate, or to make decisions (the paralysis of analysis). In the young child, a failure of splitting may result in the inability to enjoy a good feed or a warm hug, as he is unable to rid himself of the angst produced by the memory of his mother as need-frustrating. In adults, it may be evident in the partners' inability to set problems temporarily aside so that they may enjoy a nurturing time together. Where there is a failure of splitting, the individual is unable to safely think thoughts or feel feelings. "Every facet of emotional life is contaminated or about to be contaminated" (Ogden 1986, p. 54), as thoughts and feelings, fantasy and reality, become disturbingly intermingled. A failure of splitting leads to the fear of one's subjective experience.

Splitting has a developmental line from simple to complex, from pathologic to healthy. Gross idealization and devaluation; part-object relatedness; and absolute, all-or-nothing ways of perceiving and relating signal primitive splitting. Primitive splitting always entails the near total denial or disavowal of that which has been split off. Primitive splitting is evidenced whenever universal human feelings such as love, hate, aggression, envy, jealousy, and greed are absolutely and completely denied. Richard's splitting-off of his feeling of hatred is evident in his denial that his intensely stated "I can't wait for my mother to die" suggested to me both that he hates her and that he wants her to die.

Mature splitting is differentiated from primitive splitting in that it does not involve the absolute disavowal of that which has been split off. Both sides of the divide are available to awareness. Healthy splitting allows for making difficult and complex decisions and acts in service of a greater good. Thus, a surgeon is able to cut on the human body, a hospice nurse learns to work with the dying, and a general is able to maneuver his troops in combat knowing that he is putting them in harm's way. In daily life, splitting allows one to prioritize and to forego immediate gratification, such as in going to work or taxiing children when tired. Healthy splitting permits concentration, the timeless experience of genuine leisure, or a good book by temporarily setting aside other concerns.

The complexity of splitting reflects the paradox of human existence. On the one hand, where splitting is relied upon to the extreme, integration, the development of whole-object relationship to self and other, is not possible. On the other, adequate splitting is necessary to "the eventual integration of part-objects and parts of self into whole-objects and a continuous sense of self. The reason for this is that only when one has achieved relative freedom from the anxiety that loving experience is, or is about to be, contaminated by hating experience, and vice versa, that one may dare to bring these different facets of experience into closer relationship with each other" (Ogden 1986, p. 59).

QUALITY OF RELATEDNESS TO SELF AND OTHER

The quality of relationship to self in the paranoid-schizoid mode is as to a passive object, a "that" or a thing to which things just happen. The other is also seen as an object, a that or a thing, a commodity or a resource that the individual may use to regulate self-experience. This is an object-to-object relationship of a "that" to an "it."

In the paranoid-schizoid mode, the individual projects the locus of his self-experience into the other, and his perception of the other is defined by his self-experience. In rudimentary form, he attributes his feeling of deficiency to the mate, perceiving the mate as a deficient selfobject: "If you loved me I would be happy." Conversely, if feeling okay on a particular day, he expects this as his due. The personality-disordered individual is also ahistorical. His experience of the moment continuously rewrites the "truth" of self and other, as well as their history (Ogden 1989). In this circumstance, positive past experiences are forgotten or seen as deceptions in the midst of current disappointment.

Personality-disordered relationships are primary object relationships, akin to humanity's relationship to air or water (Balint 1968). The spouse views the mate as a resource or a thing, whose own needs and wishes are not felt to be important. Just as we pollute air or water and yet fight fiercely in the face of the loss of either, so personality-disordered spouses may treat their mates abusively and yet fight to prevent their leaving.

Personality-disordered relationships are characterized by ruthless aggression and an often remarkable absence of compassion or gratitude. Each spouse, due to primitive splitting, is in affective relationship to two mates, one a "good" need-satisfying mate, and the other a "bad" need-frustrating or hostilely invasive mate. Consequently, the "bad" mate can be ruthlessly attacked without concern for harming the "good" mate.

The Motivation for Relationship

Given the internal world of persecutory self and object relationships and the precariousness of the personality-disordered individual's self-organization, the primary motivation of the relationship is the pursuit of survival, rather than fulfillment. Accordingly, energy is devoted to defense rather than to development, as relationship is lived along an axis of dominance and submission, that is, toward usage rather than affiliation.

Vignette: A Hug Is Just a Hug

Beset by anxieties, Gail suffered from early morning awakening. In need of soothing that she was unable to provide herself, she would awaken Lee and pester him until he would agree to hold her. Understandably, he was filled with resentment. However, Gail ignored his feelings, insisting that if he loved her he would want to help her in any way he could. Of course, she totally ignored the thought that if she loved him she might take his needs into account. Although she claimed otherwise, it was apparent that it did not matter that Lee's hugs were not freely given. For her, all that was important was the hug itself and the usage of Lee as a self- or transformational object.

CONCLUSION

In the paranoid-schizoid mode, the perceptual process is governed by reality-distorting primitive defenses based on splitting and disavowal. Consequently, perception becomes a self-reinforcing circularity in which internal world is superimposed upon, rather than in interactive relationship with, external reality. The perceiver projects upon external reality, then re-internalizes that which was projected, reaffirming internal world at the expense of relationship to external reality. Learning from experience is impeded. This "morphing" of reality to fit internal world schemas leads to the knitting of internal world self and object relationship patterns in the relationships of the present. External reality thus becomes constructed by internal world, or, at least, shaped and selected in the direction of concordance with the inner life, its structures, objects, and dynamic themes.

This psychological situation tyrannizes the patient, the marriage, and the treatment. Interpretations that do not coincide with the patient's are viewed as twisting the facts (Ogden 1989) and thinking about different subjects may be felt as taboo. Yet, if the therapist is unable to develop the space for an intermediate area of relatedness, in which one can think one's thoughts and feel one's feelings in the service of understanding, growth and development can not occur. In health, perception is in interactive relationship with reality, allowing internal world and external reality to enter mutually enriching relationship. Perception, in this way, is a circular process of painting the world and being painted by it; of taking things in, rapidly sorting, putting things out, and taking them back in again through all the senses. The individual attends to, is limited by, learns from, and constructs new pathways toward fulfillment (development of a personally meaningful life), simultaneously shaping external reality as he is shaped by it. This is life as art, an interactively creative and generative process. This capacity, the capacity for subjectivity, is attained in the third mode of organization, the depressive.

10

The Depressive Mode

Vignette: The Capacity for Love and Loss

George sought individual therapy when his wife Suzanne was diagnosed with terminal cancer. Their relationship through the ensuing excruciating two-year process of her dying was a tribute to the power of love and of loss. In the two years following Suzanne's death, George grieved her loss. He took trips around the country to spread her ashes where they had spent time together. He also arranged memorial services at a park they had often enjoyed, he and their friends planting trees, singing songs, and reading poetry written in her honor. In this way, George gradually laid Suzanne sufficiently to rest in his own mind to begin moving on with his life.

George began dating and eventually fell in love with Bonnie, reveling in the passion and intensity. After several months of enthusiastically reporting on his romance, George began the session saying, "There was trouble in the Garden of Eden." He explained that he awakened one morning to find Bonnie cold and distant. He tried to speak with her but she said she was "too angry to speak."

Though concerned, he respected her wish to be left alone, while expressing his desire to know what was wrong when she was ready to talk.

After two days, Bonnie told George that she was upset because he had fallen asleep during their lovemaking. He had been up late that night, partying with her friends. He felt bad that her feelings were hurt, apologized, and assured her that his falling asleep had nothing to do with his feelings for her. Bonnie accepted his apology and the relationship resumed its ecstatic thrall, until a month later when George came to the session deeply troubled. He explained that he and Bonnie had visited friends of his on Easter day. While there, he remembered that the last time he had been with these friends was on Easter day three years earlier, with Suzanne. Saddened by the memory, George shared his feeling with Bonnie in a quiet time apart from his friends. She listened and shortly after initiated a "quickie" sexual interaction. However, George, uncomfortable with his friends in the next room and not really in the mood, was unable to perform. That evening Bonnie was watching the television show *ER* and invited George to join her. He replied that he had had a lifetime full of hospitals, but would like to lay his head upon her lap as she watched the show if that was OK with her. Bonnie was agreeable and George fell asleep as she stroked his hair.

The next morning, George awakened to find Bonnie cold, aloof, and again "too angry to speak." After several days, Bonnie accused George of being "maudlin and not much fun" on Easter day. She insisted that his mood was due to his having drunk wine and not to Suzanne's death. She demanded that he not drink wine in the future, adamantly ignoring George's protest that he had had only two glasses of wine the entire evening and at six-foot-five and two hundred forty pounds was hardly under the influence.

Bonnie's tone and attitude stunned George. She completely discounted his feelings related to Suzanne and treated him as if she knew him better than he did. He felt that what she was really saying was that he could not be sad around her. If this were the case, he did not want such a relationship.

From George's description, Bonnie appeared to experience

George's sadness as taking him away from her and she found that separateness intolerable. George recalled that in the past Bonnie had bitterly described her mother as a "depressed wino." We theorized that her anger, so out of proportion to any event that had occurred, and her insistence on attributing his sadness to his having drunk wine might be linked to her relationship to her wine-drinking mother. Perhaps she was equating his sadness with her mother's "maudlin" depression. We also considered the possibility that Bonnie may have felt she had lost George to the ghost of Suzanne, as she had lost her mother to alcohol. Finally, I wondered if Bonnie's mother may have treated Bonnie's sense of loss and abandonment as Bonnie was now treating George's, that is, in angry discounting fashion. If so, Bonnie's difficulty in identifying with George's loss might be related to her difficulty in accepting her own feelings of loss, which had been defensively denied.

In any case, Bonnie's harshly strident and dissonant response to George's feelings could be manifesting her fear of the return of the repressed and her subsequent re-envelopment in the "maudlin" world of internal self and object relationships of her childhood. If this were the case, the challenge to Bonnie would be considerable in that the return of the repressed is often terrifying, enveloping the individual in the totality of the sensori-cogni-affective memory of the repressed experiences in childlike form, the form in which they were initially incurred. Consequently, regression includes the loss of adult cognitive and affective capacities to abide with and think through experience. When the repressed is evoked, relatively minor occurrences become gross misidentifications, infused with all the sensations, affects, and cognitions of the repressed situation. Furthermore, the timing of Bonnie's need of a "quickie" at George's friends' home and her relatively constant need to have "fun" could represent her efforts to defend against dysphoric feelings. It also struck me that the other time Bonnie had been "too angry to speak" had occurred when George had fallen asleep in the midst of lovemaking the previous month. Her nightly need of lovemaking, set apart from whatever else was going on, suggested that Bonnie had been unable to internalize a soothing object in childhood and consequently required the physical act of intercourse and orgasm, a literal soothing hold, to feel connected. It was plausible that Bonnie's "perfect knowledge" about what made George tick was born of her direct experience in relationship to a maudlin primary caregiver in childhood.

Of course, such considerations, without benefit of Bonnie's perceptions, were highly speculative and the conversation turned to the importance of George's discussing his concerns with Bonnie. Uncharacteristically, George was reluctant. He expressed dread, revealing for the first time that Bonnie had often been "not nice" to him and often screamed at her ex-husband. At these times he had thought, *"If she treats him that way, won't she do the same to me?"* George's omitting these observations from therapy until now suggested that he had feared them as a threat to his "Garden of Eden" fantasy of the relationship. To maintain the image-inary relationship, he had denied its disillusioning elements rather than attending to them in reality. Now, in touch with these previously denied elements, he feared Bonnie would respond in attacking manner. Nonetheless, he was more apprehensive of continuing in a relationship in which he was not recognized and decided to address these issues with Bonnie after their vacation scheduled for the following week.

Upon his return, George described Bonnie as having become increasingly distant and self-isolating during their vacation. On the first leg of the trip, they had visited her mother, who "smoked and drank orange juice and vodka from morning to night." Bonnie and her mother sat together at the kitchen table for hours, virtually ignoring him. One night her mother cooked dinner, but, under the influence of alcohol, forgot to serve it, serving dessert instead. On the next leg of their trip, Bonnie became more distant and uncommunicative. Without explanation, she slept with her clothes on and George felt a deepening chasm between them. On the flight home Bonnie was finally able to speak. They argued and mutually agreed to end the relationship. George was both disappointed and relieved—disappointed that his dream of relationship with Bonnie would not materialize, and relieved that he was not going to be a continuing part of a relationship in which he was not recognized for himself.

The next day, to George's dismay, Bonnie began a campaign of phone calls, asking him "What's wrong?" and begging him to talk to her. She also called mutual friends to recruit them to speak to him on her behalf and camped out in front of his home with her five-year-old daughter, alternately calling from her car phone and banging on the door, yelling for him to come out. George felt physically threatened by the desperateness of her behavior and told her through the door that he would call the police if she did not leave. She maintained her telephone campaign for a number of days, filling his answering machine with messages, before finally giving up.

Upon hearing this alarming news, I speculated that Bonnie had been swallowed up by the return of the repressed. With the loss of her capacity for self-observation and self-reflection, she was reduced to acting out her feelings rather than thinking them through. Her behavior conveyed a palpable sense of panic akin to that experienced by a child threatened by the loss of a parent. It seemed to me that for Bonnie past and present, internal and external, fantasy and reality were now one.

SUBJECTIVITY AND RELATIONSHIP

The "I" of the interpreting subject arises in the same space that is necessary for the formation of the "we" of relationship, that is, the thirdness of the "potential space." The potential space is a hypothetical area in which internal world and external reality are in inter-enriching co-mingling relationship, rather than polarized and adversarial co-mangling relationship. The potential space is the space of symbolic activity—thinking, play, creativity, metaphor, poetry, art, philosophy, and spirituality—in which the complex and paradoxical nature of life can best be fathomed and through which surface experience derives meaning and depth (Winnicott 1971). Real, as opposed to image-inary, relationship occurs in the thirdness of the potential space. In this conceptual area, relationship is conceived and evolves, forms and reforms, impelled by the single constant of life; change.

In the depressive mode relationship is an intangible, conceived in the mind of each partner yet also existing outside of the partners, comprising a "third" that simultaneously borders upon, connects, and separates them. In early developmental form, "relatedness" is misconstrued as "relationship" (Shapiro and Carr 1991). At this level we feel we "know" our others and ourselves when much of what is known is derived from internal self and object representations internalized in childhood. With continuing development, internal self and object representations are distinguished, and along with them internal world is distinguished from external reality and past is distinguished from present. Learning from experience is then possible, as the "what was" of past experience may be distinguished from the "what is" of contemporary reality, thereby opening the possibility of the "what can be" of future imaginings. In this process, the individual becomes a subject, the author of his life and the interpreter of his own meaning, rather than merely an actor in an intergenerationally scripted family play.

Tragically, Bonnie seemed unable to differentiate between the "what was" of her childhood and the "what is" of her contemporary relationship to George. Consequently, there could be no consideration of alternate futures. Bonnie had never differentiated herself from her childhood and thus remained defined by it, so that her present was foretold by her past.

To the extent a relative lack of differentiation continues between self and other in contemporary reality, the individual will maintain a pathological self-relationship manifested in self-attacking internal dialogues (how we speak to ourselves) and self-defeating behaviors.

Vignette: Differentiation

Monica, an artist in her seventies, entered treatment financially and emotionally impoverished, in part because even the thought of exhibiting her work generated disabling colitis and nightmares. Monica was the older of two daughters. Her father was a self-centered workaholic who alternately loved and then rejected with disparaging criticisms. Her mother, a talented musician, had never achieved success and pushed Monica to excel in classical dance, an area in which she had little interest or ability. Monica recalled her mother's disappointment in her performances and her own depressing "doing what was expected."

One day Monica, reminiscing, recalled a time that her mother had watched a modern dance performance that Monica had choreographed. She spoke with anger and then guilt about her mother's lack of enthusiasm for her work. When I inquired as to the content of her guilt, Monica remembered that it was just after this incident that her mother was diagnosed with leukemia, from which she died several months later. Monica then associated to visiting her mother in the hospital and the shock of seeing her mother's swollen body, distorted by internal hemorrhaging. Monica whispered, "She didn't deserve to die that way," and then, after a pause, added in guilt-ridden voice, "That's not true. I had the thought that she did deserve to die that way, poisoned from within by her own bitterness that tore up her insides."

After her mother's death Monica pursued her ambition to be a visual artist, albeit with some guilt. However, although her work was praised, it did not sell. She felt "torn up inside," ever disappointing and disappointed. At these times she would berate her work and consider herself foolish to believe she had talent. Nonetheless, Monica doggedly pursued her dream, maintaining peripheral jobs with some financial help from her sister. She complained of friends and family constantly encouraging her to market her work and frequently advising her on how to go about it. Monica resented their encouragement and advice in that she became confused as to what was her ambition and what was theirs, as if she were still in relationship to her mother. In addition, she noted a coterie of friends who did not treat her well. For example, her art dealer was a friend, who, Monica complained, "promises the world but does nothing." On one occasion, Monica had actually observed her interfering with a sale, realizing then that her friend had a personal investment in her not being successful and thereby independent of her.

As treatment continued, I wondered about her contribution to these recurring dynamics. A possible answer was found in my observing instances when I would become activated to make suggestions to her. At these times, she presented in extremely passive and helpless fashion. In exploring this issue Monica felt that through her passivity she sustained the illusion that someone would step in and take care of her, as if she were entitled and needed to be treated like a little girl, to have the parent she felt she had never had.

During a weeklong family reunion, Monica's family, especially a cousin, persistently urged her to market her work. Monica immediately felt stomach pain and then visualized her mother, in witchlike form, within her, tearing at her insides with long talons. Monica reported, "She was so alive inside me that I could see and feel her. I felt that I was in contest with her for my soul."

Monica told her cousin that she needed to find her own way to exhibit her work and that further discussion was not helpful. Nevertheless, he continued offering suggestions. Monica recalled, "It was as if he didn't hear me. That alone reminded me so much of my mother. I'd suddenly had enough and shouted, 'That's it! No more! Shut up!'" Nothing more was said concerning Monica's work.

Near the end of the reunion, Monica, in clearer understanding of her own desires and strengthened by her ability to assert herself, invited her cousin to go with her to explore the possibility of exhibiting at several galleries. The first gallery turned Monica down, but to her own surprise she felt undeterred and contacted two more galleries that expressed interest in her work.

On her return to Baltimore, Monica felt overwhelmed by the details of preparing exhibits and meeting other commitments. At this time her art dealer called, asking her to fill in for an employee who had taken ill. Monica declined, given the demands upon her time. She trembled as she heard the disappointment in her friend's voice, shadows of her mother's disappointment. "It was so hard to do and to feel, but I knew I didn't have the time and that I needed to take care of myself. I was worried that my refusal would hurt my friendship, but I knew I didn't want it if it had to be based on meeting her needs to the point of disregarding my own."

Though these interactions were difficult, Monica met with good results and most of her relationships deepened. She eventually ended her relationship with her dealer and within a year had located a dealer who was enthusiastic in marketing her work, and several exhibits were arranged.

In experience-near fashion Monica recognized that her mother had aspired to personal fulfillment through her, thereby treating her as both an extension of herself and as the cause of her own disappointment. It was when Monica began thinking about her stomach ailments and nightmares in symbolic, rather than literal or concrete, form that she recognized their relationship to the internally attacking object representation of her mother and began differentiating herself from it. Subsequently, she was able to begin constructing a life of her own, in place of the one that had been created by her parents. Her art became more deeply expressive, her work began to sell, and her income more than doubled, although it is too soon to know how financially successful she will be. Monica now travels far afield from the gut reactions of her past, deciding for herself the worth of her work.

In the depressive mode, the individual is aware that she is evolving and remains at least a partial mystery to herself and to her others. This is a happy circumstance in that it allows for continuing growth and discovery, a generative staying young at heart, an always "coming to know." In addition, coming to know another entails the ability to "I"-dentify with them, that is, to find ourselves in the other and the other in ourselves. In this sense, we cannot know another beyond our knowledge of ourselves. Coincidentally, we can know ourselves only to the extent that we are the object of our own curiosity. Self-observation and self-reflection—the ability to identify our thoughts, feelings, and perceptions and to reflect upon them—

comprise the soil from which subjectivity (being the architect of one's life and the creator of one's own meaning) and both self- and object relations emerge.

To become subjects it is necessary, but not sufficient, to be aware of our thoughts and feelings. We must also be able to think about them and to interpret their meaning to us. Thoughts and feelings are "no-thing" in themselves; they are referents, referring to experience. It is in the determining of that to which they refer that we determine their meaning. This is the essence of subjectivity, the "I" that is capable of thinking (processing) the thoughts and feelings that occur to the "me." Via this capacity subjects come to live life in a self-directed and, thereby, personally meaningful way. Other people's opinions, feelings, and ideas are taken into account, but they are not governing. True subjects are self-responsible, that is, they realize that they are responsible for their decisions and that their decisions have consequences that influence the sense of self and shape the relationship to reality. It is in the continuing-on-becoming of subjectivity, rather than relegating oneself to the status of a final product that is fated to live a scripted life (Bollas 1987), that life is lived fully.

Bonnie did not relate to George as a subject, a separate person in his own right, but as an object or thing characterized and carica-turized by her static internal representation of him. George decided to end the relationship (self-direction) rather than live in Bonnie's internal world of petrified and petrifying objects (self-responsibility). It seemed that Bonnie was fighting a long-lost battle with her mother (transference relating) in her relationship with George. She did not differentiate George from her internal (m)other and thus was destined to repeat her past in the present, thereby ensuring the return of the repressed, the loss of the object—on this occasion, George.

The importance of attaining the capacity to abide with one's thoughts and feelings and to be able to think about them, as opposed to acting them out, in service of self-direction and self-responsibility is further illustrated in the following case.

Vignette: Developing Self-Relationship

Donna, a promiscuous young woman, had lived her life governed by her impulses. After three years of therapy, she was gradually developing the capacity to identify her thoughts and feelings (self-observation and self-awareness) and to begin understanding to what they referred. After much consideration (thinking her thoughts and feeling her feelings), she decided to end a year-long relationship with an older man that was stagnant. Within days, a married man invited her to his home while his wife was away. Donna was intensely excited by the thought of "walking the edge" of this taboo. Nevertheless, once in his home, she became aware of conflicting thoughts and feelings. Instead of sloughing them off as she would have done previously, she allowed herself to abide with them and to think about their meaning. Eventually, dry-mouthed and weak-kneed, she left, without acting out the fantasy (self-direction). She reported, "I just couldn't do it. I knew that the reality would be awful for me. Everyone would be hurt: me, the guy, his wife, his children, and I would feel terrible. I feel really good that I didn't go through with it. It almost wasn't even a decision. I knew how I would feel afterward and it changed everything. I didn't want to feel that way (self-responsibility)."

Later in the session Donna noted, "I realize that I use sex with men to get away from feeling unattractive. But, I know that being with a man is only a passing relief. Then, I feel ugly again. I use the guy and he uses me. There's no love or caring. That just doesn't work for me anymore. I've got to deal with feeling ugly. No one else can fix that for me. I've got to change the way I feel about myself. I discovered that it's possible when I left that guy's house."

Donna discovered the possibility of shaping her sense of self (creating her own meaning). She recognized that her actions registered upon her sense of self, for good and for ill (self-responsibility). She no longer related to herself or to others as static objects or things that could not be injured. Subsequently, when she gave in to impulsive behaviors, she had more awareness and looked more deeply into the feelings she was acting out and the causes behind them. Moreover, as she recognized that she was not a once-and-for-all "final product," she entered more compassionate and patient relationship to herself, accepting that her going-on-becoming would not be "all at once," nor once-and-for-all, but would be an ongoing process.

With the development of subjectivity we realize we have a choice about how we live our lives and how we feel about ourselves. We also discover why we have not learned this sooner. To be an individual, an "I am," is often inconvenient, awkward, uncomfortable, and even dangerous at times: we may not be accepted, we may lose relationships, and our decisions may hurt others—even though this is not the intent. Having one's own mind leads to willingness to "rock the boat," rather than maintain an illusion of harmony at any cost. The words "I am" are the two most aggressive words in the English language (Winnicott 1957), yet if we ignore them we remain governed by a self-repressive internal regime that stifles freedom of thought and creativity, emptying us of vitality and personal meaning.

In the movie *The Bridges of Madison County*, Jessica writes of her brief affair with Robert, "Whatever I felt, whatever I wanted, I gave myself up to. I was acting like another woman, but I was more myself than ever before." Although Jessica soon decides she cannot live her life in hedonistic fashion, the freedom and sense of aliveness she discoveres in paying attention to her needs transforms her relationship to her self. Subsequently, she develops a friendship with another woman with whom she can be herself. Jessica later writes a letter to her children, stating, "As one gets older what is important is to be known."

THE CHARACTERISTICS OF THE DEPRESSIVE-SUBJECTIVE MODE

The Leading Anxiety: Concern for the Other and Concern for the Self

The capacity for empathy is a developmental achievement. It arises from whole-object relating, that is, the realization that the "good" and "bad" object are one and the same and, therefore, that attacks on the "bad" object threaten injury to the "good" object. Consequently, loving and hating feelings enter relationship to each other, leading to the capacity for concern and empathy. Compassion then supercedes the ruthless aggression that predominates in the midst of primitive splitting and part-object relatedness.

The Bridges of Madison County also illustrates the functioning of genuine concern and the capacity to manage conflicting feelings without primitive splitting and denial. Jessica's genuine concern for her self, her husband Richard, and their children is evident in the thoughtful and heartrending process by which she comes to her decision to remain with them. She understands that Richard could never satisfy her dreams, but also that he is a good man and that she cares about him. She recognizes that he could "never get his arms around" her leaving him and that her children continue to need her. Because she cares about each of them and is able to identify the impact her leaving would have upon them, she understands that to leave with Robert would "destroy everything that has been," and that her ensuing guilt would destroy the love that she and Robert shared. She recognizes that either decision—to leave or to stay—entails loss, but only the decision to leave would be destructive. Consequently, staying is the only decision with which she could live.

In the relationship of George and Bonnie, George anticipated that ending the relationship with Bonnie would cause pain, but also recognized that remaining in the relationship would lead to escalating conflict that would be destructive to them both. George's compassion was evident in his sadness and in his unwillingness to engage in retaliatory attacks, despite Bonnie's behavior. In contrast, Bonnie related to George transferentially as a maudlin and unavailable object and attacked him ruthlessly as a "bad" object when his behavior disappointed her and cued associations to her neglectful mother, and later exerted tremendous pressure on him to remain in the relationship when she was confronted with his leaving (loss of the object). Concern for George as a separate person was not evident.

Method of Defense

The realization of the self as an "I"—a self-aware and self-reflective subject—and the awareness of the other as an "I" emerges simultaneously with and contributes to a decrease in reliance upon primitive defenses based on splitting and denial. As the subject enters relationship to the previously denied aspects of self, she enters whole relationship to self and other.

More sophisticated, less reality-distorting, defenses emerge as a result of the integration of the various part-object perceptions: intellectualization, rationalization, repression, conversion, displacement, and sublimation. The establishment of a consensual reality and a mutuality of concerns are then possible. This is a monumental achievement, entailing the capacity to tolerate the tension of ambivalence. As the spouses shift from the defensive pursuit of power and control to the pursuit of meaning and understanding, thinking through comes to predominate over acting out as the primary means of dealing with endangering experience.

This distinction was evident in George and Bonnie's relationship. George's efforts were oriented toward the exchange of mental contents in the service of developing a mutuality of understanding. Unfortunately, Bonnie was so narcissistically injured and enraged that she was "too angry to speak," and when she did it was in attacking fashion and to impose control upon George. Her all-knowing stood in opposition to his wish to understand and to be understood: Since she was certain of everything, nothing needed to be understood.

Quality of Self and Object Relationships

With the development of subjectivity life may be lived three-dimensionally, surface and depth distinguished by the interpreting subject. In addition, the subject "I" can recognize the other as an "I" who is both similar and different and whose needs are of importance. It is then understood that at times the other will—and at times will not—meet our needs. What is important is not the perfect meeting of our needs but a preponderance of good results that lead to a sense of connection or couple-ness.

The quality of relationship emerges through evolving mutual "I"-dentifications. The more the partners understand and have genuine concern and empathy for each other, the more likely the need of attachment will be met and the greater the capacity to tolerate inevitable disappointments. In this sense, intimacy is the recognition of oneself in the other and the other in oneself, while valuing the differences that exist between the two.

Genuine relationship includes the capacity to be one's self vigorously, which includes not only the willingness to say "yes" to the needs or wishes of the other, but also the willingness to say "no" if saying "yes" would involve a betrayal of the self. Too prolonged or too frequent submissions of the self are "soul murders" (Shengold 1989), stifling development and fostering malignant resentments. Genuine human connection can be realized only to the extent that we are true to ourselves and represent ourselves truly. Integrity (true-self-ness) is the highest form of integration. "Being oneself" involves the integration of, the ongoing dialogue between, the various aspects of the self. Conversely, incongruities between thoughts, feelings, words, and actions reflect dis-integrities, which promote disintegrating effects including anxiety. Furthermore, "being in relationship" involves the integration of and the ongoing dialogue between (dialectic) the two subjectivities that comprise the relation-ship.

Vignette: Don't I Have the Right to Change My Mind?

Zelda personified incongruity in self and other relations. It was not so much that she lied, but that she suffered from a lack of integration between her thoughts, feelings, words, and actions. She repeatedly said one thing and did another. Her husband, Pierre, increasingly frustrated and insecure in his relationship with her, commented, "I feel driven crazy. I cannot rely on what she says.

When we discuss something I think it's resolved and then she doesn't follow through." Zelda, unfazed by what she perceived as his need to control her, commented, "Don't people have the right to change their mind?" ignoring the fact that for her this was the rule, not the exception.

Eventually, Pierre, noting that "love is like an apple out of which you can only take so many bites," separated from Zelda several months after she unilaterally declared she was ending couples therapy. Zelda was furious with Pierre and felt "dumped" by him, ignoring any connection between his leaving and her own behavior, about which he had so frequently complained. She raged at the unfairness of it all: "I was happy in the relationship; he was the one who had a problem."

Soon Zelda began having severe somatic complaints, most notably the loss of feeling on the right half of her body and shingles. A neurologist confirmed that her numbness was psychosomatic. However she was again unable to consider the possibility that the dis-integrated way she related to self and other manifested itself in disintegrative anxiety and conversion symptoms. On occasion, she would speak of how sad and lonely she felt, and of how other men did not provide her with the security Pierre had. Yet such awareness would soon be shunted aside, as she continued to deny her part in making the marriage an insecure one for Pierre. Unable to learn from her own experience, she foreclosed the opportunity to salvage the marriage or to learn from it. As long as she continues in this way, her future is as certain as her past.

The importance of the recognition of the other as a separate "I" who cares about "me" is crucial. This is the feeling that bounds and keeps the couple coupled through difficult times. Ironically, perhaps the greatest tribute to the quality of a relationship is when both partners can be miserable together without either blaming the other. Each understands and accepts their separateness and his or her own miseries as sometimes unrelated to the other, and neither holds the other responsible for his or her own mental state.

Bonnie, in the opening vignette, had not attained this understanding. She was unable to allow George his own feelings of loss and sadness that stood apart from her, and consequently felt threatened by his separateness. She became angry with George when he was not completely available to her, acting as if he were the problem. She was unable to relate to George as a separate person, whose needs could legitimately diverge from her own. Swallowed up by her own abandonment anxiety and internal world of pathological object relationships, she equated George with her internal mother, juxtaposing his drinking wine with her mother's drunkenness, his sadness with her mother's maudlin depression, and his separateness with her mother's abandonment and neglect of her.

With the development of subjectivity, relationship is recognized as both a creation and a potential. Each spouse functions as a co-sculptor of its evolving form, giving and receiving and investing it with loving and aggressive drives. The sharing of feelings and perceptions may be satisfying or painful, but in either event is valued as the vehicle through which continued coming-to-knowing takes place. Integrity prevails. Relationship becomes not a one-plus-one that equals two, but a one in relationship to another one, two "I's" that form the thirdness of a "we."

The Primary Motivation: The Pursuit of Fulfillment

With the development of relative independence and autonomy of the depressive-subjective mode, the survival-threatening fear of the loss of the other and of the self is surpassed with a valuation of the self and concern for the other. As concern for the survival of the self ebbs, concern with the quality of life and of relationship flows.

Developing subjectivity is both liberating and frightening, for with it comes the realization that we cannot viably treat ourselves as things and force ourselves to live life in a scripted way without expense to the sense of self. Consequently, we are faced with the uncertainties and losses that this entails.

Vignette: Self-Navigation

Josh, a twenty-four-year-old man who had struggled for years with
bipolar disorder, narcissistic personality disorder with explosive
features, drug and alcohol abuse, and suicidal behavior, had made
substantial progress over a four-year course of individual therapy. He
commented, "As I get stronger within myself I'm real clear that I
want to attend college. But I don't think Dave, my best friend, is
happy for me. He always has something negative to say when I talk
about my plans and keeps pushing me to go out drinking and
partying every night. I'm afraid we'll grow apart and that makes me
sad. I know he is as afraid of life as I am, but he is too afraid to admit
it. He keeps partying, pretending to be cool and not worried about
the future. . . . I'm really afraid too, but I want to make something
of my life and not wind up ten years from now where I am today.
And, I know now that being afraid isn't a reason not to face it. That
would just keep me more afraid."

Josh, in acknowledging and struggling with his human imperfections, including his fears, was able to identify with those of his
friend. He empathized with Dave while maintaining his own course.
Previously, the possibility of the loss of this relationship would have
blown Josh completely off his own course. Now he understood that
such possibilities are an ever-present part of life and that he could
choose to be controlled by them or decide to make his own way.
Now, he rights himself repeatedly, as he moves toward what he wants
to become and how he wants his life to be.

With a decrease in reliance on primitive defenses and the
integration of feelings of love and hate, there is a growing ability to
accept human foibles and limitations, both in oneself and others.
Instead of a looking "down on" the other or a looking "up at" the
other, there is a self- and other-identifying looking "over at" the
other (personal communication, 1995). The recognition of similarities, differences, boundaries, and limits entails a sense of freedom
and relief. We recognize not only the responsibility for our own life
and the power to shape it but the growing realization that perfection
is not attainable and that we are not responsible for everything that

happens. Accordingly, the achievement of a preponderance of good results, in life and relationship, becomes understood as a far more realistic and realizable goal than the pursuit of perfection, the surest route to unhappiness and to the spoiling of what might otherwise have been.

The Capacity for Reparation

With the emergence of genuine concern, adult-to-adult relationships realize a mutual interdependence, each partner being both giver and receiver—each giving and accepting parts of self and other, literally and figuratively. Healthy adult relationships entail a *will toward vulnerability*, in which each spouse gives without guarantee of acceptance, and each risks taking in what is given by the other to experience its fulfilling potential.

Giving from and receiving into the heart is a risk-taking in that the psychological walls erected against the possibility of loss and pain must come down without guarantee. The risk of vulnerability is particularly difficult when it is needed most: when a relationship is not going well. One feels exquisitely vulnerable to being "cut to the quick." Continuing to invest oneself in becoming known may be felt as equivalent to walking up a slaughterhouse ramp. The spouses often say, "I can't do it. It makes no sense to me. I can't let my guard down. I've done it before only to be hurt again and again." Yet for the relationship to evolve the partners must, as described in Rudyard Kipling's (1910) poem "If," risk all they have, lose, and risk all again, in pursuit of the "coming to be known" of real relationship. Even if this effort fails, the relationship to ourselves deepens and clarifies the obstacles to real relationship.

Of course, a line must be drawn somewhere. On one side, we must thoroughly understand our contributions to the problems in the relationship, differentiating between legitimate and realizable expectations and those that are not. On the other side, if all avenues of resolution have been explored and a preponderance of bad results continue to occur, then a sea change may be warranted, involving a change in the object of desire rather than in the desire itself. Such realizations are painful and sad, not angry and hostile, for the self-responsible individual does not hold the mate accountable for his own fulfillment or for what the mate can or cannot give.

Unfortunately, people who have encountered generally bad results in childhood relationships experience vulnerability only as terrifying. They continuously project past hurts and basic mistrust around every bend in the road and often prefer to remain with the "devil that is known." Those fortunate enough to have experienced the good-enough holding that led to faith in themselves are more willing to risk pain in the pursuit of the object of their desires.

Relationship to self and other in the depressive-subjective mode is multifaceted. With the continuity of self-relations across time and changing circumstances, each moment emerges from the last and toward the next. Far from a devotion to the Golden God of Olympian Omnipotence, which leads to the effort to concretize and absolutely control life and relationship, there is recognition of finiteness: time, boundary, and space. The complex and paradoxical nature of life is given meaning by the acceptance of finiteness, including one's mortality. We come to recognize that not every story has a happy ending, and that the only thing over which we have some control is how we relate to life's events in the service of our own becoming.

A major part of the never-ending road of growing up involves the gradual introduction to reality and the ensuing realization that we cannot remain in childlike relationship to the world. In failing to heed the curbs that reality provides we ride off the road and over the cliff, for fantasy without reality is akin to having an accelerator without brakes. For individuals in the pursuit of symbiotic relationship, reality is not seen as a Terra Firma upon which to stand, but as a Terror Inferno to be avoided. The individual moves away from thoughts and feelings, which carry anxiety, rather than toward them in the service of understanding. Conversely, individuals in the depressive mode sense that health does not equal happiness, that life and death, gain and loss, satisfaction and frustration are dancing hand-in-hand all the time: duality equals totality. They understand that every decision entails loss—even when it is a good one—and that losing is not something to be avoided at any cost.

Whole relationship to self and other is of whole cloth. Its threads are multicolored, changing in hue across time and circumstance while maintaining, more or less, the continuity of the whole. This is not a constant awareness, but is won, lost, and won again in the never-ending interplay between the need for separateness and the need for relationship. From time to time we can all become swallowed up by ourselves, or lost to ourselves, in one circumstance or another. It is in the ability to be aware of and think about these shifting states that we navigate the diamond shoals between self and other.

As with most things, this is easy to say and hard to do, particularly when the journeyers, already adults, must begin near the beginning. In any event, the outcome is never known ahead of time. All that we can do is aspire to some understanding of how to go about the journey. It is never too late to begin—in fact, whenever one begins is just the right time.

III

Treatment

11

Treatment Overview

The treatment of personality-disordered couples is devoted to helping the spouses develop the capacity to relate in more normal/neurotic fashion, that is, in real as opposed to image-inary relationship to self and other. It is important to keep in mind that all humans experience some degree of deficit in early development and that image-inary relatedness (projection and transference) is found to varying degrees in every marriage. Normal/neurotic marriages (Figure 11–1) also face regression, acting out, and less-than-empathically-attuned responsiveness. The difference in normal/neurotic marriages is that when the spouses tumble into areas of blurred identity, they are more capable of processing the resulting dissonance in the service of deepening relationship. This generative processing of experience returns the couple to mutually attuned and responsive relating, with the possibility of even greater integration of self and relationship.

In contrast, personality-disordered spouses have a deficit in the capacity to observe or reflect upon their experience and continue to generate transference-based perceptions of self and other. Resolu-

Figure 11–1. The Normal/Neurotic Couple

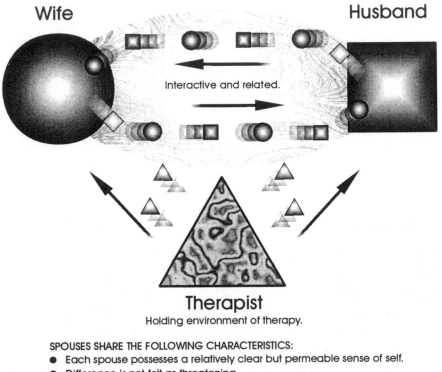

Wife

Husband

Interactive and related.

Therapist
Holding environment of therapy.

SPOUSES SHARE THE FOLLOWING CHARACTERISTICS:
- Each spouse possesses a relatively clear but permeable sense of self.
- Difference is not felt as threatening.
- A mutuality of understanding evolves.
- Direct spousal interaction is possible without frequent regression to the use of primitive defenses.
- The couple is able to maintain the holding environment of the relationship without frequent interventions by therapist.

tion of conflict and evolution of relationship are impeded. The personality-disordered relationship remains in more primitive, polarized, and complementary part-object relationship form, typified by each spouse's failure to relate to self and other as whole persons. Instead, each maintains disavowing relationship to aspects of self and projects these aspects onto the mate, and then rejects the mate.

As a result, blaming and shaming interactions prevail and the perception of self and other exists largely in fantasy rather than in reality. There may be truth to the projections, but it is far from the whole truth (Figure 11–2).

The central challenge to the treatment of the personality-disordered couple is that the partners are psychologically ill-

Figure 11–2. The Personality-Disordered Couple

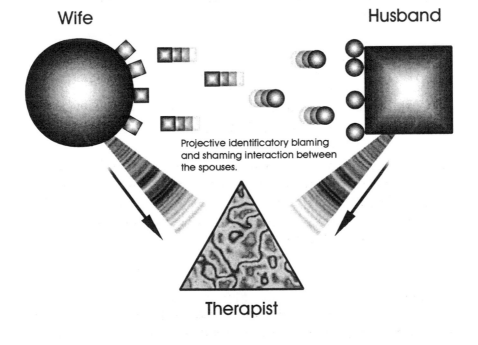

Each spouse is intent on convincing the therapist of his or her own reality.
Oriented toward control, not exploration or understanding.

Wife   **Husband**

Projective identificatory blaming
and shaming interaction between
the spouses.

Therapist

SPOUSES SHARE THE FOLLOWING CHARACTERISTICS:
• Little infrastructure or interiority.
• Communication is blaming and attacking or withholding and withdrawing.
• Motivation to control and change the other; not to understand.
• Interaction is co-mangling, not co-mingling.

equipped to process and learn from experience. The capacity to think through, a relative given in normal/neurotic relationships, is in fact a developmental accomplishment of the highest order, on par with the evolution of the self from single cell to whole subject. Accordingly, traditional models of marital therapy—presuming the use of language as symbolic process, the capacity to abide with painful experience, the ability to use abstraction and metaphor, the importance of exploring interactional patterns and meta-communications, the sharing of thoughts and feelings, the alleviation of repression, and the pursuit of conflict resolution—radically overestimate the rudimentary development of the personality-disordered individual.

THE HOLDING ENVIRONMENT AS AN ESSENTIAL TREATMENT CONSTRUCT

The advocated approach concentrates on fostering each spouse's journey along the developmental road toward independence. It is in the journey of separation, individuation, and differentiation that the capacity to sort through and learn from experience develops and that relationship to self and other evolves.

Winnicott (1960b) believed that every human being intrinsically contains momentum toward emotional growth, and that growth would naturally occur given a good-enough holding environment. Winnicott defined three stages of development: absolute dependence, relative dependence, and toward independence (Davis and Walbridge 1981, Winnicott 1956, 1958b). Each of these stages requires different functions and aspects of the holding environment as it evolves in relationship to the developing self.

In the stage of absolute dependence, there is a valuing of being versus reacting, to provide space for self-experience. For example, an infant's exploratory movements are different than movements prompted by being stuck with a pin. The motivation for the former is internal, while the latter forces the infant to react to an impinging environment. Winnicott believed that when the baby acts, it should be due to its own initiative and thus represent an expression of self

(Davis and Walbridge 1981, Winnicott 1956, 1960a). In turn, a series of self-expressions results in an emerging pattern of self-experience and self-organization.

In the stage of relative dependence, the focus is on ego support versus ego impingement. The emphasis of the holding environment is on helping the individual to process and learn from experience, the development of mastery and competence.

Finally, in the stage of toward independence the focus of the holding environment is on reparation versus annihilation. As the individual learns from experience, she learns that need-satisfying and need-frustrating objects are the same. Consequently, ruthless attacks upon the latter are understood to endanger the former. Genuine concern and empathy are fostered. In addition, the holding environment of reparation versus annihilation cultivates the realization that repair for damage done is possible when concern is genuine and learning from the experience has occurred.

To the extent that there is an absence of an adequate holding environment, the evolution of the self toward independence goes awry. The development of autonomy is encumbered. An internally derived and secure sense of self does not become consolidated. Anxiety, mistrust, and pessimism prevail. When stressful events or even disappointments occur, the relatively precarious sense of self is threatened and the legacy of impingement, abuse, or neglect is re-evoked, leading to catastrophic or worst case thinking and feeling. The amplified concerns with survival result in further reliance upon primitive defenses, promoting further regression.

To offset these difficulties, the therapist works to create a holding environment that fosters the safety of the self of each spouse. The holding environment is prerequisite to the development of the potential space. Thinking, versus acting out, occurs within the potential space. The holding environment is created in the marital therapy by the therapist's intervening between the spouses when they enter primitive projective identificatory relationship to each other (Figure 11–3). This is typically signaled by the onset of blaming and shaming interactions. At this point, the therapist engages each spouse in separate dyadic interactions, each

Figure 11–3. Beginning Process of Separate Dyadic Interactions

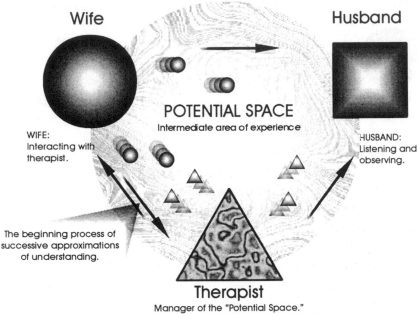

Wife

Husband

POTENTIAL SPACE

Intermediate area of experience

WIFE:
Interacting with
therapist.

HUSBAND:
Listening and
observing.

The beginning process of
successive approximations
of understanding.

Therapist
Manager of the "Potential Space."
Creating space for observation and reflection.

in the presence of the other, with the focus on processing that which resulted in the onset of the use of primitive defenses in the pursuit of understanding. Via reliance on clarification and tentative interpretations, the therapist develops a series of successive approximations of understanding toward the end goal of developing mutual understanding. In this way thinking through, versus acting out, is fostered in the experience of the session itself (Figure 11–4).

As the self develops and concerns with survival ebb, valuing of the quality of life and of relationship flows. In marital relationship, concern with the survival of the self is evident when the couple is in pursuit of the absence of the "bad." They declare a "good week" when there has been an absence of fighting. In contrast, the

Figure 11–4. Understanding by Successive Approximations

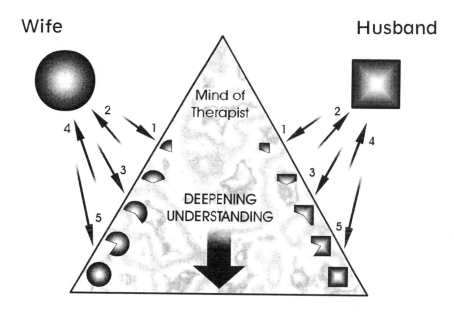

Developing an understanding of each spouse's experience through a
process of tentative interpretations and successive approximations.

couple's transition to concerns with the quality of life and relationship is witnessed in the pursuit of the presence of the "good." The
spouses declare they have had a "good week" because they have
been able to talk to and understand each other leading to the
experience of connection.

THERAPIST'S CONTRIBUTION TO
THE TREATMENT EFFORT

The evolution of the self is an arduous journey at any time. However,
it is particularly so in adulthood when much has gone awry in early

development. The personality-disordered adult is reliant upon all-or-nothing defenses and wedded to the pathological world of self and object relationships. His psyche is permeated with lacunae from developmental deficits. There is a resultant schism between internal world and external reality. This leads to either the superimposition of internal world upon external reality, in defense against the experience of external reality as impinging, or the superimposition of external reality upon internal world as manifested in those individuals who hold that if everything looks all right, it is right. Perception is distorted and learning from experience is impeded.

In therapy, the therapist is the manager of the holding environment and also represents and cultivates the area for potential space in which thinking can begin to develop. In this role, the therapist values internal world *and* external reality and endeavors to construct a forum, the potential space, in which the two may enter mutually enriching relationship. Common sense tells us that the potential space cannot be developed if the focus of treatment is exclusively on manifest content, reason, and logic, any more than a child's panic can be calmed by reason alone. Nor can it be achieved through attending to feelings and fantasies, without regard for reason and contemporary reality. What this means for the therapist is that, just as child rearing is a full-contact relationship between parent and child, so too is the relationship between therapist and spouses a multidimensional one.

The phrase *treatment from relationship* speaks to the therapist's use of her whole self in working with the couple. Treatment from relationship occurs in the following way: As one spouse attempts to rid himself of threatening parts via denial and/or primitive projective identificatory processes, the therapist uses countertransference awareness to identify with that which is being denied and/or projected. The existence of denial or projection is manifested in "dis-integrities" or incongruities in the presentation of one or both spouses. In contrast to the spouses, the therapist aspires to identification with that which is denied or projected. The therapist attempts to introjectively identify and contain the spouses' projections, so that she may abide with, organize, identify, sort through, and return

them to the spouses in modified form. Through introjective identification, the therapist labors to understand the nature of the
spouses' intrapsychic struggles as they are interpersonalized within
the treatment relationship, between either spouse and the therapist
and in the marriage. Using self-experience, the therapist strives to
enter real, that is authentic, reality-based (internal and external),
and personally meaningful relationship to the spouses. In essence,
the therapist practices what she preaches. She does what she is
asking the spouses to do: abide with, sort through, and process
experience so that the experience becomes identified and understood and the process itself becomes available for internalization.

This is a time-consuming, difficult (mentally and emotionally),
and nonlinear process. The spouses' mental contents are not easy to
organize and identify. Often in bits and pieces and prethought
form, such as sensations, the spouses' projections are confusing and
elusive, sometimes best sensed or intuitively grasped through the
therapist's reveries in relationship to the couple. As the therapist
abides with her confusing experience in relationship to the couple,
rather than trying to get away from it by excessive activity or
organizing of the session, the experience percolates and is filtered,
consciously and unconsciously, through the therapist's psychological matrix, where it becomes subject to the natural organizing
tendencies of the therapist's self. In turn, this makes the experience
available to her capacity to think. As the therapist forms partial and
trial identifications, they are shared with the spouses through
exploratory questions and tentative comments and interpretations
(speculations). The therapist does not equate her experience with
that of the spouses, but verbalizes her attempts to understand her
experience in relationship to the spouses. She clearly labels her
thinking as partial or tentative, and actively encourages the spouses
to correct or modify her perceptions. Through a series of these
partial identifications the therapist achieves "successive approxima-
tion" (Stern 1985) of the spouses' experience (Figure 11–4).

This nonlinear process involves associative thinking and the
therapist's reveries in effort to understand the couple's experience.
The incongruities of the spouses' presentation are understood to be

"ill-logical" in terms of external reality, but profoundly "psycho-logical" in respect to internal reality. Surface incongruities are understood to have subterranean coherence, embedded within the dynamic unconscious of each spouse. While surface incongruities frustrate the therapist's attempts at understanding through reliance on linear thinking, the therapist's reliance on associative thinking and reveries—her own subterranean connections—can yield understanding, or confusion that may lead toward understanding of the spouses and the relationship between them.

The therapist's interpretations are usually tentative because they are acknowledged speculations. Accordingly, spouses are encouraged to modify or reject the interpretations to the extent they don't "feel right" or "fit." *Rejectable interpretations* are less inviting of persecutory anxieties and easier for the spouses to consider. They are not given from on high, but from across, as the therapist attempts to sort through and understand shared experience. The tentative nature of the therapist's comments conveys that she does not "know," she is "only thinking." As the therapist explores her thoughts, feelings, and perceptions in relationship to the spouses, the couple is led to think about their experience as it is "held" by her. This fosters self-reflection, through reflecting on the experience of the therapist. In this way, the therapist partially internalizes the illness (projections) of the spouses. As these are processed and understood, they become available for re-internalization. In this way, the spouses begin to nibble away, in start-and-stop fashion, at endangering aspects of self and other. Often, before they themselves recognize it, they come to better observe and think about their own experiences as these are held, identified, thought about, and clarified in relationship with the therapist. As understanding is achieved, previously denied aspects are put into the perspective of the whole, thereby becoming less powerful, less endangering, more understood, and more manageable—and therefore more available for reintegration.

As a result of this process of struggle among equals, in that the therapist is struggling to understand rather than speaking all-knowingly from on high, security and trust are enhanced and the spouses' persecutory anxieties and reliance upon primitive defenses decrease. In that the therapist works with (i.e., brings to awareness) impingement and the focus of therapy is upon the therapist's puzzlement and her own experience, as well as the spouses' experience, the spouses are less threatened and their capacity for observing ego is maintained and nurtured. Learning from experience becomes possible.

This is a labyrinthine, confusing, and sometimes painful journey, often more so for the therapist than the spouses. The spouses, whose defensive needs must be respected—signaling as they do the fear of dissolution of the self—largely set the pace of the process. If the therapist's thoughts are rejected, alternative explanations are explored. If alternatives are not forthcoming, the issue is put on hold until it comes up again, as it inevitably will.

THERAPY TAKES PLACE IN THE MIND OF THE THERAPIST

The process of successive identifications between the therapist and each spouse results in the development within the therapist of evolving internal images of each spouse and of their relationship. These images are amalgams consisting of all the shapes, forms, hues, values, affects, tones, themes, perceptions, impressions, attitudes, intensities, and judgments that together form the sensory, cognitive, and affective structure of the therapist's perception of the spouses (image-in-action). Inevitably, the therapist conveys her evolving image of each spouse and the couple back to them in conscious and unconscious ways throughout the process of therapy. As the therapist strives toward real relationship, as opposed to *image-inary* relationship, with the spouses, the obstacles to real relationship are explored and the ability to identify with the spouses deepens. In turn, each spouse develops a deepening identification with the therapist and with the therapist's identification of him or her, of the mate, and of the marital relationship.

The therapist's internal image of each spouse and of their

relationship stands in modifying or confirming relationship to those held by the spouses. Whereas the spouses' internal images of each other and of the relationship tend to be fixed and concrete, the therapist's may be more abstract and symbolic. Where the spouses' views are immediate and reactive, the therapist may maintain perspective and creatively imagine future possibilities, expanding the couple's horizon. Just as each spouse reads the therapist's internal image of him- or herself in the way she relates to them, so each reads the therapist's internal image of the mate and of the relationship, images that may stand in competing relationship to his or her own. The therapist's mind and her capacity for creative apperception, a view of what may be possible as opposed to what is, can serve as a bridge that connects each spouse to a modified image of self and other. In other words, the spouses meet not only in direct interaction, or in observing each other in relationship to the therapist, but also in the mind of the therapist (Figure 11–5).

The therapist's projective processes can be liberating or incarcerating, working for good or for ill, in either confirming the spouses' pathological perceptions of self and other, or in standing in modified and competing relationship to such perceptions. When the therapist's view of one or both spouses becomes caricaturized, often manifested in flat, two-dimensional image form, without depth or elaboration, the therapist should consider the possibility—if not the probability—that she is failing to identify, understand, and metabolize the spouses' unidimensional and concretized perceptions of self and other. This problem is magnified by the countertransference difficulties the therapist will encounter as the couple resists her expanded formulations and as she becomes caught up in the vortex of the spouses' projections of each other.

The "known," typically a persecutory view of the other of the paranoid-schizoid mode, is preferred to the vulnerability of the "not-known," which threatens the spouses with the reexamination of their constructions of self and other, including the possibility that they are part of the problem. In their all-or-nothing world they cannot tolerate being part of the problem, for that is felt as being the entire problem. From their perspective, in that they have little

Figure 11–5. The Couple Meets in the Mind of the Therapist

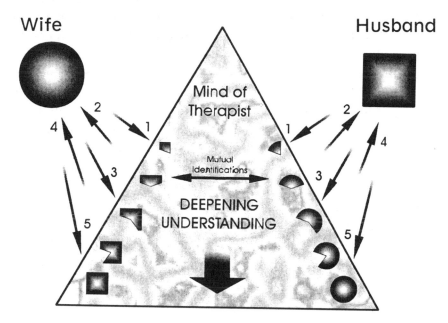

Each spouse meets aspects of the self and aspects of the partner as each
develops mutual identifications with the therapist.

experience of thinking through or of repair of damage done being
possible, it is best to not recognize wounds or wounding. Consequently, the spouses relate circularly, in a recurring sequence of love
(need-satisfaction), hate (need-frustration), and aggression (attack
or withdrawal) (Klein and Riviere 1937). It is through understanding that the need-frustrating and the need-satisfying person are the
same that wounds and wounding can be recognized (empathy) and
that repair becomes possible. The circularity of love, hate, and
aggression may then be replaced with an evolving spiral, the benign
circle (Winnicott 1948, 1954) of love, hate, and reparation.

Throughout this process, the therapist understands that pushing the couple to change fosters unconscious resistance. In that the

spouses rely on primitive splitting, denial, and projection, the therapist recognizes that if she becomes identified as a transformative force, the spouses will tend to identify themselves with homeostatic forces (Andolfi 1983). Thus, the therapist works with the couple without the edict to get better (Giovachinni 1981), knowing that the motivation for change must come from within each spouse; that much of treatment entails the discovery of the spouses' unconscious motivations; and that her capacities are limited, at best, to the development of understanding. Indeed, any acted-out wishes to "fix the couple," on the therapist's part, only support their magical fantasy that "things will get better" without their having to change. In such circumstances, the therapist tends to assume responsibility for the spouses' difficulties instead of returning the difficulties to the only place they can be resolved, that is, in and between the spouses. With this overview in mind, we will now begin the therapeutic journey with the therapist's creation of a holding environment that protects the self of each spouse.

12

The Creation of the
Holding Environment in Treatment:
Being versus Reacting

In a safe environment, the self emerges in fledgling form. Sensations (autistic-contiguous), feelings, and/or thoughts (paranoid-schizoid) arise unorganized, unelaborated, and unsynthesized. Given sufficient time and space to "be," the self, due to its inherent organizing tendency (Stern 1985), pulls its various elements together in more integrated form. This is the self as process. It is for this reason that Winnicott (1960b) praised the capacity to flounder, that is, to abide with unorganized experience, because it allows for the emergence of an internally derived organization of self.

THE EARLY HOLDING ENVIRONMENT

A prerequisite to the emergence of the self is a holding environment that protects the tender shoots of the self from impingement, much as a hothouse protects new plantings from cold weather. The self emerges as sensory experience is filtered and sorted. In this process, the need to be, as opposed to react, is primary and *must* be protected.

The creation of time and space for experience, that is, for spouses to feel their feelings and think their thoughts, is the primary task of the therapist as the manager of the early holding environment of treatment. Once the holding environment has been established it must be maintained. When breeches occur, the focus of the therapy is on the reestablishment of the protective boundaries of the holding environment to shield each spouse from impingement by the other *and* from the demands of the therapist's own ambitions. A culture of relationship is established that is qualitatively different from what either spouse has known in the marriage or in childhood. As the self of each spouse emerges and develops, the culture of the holding environment is internalized, freeing the therapist for other functions.

The successful management of the holding environment is essential to the formation of a secure treatment alliance. This cannot be established through lip service alone. The spouses must have the lived experience of the therapist's trustworthiness that is found in the way he relates to them individually and as a couple, and in the way he manages the session. The working alliance is further deepened by the therapist's collaborative approach. He does not present himself as a truthsayer or as the arbiter of reality, but as a human being, knowledgeable about human processes and invested in working collaboratively with the spouses in the pursuit of understanding. To this end, no aspect of behavior or mental content is pathologized. There is no "looking down at" or "looking up at," only a "looking over at" other human beings struggling to manage their lives. Every defensive or pathological interaction is understood as, at least in part, a communication of thwarted human need or defense against injury.

The importance of the holding environment is difficult to overstate. Its ramifications extend beyond technical considerations. Just consider that the experience of a safe and accepting environment is largely foreign to personality-disordered individuals. Often one or both parents used the child as a primitive selfobject or as a narcissistic extension of themselves (Giovacchini 1981, 1986; Sonne and Swirski 1981). In childhood these individuals encountered attack, indifference, or micromanagement in which overparenting, often mistaken for "good parenting," obliterated their signals and needs. Consequently, their signals and needs went unrecognized and unmet and importance (meaning) was not given to their gestures (Winnicott 1960a). Subsequently, in adulthood, despite whatever worldly success these individuals achieve, they experience a feeling of emptiness at the core, for personal meaning has never been developed. In essence, the experience of childhood has been internalized and their efforts are driven more by the need to stave off the feeling of basic flaw and the pursuit of survival than by the pursuit of fulfillment.

In contrast to the personality-disordered individual's usual mode of relatedness along an axis of dominance and submission, the therapist is invested in relationship along an axis of affiliation and separateness, developing a relationship based on the sharing and processing of innermost thoughts and feelings. Whereas the marital relationship is typically impinging, marked by blaming and shaming and by object usage, the treatment relationship pursues understanding and object relationship without the expectation or demand for change. Indeed, the therapist views the motivation for change as an internal initiative completely within the domain of each spouse, a personal choice that is subject to understanding, but not decree. The therapist's ambition is limited to helping each spouse become the object of their own curiosity—self-aware and self-reflective—so that they may make conscious choices in their lives and relationship.

The development of the capacity to abide with experience is crucial to integration. Much of treatment is focused on the obstacles presented by each spouse, and the couple, to the development of a safe holding environment for self and other in which things may be thought and felt, rather than denied. In addition, a primary aspect of the early holding environment of infancy is the mother's maternal preoccupation (Winnicott 1956), in which the mother is nearly one hundred percent preoccupied with the infant. The therapist enters a similar state, preoccupied with reliably attending to the experience of each spouse. The therapist follows the lead of the spouses, his questions serving to elaborate their experience so that he can identify and relate to it. The therapist avoids asking questions in rapid-fire fashion and resists the temptation to become active in the face of silence. Ideally, he sits quietly during and after the spouses' responses, to more fully absorb and experience, rather than simply intellectualize, what is being conveyed. His focus is to make room for experience. In this manner, the spouse/therapist relationship evolves from the initiatives of each spouse.

THE COUPLE EXISTS IN THE MIND OF THE THERAPIST

There is only one place a couple exists when personality-disordered spouses enter the consulting room: that is, in the mind of the therapist. Treatment in the beginning is a "project" in every sense of the word. As the therapist is subject to the spouses' part-object projections, so the spouses are subject to the therapist's whole-object projections and the projection of their couplehood. The therapist's view of the spouses as a couple is a creative apperception (Winnicott 1960a), the imaginative intuiting of potentials, of what "can be," without denying "what is." Sometimes, given the extreme resistance of a couple, creative apperception may seem to border on the delusional, but is, even when unspoken, a powerful message of "what may be" to the couple.

Creative apperception is not a mysterious process. It is known by every parent who "holds" a child not as a burden, or as a loose assortment of appendages, but as a whole person. In like fashion, the therapist "holds" the spouses in mind as two, potentially whole, selves who may enter the process of becoming in relationship to one another. The therapist struggles to maintain this view and to examine attacks upon it, regardless of how the spouses perceive and treat each other or the therapist. Thus the therapist also provides a holding environment for each spouse and the couple in his own mind.

The therapist meets the spouses and asks what brings them to treatment. In the telling of their story, they begin relying on the use of primitive defenses, signaled in behaviors of fight and flight and blaming and shaming. As soon as this occurs, their words are no longer in the service of understanding but of poking and prodding one another into familiar roles, or of blaming and shaming one another for being in or falling short of assigned roles. They speak without awareness that the problem is not only interpersonal, but also intrapersonal. Each is defensively invested in propounding his or her view of reality, with a near total inability to identify with the concerns, disappointments, pain, and losses of the other. Given the polarized and counteridentifying nature of their interaction, the spouses have little interest in exploring alternative meanings or of reowning their projections, to which they are blinded by denial. Consequently, they are unable to establish a consensual reality, much less mutual understanding.

The onset of primitive defenses signals several significant events: First, at least one spouse is experiencing a threat to his or her psychic equilibrium and thus to the survival of the self. Second, there is a simultaneous loss of observing ego and therefore of the concomitant capacity to learn from experience. As long this situation continues, the treatment environment will be unsafe, there will be a collapse in the space for experience, and the emergence of the self of each spouse will be inhibited. There will be no room for self-observation or self-reflection and learning from experience will be impeded. The therapist recognizing these problems immediately assumes the role of the manager of the holding environment and intervenes between the partners. Through entering separate dyadic interactions with each spouse, the therapist separates them and begins to establish or reestablish the time, space, and boundary for experience.

Given the intense aggression that resides within personality-disordered individuals, the therapist may need to use her own capacity for healthy aggression to form and preserve the boundaries. When impingement cannot be adequately managed through words alone, the therapist may need to revert to more concrete and literal forms of intervention: that is, she may need to meet force with force to protect the integrity of the therapy and maintain the holding environment. The therapist may have to insist that one of the spouses remain quiet, and may even shout. In extreme circumstances, the therapist may meet with the spouses separately for several sessions to establish a working alliance from which to better manage impingements.

Vignette: A First Session

Don and Gerry (short for Geraldene) were in their early thirties, had been married five years, and were childless. Gerry's individual therapist referred them for the treatment of chronic marital conflict with episodes of violence. Gerry's therapist described her as a "classic borderline": attractive, athletic, angry, depressed, and intermittently bulimic. She had been sexually abused by her father from age five until age eighteen; the abuse stopped when Gerry threatened to kill her father in his sleep if he touched her again. Don, a physician, was described as a dependent, immature, and narcissistic individual, without motivation or insight. Little was known of his family background.

Gerry and Don entered the consulting room for the first time in a strangely festive manner. Gerry was good-looking as advertised: tanned, athletically fit, casually but well dressed, and armed with an engaging smile. She introduced herself, shook my hand, made direct eye contact, and smiled warmly, before taking a seat. Don was tall, handsome, and athletically built. He entered the room buoyantly and immediately took a seat on the couch nearest my own chair, without introducing himself. He bounced around as he looked about, his behavior reminding me of a young boy not yet accustomed to social graces. He looked happily around the room, without making eye contact. I wondered if he realized that he had taken the seat closest to mine. Without his speaking a word, I had the impression that he perceived Gerry and me as the only adults in the room and perhaps felt safer with me than with her. To add to his boyish impression, he wore short-shorts and a tight polo shirt that advertised his athletic build. I became aware of my excess weight and felt dumpy. I wondered at my sudden sense of competitiveness and feelings of inadequacy, thinking they might relate to Don's own concerns and ways of dealing with them. I turned to Don to establish direct contact and to counter any idea he might have that his wife and I would interact while he remained on the periphery.

T: "I'm sorry. I didn't catch your name."

D: "Don."

T: "Well, it's nice to meet you." They both looked at me expectantly as if they thought I would structure the session for them. I looked back and forth between them, so as not to designate one or the other as respondent, and asked, "What is it that brings you my way?"

      Don and Gerry looked at each other, Don smiling and Gerry appearing defiant. They seemed in silent struggle, each trying to force the other to take the lead. I put my money on Don, who, in the role of a dependent little boy, acted clueless as to why they were there and was willing to sit forever without saying a word. He seemed the embodiment of childlike passive-aggressiveness, along the lines of "I'll hold my breath forever." As anticipated, Gerry finally broke the silence, her tone conveying anger and embarrassment over losing the transparent power struggle. In what I took as an attempt to save face, she looked at Don and laughed derisively.

G: "I guess you want me to begin?" Don, pausing as if this were in question, seemed to enjoy playing his advantage to the hilt. Finally, he nodded affirmatively. Though Gerry's disgust was apparent, he acted oblivious to it. His overacting succeeded in conveying the surface impression that he was puzzled as to why they were there and that he was simply along for the ride. This impression was immediately confirmed.

D: "You're the one who wants to be here."

G   (with another look of disgust, turning to me): "I guess this is as good a place to start as any. This is why we are here. I have to do everything, while Don sits back. He likes to think that the problems we have are all of my doing and will stop once I'm cured. He focuses on my problems rather than dealing with his own. I have many and he gets impatient with me. He talks about leaving all the time. He's been threatening that for years." After these words Gerry sat silently for some time, struggling with her thoughts, as shifting emotions passed like shadows across her face. Within twenty seconds, I had the impression of anger, frustration, futility, sadness, and confusion. She continued: "I'm never sure if he really cares about me. An example happened just last week." She explained that they had vacationed with his family for five days. She and Don had been concerned about having time to be together and planned to reserve a day apart from his family. However, his sister, Sophie, took issue with their plan, passionately asserting that the family did not get together often and that they had all the rest of the time to themselves. Although Don did take the day with Gerry, hers was a pyrrhic victory. Rather than standing by their decision from the beginning, Don never voiced his own desire and thus avoided conflict with Sophie, who was forceful and opinionated. Consequently, Gerry was left to represent their position while Don conveyed the impression of needing to function as a good husband going along with his demanding wife. After she completed her story, I responded.

T: "Have you always felt pitted against Don's family?"

G: "No. Actually, they were part of my attraction to him. It was like he had all the ingredients I was missing: a good profession, friends, and a family that seemed really normal and happy. Plus, Don was outgoing, charming, admired, and always 'up.' I wanted to be a part of all that. But I can't stand it when they treat him like a baby and expect me to follow suit. Now his family is against me. I stand up to them and he waffles. He doesn't defend me. He even takes their point of view. He's always been told what to do and what to think. His older sister Sophie did his thinking for him and she resents me." Looking at Don she said, "You're such a putz." Turning again to me she asked with great intensity, "Is he married to me or not?" The intensity of her tone was such that I felt an urge to mollify her. I became aware that she could be quite powerful. I could suddenly empathize with Don's wanting to avoid direct conflict with her. Feeling at a loss about what to do or say I fell back on the obvious.

T: "You seem very angry and hurt about this. I take it, if I'm understanding you—and please correct me if I'm not—that this way of being between you has existed for some time." Through this comment, I tried to respond to her and to begin educating both of them to the collaborative nature of how I work. I also tried to convey that I am very interested in understanding their perceptions and encourage their correcting my own to this end.

G: "That's for sure. It started a few months after we were married."

T: "What happened?"

G: "I don't know." With these words, we entered the fertile land of the "not-known," the only area in which something can be discovered. I attempted to establish time and space in which Gerry's thoughts and feelings on this subject could emerge.

T: "Take some time. Whatever comes to mind, even if it doesn't seem important to you."

G (after a few moments): "All that comes to mind is a night we went out to dinner when dating. I told Don how sensitive I thought he was and that I liked that about him. It was like a wall came thundering down. He was suddenly distant and the conversation became stilted. Our next date he stood me up. I was furious and confronted him, but he said he forgot. Every once in a while I glimpse that sensitive part again, but it's been a long time now." I did not respond immediately as I was intent on identifying with Gerry's experience. It seemed a lonely one, but for some reason she seemed driven to endure Don's aloofness in hopes of another glimpse at the sensitive side of him. I wondered about her tolerance for the preponderance of unsatisfactory results in her quest and what purpose this served for her.

T: "It sounds like Don's sensitivity touched you in a compelling way, but that it has also been far between such moments. These have been very lonely times for you. What do you find so compelling about Don's sensitivity?"

G: "That's a good question. I think it's because I can't figure out if he loves me or not. I feel it would be easy to end the relationship if I knew he didn't, but I can't get a clear answer about that. I keep hoping to see that sensitive side again. I keep wondering if the problem is of my making?"

I was impressed with her openness and capacity for self-reflection.

T: "I take it you have your own concerns about your capacity for intimacy and you fear that Don's no longer showing you his sensitive side has to do with you and not with him?"

G: "That's right."

Gerry's history of sexual abuse, reported by her therapist, came to my mind. However, I hesitated to introduce this knowledge in that it could be premature and impinging. Nevertheless, I did want to see if she was ready to bring it up herself.

T: "Do you know the source of your concern?"

G: "Yes. I know it well. My father sexually abused my sisters and me. He also physically abused my mother. Every time I have the opportunity to get into a close relationship, be it with a man or a woman, I begin to distrust the relationship, the other person. I become my own worst enemy. In my suspicion, I do things that drive the other person away. With women, I expect too much. My standards are impossibly high and cannot be met. Then I feel betrayed. With women, I give too little of myself and with men I give too much. I feel when a relationship goes sour that it is my fault, that I drive people crazy. I end up hating myself. I see other people in wonderful relationships, leading normal lives, and I want that. But I fear that I can't have it, that I'll screw things up. When I first meet someone, I think they're wonderful. Then, when they don't live up to my expectations, I feel betrayed. I just don't know if I can have a normal relationship and I don't know if I'm the cause of the problems in this relationship."

I was impressed with Gerry's voicing of the plight of many individuals whose early relationships were harsh. She idealized the relationships of other people she knew and applied the infantile fantasy that in a "normal" relationship all of her needs would be met. Her sadness was unmistakable. I put my perception of her into words to see whether she recognized her feelings within herself.

T: "That must be very sad for you."

G: In soft tone, she responded, "Yes. It is."

Despite the harsh nature of her experience in relationships, Gerry continued to struggle in pursuit of relationship, her hope outweighing her experience. I wondered what nurtured her hope that she could have a different kind of life for herself.

T: "Although you're very sad something keeps you hoping that you can have a good relationship?"

G: "Yes."

T: "What do you think it is? Have you had such a relationship?"

G: "No."

T: "Are you sure? Many people with the experiences you had growing up might not have this hope. Was help around when you were a kid, that let you know there could be different kinds of relationship?"

G   (bitterly): "No. There was no help. The abuse was a secret. Even my sisters and I didn't talk about it until we were older, and then only briefly. They insisted I not bring it up anymore. But I couldn't let it go and they see me as a troublemaker. They have kids and they want their kids to have a good relationship with their grandfather. So, I don't see them anymore. I'm completely cut off from my family."

Gerry still had not identified the source of her hope. She only punctuated reasons to feel hopeless. Accordingly, I pursued this question further because her hope suggested the presence of an internal good object relationship experience that could become a useful part of therapy.

T: "The more you tell me, the more it seems impossible that you would have even the idea of a good relationship. Take your time. Just sit and see what comes to mind when you think of people you have valued."

G: In a few moments, with warmth in her voice, Gerry recalled, "I think it was with my friends and their families. My next-door neighbor's Mom was really good to me. I spent as much time with them as I could. They had a nice family and it gave me an idea about how families could be. I often dreamed about belonging to their family."

T: "That was fortunate for you."

G: "Yes. I don't think I could have survived without it."

T: "What happened to your friends?"

G   (in a sad tone): "Oh. They moved away."

T: "Another sadness in your life." Gerry sat quietly, absorbed in her memories. I wondered about her relationship to her mother. Did Gerry internalize two bad parents or only one? I suspected two, because she had significant problems with men and women. "I've noticed that you haven't said much about your mom?"

G   (with an instantaneous look of disgust): "She was afraid of my dad. She would go along with whatever he wanted to save the marriage. She worried all the time about being left. She was a doormat. When I told her of the abuse a few years ago she told me it didn't happen, but that I should let bygones be bygones."

I could well imagine this scenario. I felt anger toward her mother, whom I pictured as a pathetic person, while I admired Gerry's strength to be able to talk and think about all that had happened to her. Simultaneously, I recognized that the internal image of Gerry's mother that I was forming was a part-object image as seen through Gerry's eyes and my own experience.

T: "I see. She didn't protect you or acknowledge you."

G: "That's right."

T: "I can see why you would have trouble trusting both men and women. So with Don you're not yet sure to what extent the problem may be yours and to what extent he is not available to you for his own reasons?"

G: "That's right."

At this point, I was aware of the need to make contact with Don. I also wanted to acknowledge Gerry's thoughtfulness and candor, before relegating her to the role of participant-observer.

T: "It's very helpful for me to know what you've told me. I appreciate your being so candid. Is there anything else you would like to say before I talk with Don?"

G: "No. I think that's all for right now."

While talking to Gerry, I had noticed that Don had little reaction. However, I had observed that when Don was the focus of Gerry's comments he became rigid, his face free of expression. "Plastic" was the adjective that came to mind. However, when Gerry focused on her past and her own issues, he relaxed and was more attentive.

T   (turning to Don): "You've been very patient. Can you tell me what's been on your mind while Gerry and I have been talking?" To my surprise and growing discomfort, he did not respond. He stared at me. I waited, remembering his struggle to avoid speaking earlier in the session, and wondered how he would handle being the subject of my attention. Time continued to pass and I realized it was becoming very important to me. I thought of the ticking of a clock, "Tick tock, tick tock," and that time was wasting. I was concerned that at this rate we would not accomplish anything. Finally, Don's expression changed, which suggested he was about to speak. I waited with baited breath.

D   (finally): "What do you mean?"

I was shocked. I thought, "After all this time what I get is "What do you mean?"" His withholding was infuriating. I

wanted to throttle him. After reining in my homicidal
fantasies, my curiosity took over. I wondered if my experience
of rage was his projection of rage, and, if so, what his rage was
about. At this time, I also recognized that his energy was far
more devoted to defense than to exploration, cueing me to
the importance of understanding his defensiveness before
exploring his conflicts.

T: "Anything at all. I think that whatever you've been thinking,
whether or not it relates to what Gerry has been talking
about, is important." In this response, I deflected his expectation that I channel his thinking. My interest was in discovering whatever was on *his* mind.

D   (after another long silence): "I don't know." I waited without
comment and eventually he continued. "I'm tired of therapy.
I don't know that it helps." I felt put on the defensive again:
first, in the competitiveness I had felt at the beginning of the
session; second, by his unwavering silent stare just moments
ago; and now with his early and direct questioning of the
value of what I had to offer. My take on this came not so much
from his use of particular words, but from the way he spoke
to me. I felt accused of being a quack. I wondered if Gerry's
feeling of inadequacy was played upon in similar ways. I also
felt that Don wanted me to launch into a discussion of what
would make therapy worthwhile. I had no interest in making
such an appeal or of establishing the kind of relationship with
him in which I had to prove anything.

T: "I see. Many people feel that way. Have you been in therapy
long?"

D   (another long pause): "Oh. I can't really remember."
        I was not willing to let him off the hook with such a lame
response.

T: "Days . . . weeks . . . months . . . years?" As I heard my own
words, the derision barely disguised in my tone reminded me
of how Gerry had sounded. After another long pause, Gerry
interjected.

G: "Group therapy for about a year and couples therapy for about six weeks."

Although Gerry's clarification was useful in content, it supported Don's ongoing hostile dependent form of relatedness and intruded into my relationship with him. I felt she was trying to reduce the tension that was mounting between Don and me. I maintained my focus on Don.

T: "Is that right?"

D   (grudgingly): "That sounds about right."

I marveled at how withholding he was. Trying to make contact with him was like pursuing an immaterial and transparent figure through dense fog.

T: "Boy, you're lucky. Some people are in therapy for years before coming to that conclusion. So you feel like you've about had it?"

D   (after a short period of hesitation): "I don't know. I'm not sure I would say that."

There he went again, refusing to define himself in any way. It was as if he were afraid of his own shadow, that defining or locating his own position on anything would be a grievous error, perhaps subjecting him to attack. Undeterred, I persisted in my attempt to locate him, or to at least define him as difficult to locate. To this end, I began confronting the incongruities in his statements.

T: "But, I gather from what you said earlier you feel kind of dragged here? That it is Gerry that wants to be here, not you."

D   (long pause): "I don't know if I would say that." After another long pause, Don continued. "But, I'm not sure how much time to give the therapy, to give you a chance." Finally, he had come out of the closet. He had put the challenge I felt from him all along into words. From his point of view, I was on trial. He wanted me to prove myself and guarantee that treatment would be useful, as if the quality of his participation would have nothing to do with the outcome.

Looking at my countertransference experience, I imagined that Don felt on trial. I wondered, in opposition to the way he presented himself, whether he, like Gerry, felt over-responsible for the outcome, highly insecure, and self-critical underneath his uncaring veneer. I speculated that he felt so bad about himself that he could not afford to perceive himself as doing wrong. Consequently, he was hostile in a passive-aggressive manner that allowed him to both deny his hostility while buttressing his sense of self at the expense of others. The only thing I knew for sure was that I had no interest in assuming singular responsibility for the course of the therapy.

T: "Ah! Quite a dilemma, but I'm not clear about something. Is it me you will be giving a chance, or you?" He looked puzzled and taken aback.

D: "I guess it's both of us." This was the first thing he had said that I agreed with.

T: "Yeah. I can see that. So, shall we see how we do? What's on your mind?" Back to the beginning. Another long pause followed during which I began to wonder whether he was going to refuse any working alliance at all.

D: "Oh. The marriage just hasn't been much fun for a long time. Gerry doesn't want sex, she often sleeps in a different room, she doesn't keep the house clean, she doesn't want to go out to the club, she's always bitching about something. She's—" Gerry broke in with a roar.

G: "You bastard. I don't want sex because I'm depressed and you try to force yourself on me when I'm asleep. You follow me around like a puppy dog, even coming into the bathroom if I don't lock the door. You want me to be your sex object, your maid, and your mother. I don't want to go to your goddamn yuppie club, with your yuppie upper-middle-class snobby friends with their false smiles, and hear you talk endlessly about your great golf game. Go suck."

I was stunned! Where was the thoughtful and reflective Gerry of only minutes ago? She continued in this way without pause. I listened with one ear as I thought about how to handle her attack on Don. Clearly, her words were not in the service of understanding, but a communication-by-impact imparting of her rage in tangible form. This attacking, blaming, shaming mode of relating signaled the onset of primitive defenses elicited by the endangerment of her sense of self. Her intrusion into Don's space suggested that she readily introjected his words, and, therefore, at least partly concurred with his view of her as a "bad," inadequate wife. It further indicated that she was unable to maintain her sense of self. Instead, she was swallowed up by his view as it reverberated with her own fears. In contrast to her earlier interaction with me, Gerry was now unable to abide with and reflect upon her own feelings. It was likely that this was the nature of their communications at home—accounting for the chronic conflict that occasionally escalated into violence.

On a process level, Gerry was impinging on Don at the very moment he began to expose his own thoughts, feelings, and perceptions. In the face of her attack (although I was sure *she* had felt attacked), Don had again withdrawn. His face had taken on a plastic, masklike appearance, and he stared into space. It appeared certain, given the difficulty of getting him to speak the first time, that he would not easily speak his mind again—and perhaps not at all, if Gerry attacked him whenever he did so. In addition, if my previous speculations concerning Don's feelings of inadequacy had any merit, Gerry's attack only confirmed to him that the external world was a dangerous place and that to define himself in it was the ultimate insanity, as it opened him to direct attack.

I also recognized that Gerry's description of Don's sexual behavior was similar to that of her father. She also perceived him as similar to her mother in her disgust-tinged description of his weak-kneed dependence. Later, when the couple had settled into therapy, it would be appropriate to explore with Gerry her experience of Don's words. However, at this point the therapeutic task was to establish a safe holding environment for Don. I attempted to interrupt Gerry.

T: "Hold it. Hold it. Let me jump in here a minute. We've got a problem." Gerry paused. "I can see that it is very difficult for you to hear what Don has to say without feeling defensive." Gerry broke in before I was finished with my thought.

G: "He distorts everything. He's like a spoiled little boy who must have everyone admire him. And if I don't, he can't stand it."

Her description supported my feeling that Don required constant admiration to offset his feeling of inadequacy and possible self-hatred. Yet, on this occasion, she was being criticized and was unable to tolerate it. Although I thought her statement was probably true of Don, it also seemed true of her, and I doubted she was aware of this. All the while, Gerry's voice was increasing in volume and intensity, which suggested that she was about to run verbally amok. Again, I attempted to establish the protective boundaries of the holding environment for both of them and interrupted her.

T: "Gerry . . ." She continued her diatribe without letup, oblivious to me. "Gerry." She was running at full throttle, careening along the tracks of her own mind, driven by welling rage, totally unaware of my repeated attempts to apply the brakes. At this point, I escalated the intensity of my voice and behavior to better penetrate her awareness. I waved my hands, whistled, and repeated her name until I got her attention. "Gerry . . . Gerry . . . Gerry . . ." She finally stopped and looked confused, as if she had just come out of a trance. "I've got to tell you something important." She focused on me and I felt I had her attention. "I'm not going to be able to do my work here if you're not able to sit for a while with the feelings you have when Don is speaking. I know it's difficult, but his being able to speak without interruption is important. Think about it. You say a lot of the problem is that Don wants you to do all the talking and the thinking and you don't like this. You can never discover how he feels. But, at the same time, you have a difficult time allowing him to voice his thoughts and feelings. I assure you, you will have time to speak. Is there any way you and I can figure out how to manage this? Otherwise, I don't think I can be useful to you."

I made the problem a collaborative one, attempting to establish the rules of engagement, forming boundaries between self and other. Until the protective boundaries of the holding environment are established, the work of developing insight and understanding cannot proceed. I could focus on the pursuit of understanding with Gerry, but this would take a long time and result in the session being totally focused on her to the exclusion of Don. This in turn would feed into Don's defensive withdrawal and the failure to create a safe place in which his self could begin to emerge. Later, once a protected space and working alliance has been established for both spouses, focusing on one partner to the relative exclusion of the other may be necessary and useful. However, in the beginning of therapy the primary focus of the therapist is upon the initial creation of a holding environment and working relationship with both spouses.

G: "But if I don't say it when I think it, I'll forget what I was going to say." This common rationale was not the problem. The problem was that Gerry was unable to abide with her feelings. Instead, she acted them out. The ability to abide with one's feelings is a developmental capacity that is essential to the emergence of the self and must be fostered. Accordingly, I offered what appeared to be a concrete solution to what Gerry experienced as the problem.

T: "What if I give you a pen and paper to write your thoughts down; would that help?" Although this is a common strategic intervention, I have rarely seen a spouse put pen to paper. I believe the pen and paper serve the holding function of a transitional object, much like a blanket or a teddy bear. They provided Gerry with something to hold on to that would comfort her. She responded dubiously.

G: "I can try it."

Her words and tone conveyed a sense of doubt and established this attempted solution as mine, not the all important ours, in which Gerry would share a real investment. This runs counter to my treatment philosophy: I am not interested in Gerry's "jumping through hoops," but in her genuine investment in the treatment process. Gerry's attempt to abide with her emotions needed to be something in which she felt a personal investment. Throughout treatment I repeatedly express my belief in the importance of the personal meaning of behavior and discourage behaviors that are simply for compliance, leading to underlying resentment. This often-expressed belief fosters the valuation of integrity, of the spouses voicing their genuine thoughts and feelings, and the importance of congruence between thoughts, feelings, words, and/or actions. Gerry's half-heartedness was an indication that my solution was experienced as something outside of her self, more an impingement or deprivation than a help. Her compliance would constitute false-self functioning. In addition, the pen and paper had to have personal meaning for her if they were to function as transitional objects.

T: "Well, I don't think you should try it unless you feel that there might be something in it for you. Can you think of any reason for yourself that you might want to try to contain your feelings when Don is speaking?"

This question resulted in Gerry entering a more self-reflective mode aligned with the capacities of the depressive position, and invited higher-level ego functioning that stands in contrast to the action-oriented, fight-or-flight way of being and relating of the paranoid-schizoid position from which Gerry had been operating. Even if successful, such attainments are small and momentary, but it is upon such gains—attained, lost, and attained again—that a therapeutic result is built. After several moments, Gerry responded.

G: "I can see how I am saying one thing and doing another. That makes sense to me. If I want to learn how he really feels I'm going to have to learn to hold my own feelings until he's finished. I think I can do this. I see the importance of it."

T: "Okay. That makes sense to me. We'll give it a try and see how it goes." I speak in terms of we, rather than you, to underline the importance of treatment as a collaborative process. I also leave room for further slip-ups on her part, recognizing the compelling nature of primitive defenses and that much of the treatment process will be oriented toward struggling with and understanding what motivates their usage.

At this point, I again turned to Don. However, I had forgotten where we were in our conversation. In addition, I was curious about what he had been thinking during the interaction between Gerry and me.

T: "So what was on your mind during all this?"

D   (for the first time, responding immediately): "It's interesting. I didn't realize how she shuts me up. That makes sense to me."

I realized with a sinking feeling why he could respond immediately. He was focused on Gerry as the problem, leaving himself in the preferred role of victim. For whatever reason, he could never be in the wrong. He denied his responsibility in the interaction. Instead of looking at his own failure to assert himself, he blamed her.

D: "What did you want to know?"

It was deja vu all over again. I felt confused, having lost the thread of our earlier conversation in the tumult of the session, and dreaded having to play hide-and-seek again. Previously obscured from my awareness, my feelings became manifest in a compelling urge to move things along and to establish the illusion of being in control. Rather than processing my mental state, I began acting upon these feelings and became directive in the session. In acting on my urge to establish a sense of control, I risked re-creating with Don a structure of relationship that paralleled that between him and Gerry.

T: "I'm getting the feeling that you would be more comfortable if I asked you more specific questions; is that right?" This statement was a dis-integrity on my part, a projection, that although probably true of Don, spoke mainly to what would make me comfortable, and was also my response to Don's disavowal of investment in the treatment process.

D: "Yes. I would be. I don't know what you want." It was with these words, "I don't know what you want," so reminiscent of my beginning interaction with Don and of false-self-functioning, that I realized my mistake. Don, in response to my becoming directive and taking control, had returned to his dependent position. It also dawned on me that the real issue was that Don had little idea of what *he* wanted. I decided to respond in global fashion, which would leave Don with the choice of what to respond to.

T: "Well, Gerry has described her concerns about the marriage, and about her relationship to both you and your family. I wonder what your thoughts are about these issues?" Don took another long pause, which I used to better assess what I was feeling. In this self-observing mode, I became aware and wondered about the substantial increase in my activity level. I felt wound up from my interaction with Gerry and realized I needed to calm myself to allow space for Don's personality to emerge. As I thought these thoughts, Don stared at me, amplifying my discomfort. Remembering the ancient story of a besieged city that threw their last cow over the wall to give the besieging troops the impression of bounty within the walls, resulting in the lifting of the siege, I commented.

T: "Take all the time you need."

Don responded immediately. My instantaneous thought was that he could not stand the idea of going along with anything I suggested.

D: "Gerry's right. I'm not an opinionated person. I guess I do have a hard time knowing what I feel and I guess I do waffle a lot."

I felt ridiculously pleased by his articulation of these foibles and his bringing up the issue that he does not know what he wants. Finally, he had provided his own theme to follow and explore.

T: "What are your thoughts about having a shortage of your own opinions?"

D: "I don't know."

T: "Take a minute. See what comes to mind. Don't worry if it makes sense or not to you. Trust that what comes to mind is important." With these words, I encouraged Don to flounder, to free-associate, to discover what emerged from within him.

D: "My mother and father were very absorbed in their own careers. It's like they were there, but not there. We didn't do anything together." His voice is constricted with emotion. "My older sister basically raised me. She is my rock. She would always tell me what to do."

Surprised by the suddenness of this very personal revelation and the "feelingful"-ness of his tone I was more hopeful about Don's prognosis.

T: "So, you're close to your sister. She helped make sense of things for you. When she challenges what you want to do, like on the vacation, it's a real dilemma. You then get confused about what you want to do?"

D: "Yeah. I hadn't thought of it that way, but I guess that's right."

T: "About this waffling, does that mean that your opinion tends to be influenced by whomever you're with at the moment?"

D: "No . . . I don't think . . . well, maybe . . . yeah, I guess it does, a lot."

Instead of responding counter to my statement, as had been his pattern, Don acknowledged it, albeit with some effort. This may have been evidence of a growing trust in our relationship. I also associated his sister with Gerry, with whom she seemed to share a proclivity toward strong opinions.

T: "I get the feeling you're not comfortable with conflict, nor with feeling unable to arrive at your own position on things."

D: "That's true. Who needs conflict? I don't see the point of it. I don't see how it's useful. I like getting along with people."

His response emphasized interpersonal, rather than intrapsychic, conflicts.

T: "I can appreciate that, but what about your feelings, having your own position on things?"

D (in forceful and dogmatic tone): "If other people are happy, I am happy."

I imagined he had held this credo for years. He interpersonalized his self-experience as if his sense of self was totally located in the way others reacted to him.

T: "Wow. You have a clear opinion about that."

D (with a laugh): "Yes. I guess I do."

I then pointed out the incongruity between his voiced preference and the reality of his relationship.

T: "It's interesting you have such a clear preference to please people, and yet Gerry doesn't appear pleased at all. Ironically, what displeases her seems to be that she doesn't know where you stand in regard to her. It seems a relationship in which your opinion is very important."

D: "I didn't know about Gerry's history before the marriage. If I had, maybe I wouldn't have married. I've just hoped that she could work her troubles out, but they are just getting more and more."

Don, reliant on splitting and denial, perceived the difficulties in the marriage as entirely Gerry's responsibility. He also failed to attend to her complaints about his behavior.

T: "What first attracted you to Gerry?"

D: "Oh. That's easy. She's very good-looking and sexy. And, she was very caring. I liked the way she cared for me and the way she could talk about her feelings. She helped me think about things. But her troubles are so big I just don't know."

This comment supported my earlier impression that in Gerry Don recognized another version of his sister, his "rock," who would take responsibility for, direct, and make sense of his life. However, he also put the blame for their relationship problems upon her, relating to her as a deficient self-object. I wanted to fathom the level of his splitting and denial and so asked my next question in such ludicrous all-or-nothing fashion that most people would qualify their response, unless excessively reliant upon primitive defenses. If he responded with a qualified answer, then the opportunity was open to explore the situation further using his own experience.

T: "Are you saying that prior to your relationship with Gerry, you've never had conflict in any relationship?"

D: "That's right. I get along with people."

Don's splitting and denial were pervasive, suggesting that his sense of self was marginal and precarious. Consequently, he psychologically could not afford to consider his contributions to the difficulties in the marriage. I speculated that in his all-or-nothing world to acknowledge any responsibility entailed his feeling totally responsible. To better understand the genesis of his lack of self I decided to explore his family history.

T: "That's very interesting. I've never met anyone who has never had one kind of relationship conflict or another in their life. What was your family life like?"

D: "What do you mean?"

T: "You know. Growing up, was there any conflict there?"

D: "No. My family was perfectly normal." Don espoused a naive notion of a "normal" family as one devoid of conflict.

T: "Can you tell me a little more about your family? Your parents: what were they like?"

D: "My father was a businessman. He spent most of the time in his study. I guess you would call him quiet and reserved. My mother was a very social person, involved in many clubs and charities. She was busy." Don conveyed an image of family life in which his parents were essentially removed.

T: "Were you ever disciplined by them?"

D   (after a long pause in which he seemed to have never considered this question before, further indicating his lack of reflection upon self and other): "No. I think the main thing in our house is that everybody went about the business of their own lives."

    I tried to assess his feelings about this.

T: "Did you feel loved and attended to?"

D: "I guess so." A pause followed in which Don seemed lost in memory.

T: "You seemed to be thinking about something. Can you tell me what it is?"

D: "Oh. I was just remembering eating dinner together. There was always all the food you wanted and my brothers and I ate like piranhas." He laughed.

    The timing of this association was remarkable in that it followed my question about whether he felt loved. His associative response was to eating food, a concretization of his dependency needs and a substitute form of their being met. He also painted a picture of voraciousness, which suggested underlying hunger. I associated to his emotional choking up when speaking of his relationship to his sister as his "rock." I realized that it was with her that he had the clearest sense of human connection.

T: "That sounds like it's a pleasant memory."

D: "It is." He became lost in thought again and I waited until he came out of his daydream before I spoke again.

T: "You seemed to have another thought."

D: "Yes. I was just remembering that I was obese until age thirteen. I guess I lost weight then, when I began exercising and got involved in sports." After a long pause, he continued. "I wonder if that was a symptom of depression?"

T: "What is your thought about that?"

D·   (speaking suddenly in clinical tone, as if about someone else): "It's just an observation. I don't have a personal opinion on that." Again, his reliance on avoidance and denial were manifested. He depersonalized his experience, as if it had happened to someone else.

    We were nearing the end of the session and I did not want to end on this sour note.

T: "I would like to hear more about this—perhaps next week, if some other issue hasn't arisen that is more pressing. Is there anything else you would like to say before we end?"

D: "No."

T: "Gerry. You've been very patient. How was it sitting there and listening?"

G: "It was okay. The paper and pencil didn't help me remember the thoughts I had along the way. I forgot to use them. But, it was interesting to see how much you had to struggle to get anything out of Don, just the way I do. It's very tiring."

I did not want to end on a note critical of Don, particularly after he had shared much during the session.

T: "Well. People generally have to feel safe to say what's on their minds. I guess to even have their opinions. But, it's so important because otherwise you'll never know what's on the other person's mind. You're very verbal and Don will need to have time to come to better verbalize what's on his mind. It's like a snowball; It's hard to get started, but once underway it gathers momentum. We're out of time for today."

DISCUSSION

In this vignette the holding environment was temporarily established and, when breached, reestablished. Space was created for each spouse to identify and verbalize mental contents. They spoke of the marriage, themselves, their histories, each other, and treatment in general. No attempt was made by the therapist to resolve conflicts, while much was done to begin establishing protective boundaries and the therapist's working relationship with each spouse. The therapist's efforts were based on the premise that until the protective boundaries of the holding environment are in place, and the therapeutic relationship established, the personal meaning of events to each spouse cannot be adequately explored and understood, freeing the spouses for further development. The session was successful in eliciting information from each spouse that enabled the beginning formulation of working hypotheses. These are not held as truths, but simply as the therapist's beginning speculations about the couple. Let us examine these hypotheses in detail.

The Intrapsychic Structure and Marital Relating of Gerry

Gerry internalized her parents as "bad" objects and a sense of self as "bad" and unlovable in relationship to them. This was suggested in her not knowing to what extent her relationship problems were her fault and by her becoming enraged when criticized by Don. She also acknowledged an inability to trust both men and women with whom she developed close relationships.

Gerry revealed that there was a pattern to her relationships. They began with an initial idealization, as she idealized her friend's family during childhood. However, when closeness threatened, so did the return of the repressed. At this point, rather than remaining differentiated from her internal world of self and object relationships, the other was perceived through the psychological matrix of her childhood and became confused with her "bad" internal objects. She was subsequently unable to differentiate the contemporary object from the primary objects of her past. Hypervigilance, idiosyncratic interpretations of reality, and repeated testing of the relationship ensued, in the attempt to defend her self against the other as potentially endangering. Sadly, these paranoid defensive maneuvers "drive people crazy" and lead to exactly what she fears, that is, the loss of the relationship, which she then perceives as due to her "badness."

Though cognitively aware of her pattern, she was unable to change it, caught up as she was in her internal world of persecutory object relationships. Endangered by her need for attachment to others, in that this need put her in danger of further injury in relationship, her survival instinct was triggered. At this point, feelings overwhelmed cognition and she was no longer able to differentiate past from present.

These interpersonal dynamics would likely continue until she was able to differentiate between her internal self and object representations *and* between internal world and external reality. Until this occurrence, intimate relationships would probably continue to trigger her defenses against the return of endangering objects. In hypervigilant and paranoid relationship to others, she will compulsively test others to reassure herself of her own loveableness and of their trustworthiness, "driving them crazy." In that her issues are intrapsychic they cannot be assuaged on the interpersonal plane. In that she does not feel loveable, she cannot trust an other as loving. The problem is inside, not outside.

Gerry felt herself to be worthless in relationship to a neglectful, unloving, and insubstantial love-object, her mother, and an abusive and sadistic father. She internalized the "badness" of the situation. She fought against this feeling by holding her mother in contempt and counteridentifying with her mother's passivity and submissiveness. To remain in relationship to this neglectful and nonprotective object (the alternate being no relationship at all), she married a man who shared many of her mother's characteristics. Don possessed a diffuse sense of self, was conflict-avoidant and indecisive, treated Gerry's needs as unimportant, and didn't stand up for her or to her. Instead he was passive-aggressive, exhibited a pathologic inability to define himself or to reassure her of his love, and failed even to take a stand with his own family. He tolerated Gerry's verbal abuse much as her mother tolerated the verbal and physical abuse of her father. In essence, Don was a parody of her mother and was held in equal contempt.

In the attempt to master the original abusive situation, Gerry unconsciously identified with the aggressor, her father, in her marital relationship. She berated Don ruthlessly and seemingly without fear, although I doubted that she was so much fearless as impelled to intense onslaughts in the need to defend her sense of self. Gerry also tried to defeat her father, represented by Don, in the marriage. Typically, she verbally castrated him and held him in contempt. In such fashion, she temporarily vanquished her feelings of helplessness and vulnerability while expressing her hate and aggression, castrating the man, the father perceived in Don, who had repeatedly raped her.

Gerry's internal father was a violent, aggressive, invasive, sexually and psychologically abusive figure, frightening to the extreme. In relationship to him, Gerry felt dehumanized, only a thing, a sexual object the worth of which was limited to her meeting his sexual and sadistic needs. Don was a compromise object choice. Although not typically violent, he shared some of her father's characteristics. He complained that Gerry did not want sex, slept in a different room, did not keep the house clean, did not want to go out to the club, and was "always bitching about something." He treated her like an object, without compassion, ignoring the relevance of her depression and the impact of his attitude toward her. He also ignored her complaints concerning the absence of emotional connection, warmth, or affection. His object-to-object relationship to her is captured in his attempts to have sex with her while she is asleep. Not surprisingly, in addition to her own sexual issues, Gerry felt like a "sex object, a maid, and a mother," in relationship to Don, that is, not recognized as a person in her own right.

Nonetheless, because of his passive-aggressive and conflict-avoidant style, he protected Gerry from the risk of the primitive, unbridled aggression and loss of control she experienced at the hands of her father. Although he could be provoked into violence from time to time, as indicated by Gerry's individual therapist, his violence was largely under Gerry's control. She could provoke it and she could appease it. I imagine that when she felt sufficiently ignored she created the experience of "warmth through friction" (Lewin and Schulz 1992) by provoking him. At the same time, his violence did not appear to frighten her, at least on the surface, as evident in her verbally abusive, denigrating, and castrating attitude toward him in the session, and by her not raising his violence as an issue. Through Don she maintained the illusion of mastering her father's violence.

Gerry's sense of self was contaminated. She could not get away from the core sense of herself as responsible for that which had befallen her. She was aware that she drove people crazy and was profoundly concerned with establishing her own worth. This issue was voiced on the interpersonal level when Gerry asked, "Is he married to me or not?" and when she described her need to know, "Does he love me or not?" To get these questions answered seemed like a senseless reason to stay in a relationship. However, if we understand the tyrannizing power of Gerry's need of reassurance it makes more sense. She was compelled by two profound intrapsychic questions to which she hoped to find the answer in the interpersonal world of the relationship: "Is it my fault?" and "Am I loveable?" Despite her apparent power during the session, she was held hostage by her need for Don to confirm her goodness, which for her was so in doubt. She also needed his refusal to answer her questions, so that her self-doubt could continue to be interpersonalized in the relationship and, thereby, placed at a safe distance from her inner world.

Don was an object with whom Gerry could interpersonalize her intrapsychic conflicts. She projected her neediness into him by frustrating his need for contact, so that he ended up in the desperate position of following her around "like a puppy dog." Alternately, she also counteridentified with his neediness, so reminiscent of her own, which she found disgusting, and attacked it and his sense of self. The heartrending quandary for Gerry was that she equated intimacy with invasion, neglect, betrayal, and the eradication of her self. Don's difficulties with intimacy, which kept him from offering her the sense of affirmation for which she so yearned, also protected her from the risk of real relationship and the vulnerability that entails. On the one hand Gerry blamed Don for their lack of intimacy, while on the other she acknowledged destroying relationships when they become intimate. Gerry could view Don as the obstacle to the relationship. She implied that their relationship would have been better if only he could commit to her. I believe that it is likely that at times when Don was more vulnerable and available, Gerry, frightened of closeness and vulnerability, would tend to function in ways that pushed him away.

Perhaps we can now partially answer the question, "What was it about Don's sensitivity, so briefly glimpsed in the beginning of their relationship, that spurred Gerry on?" I think Don's sensitivity served two functions: First, in it Gerry glimpsed herself. She identified with Don's vulnerability, and felt that if she were successful in drawing him out that she would vicariously cure herself. Second, the obverse is equally true. The maddening effort to draw him out maintained her love of hope for the possibility for redemption, but without the risk of losing hope given Don's withholding or of discovering that his answer was not sufficient to alleviate her concerns.

The Intrapsychic Structure and Marital Relating of Don

Don appears more difficult to define until we focus upon his interpersonal interactions and the countertransferential experience of him. Don had two primary ways of relating, one marked by elusiveness and the other by his infantile dependent little boy presentation. Paradoxically, his elusiveness was his most substantial quality, constituting the "presence of absence" (Winnicott 1951). Trying to engage Don in relationship was akin to "pursuing a transparent and immaterial figure through dense fog." We might wonder if this experience of him was the internalization of his experience in relationship to his parents. Don himself used a wonderful turn of phrase to describe his parents as "there but not there," and of the essence of his family life as "everyone going about the business of their own lives." He described a total absence of conflict and equated conflict with abnormality.

As a "present absence," Don was identified with the aggressors, his parents, who were "there but not there." As Don identified with his non-nurturing objects, he projected his needy and dependent self into Gerry, thus interpersonalizing his internal world of object relationships. Gerry provided fertile soil for such projections given her intense needs both to feel loveable *and* to be in relationship to a rejecting object. The resultant relationship configuration was of

Gerry in hostile dependent relationship to Don, as Don was in hostile dependent relationship to his parents. At these times, Gerry carried the yearning for attachment in the relationship while Don functioned as the elusive, here-and-then-gone object.

In this relationship, Gerry "carries" the frustration and rage that Don associated with the pursuit of attachment with his parents. The extent of his feelings in this area was evident in his memories of the dinner table. Food was the concrete manifestation of nurturance. Eating like piranha conveyed a highly aggressive and voracious image that spoke to both Don's hunger for attachment and the aggression associated with its not being met. Don's image also promoted a delusional conviction of fulfillment via feeding frenzy, a being filled "all at once" and "once and for all." He defended against the feeling of his experience of neglect by identifying with his parents and projecting and then rejecting his own neediness, which was now located in Gerry. He treated Gerry as he had been treated and the way he treated his own needs now. This was partly the reason why he had difficulty identifying and expressing his wants, needs, ideas, and opinions.

Don had little room within himself in which to identify and express his needs. Not only were they frustrated and subsequently repressed, but he had also internalized the family edict that conflict was "bad." Since the appearance of harmony was primary, Don was unable to pursue his need of attachment with its potential for conflict. Instead, he communicated his needs in indirect and displaced form, such as in food, sex, or a clean house, and he expressed his anger in passive-aggressive and deniable form, which maintained his golden-boy image. He further protested his golden-boy innocence by directly stating that all the problems in the relationship were of Gerry's making. Simultaneously, he failed to mention his clinging dependency, evident in his following her around like a "puppy dog," including into the bathroom, and trying to have sex with her when she was asleep. His narcissism was a defense against his inadequate sense of self. He could not tolerate the recognition of his own contribution to the marital problems

because he perceived his world and himself in largely undifferentiated, all-or-nothing ways. For him to be at all responsible was to be
completely and unbearably responsible, so he sustained a golden-
boy image of himself, in which he could do no wrong, that was
highly supported in his family of origin.

The marriage with Gerry provided Don with the illusion of
mastering the original traumatic situation. Instead of being power-
less and helpless, he was in the role of the aggressor. He felt both
desired and powerful in his ability to frustrate Gerry's needs, as his
own needs were frustrated in childhood. He took sadistic pleasure
from this reversal, presented Gerry with his original dilemma, and
observed her attempts to resolve the problem while he remained
omnipotently protected from it.

All the while, some of his dependency needs were being
perversely met. He was the object of Gerry's negative attention and
felt valued by her intense need to be loved by him. His capacity to
get under her skin and torment her, often effected through his
repeatedly threatening to leave and his refusal to tell her he loved
her, gave him a sense of power and importance, feelings he lacked
in childhood.

However, when Don was overcome by his dependency needs, he
related in infantile-dependent form. Then he was clinging and
followed Gerry around, compelled to pursue a primitive, sensory-
dominated core relatedness through his attempts to have sex with
her when she was asleep. He was unable to see that the rejection of
his needs was, at least in part, a function of his refusal to connect to
Gerry in a "feelingful" way, thus reducing her to the status of an
object, which she resented. Again, this aspect of Don's internal
world of relationships is interpersonalized within the marriage.
Overcome by his infantile dependency needs, he found himself in
relationship to a highly rejecting, denigrating, and castrating object
that both refused to meet his needs and ridiculed his pain.

Finally, there was Don's internal relationship to his sister
Sophie. From the initial interview, it was clear that Don's attraction
to Gerry was in part due to her similarities to Sophie. He described

Gerry in similar terms as his sister: "feelingful," caring, and able to help him "think about things." Gerry was also strongly opinionated and a forceful presence. As his sister was his "rock" in childhood, Gerry was his "rock" in adulthood. In light of this need, we witnessed Don acting like a little boy in relationship to a parent, and heard his expectation that she be his sex object, maid, mother, and greatest fan. He wants her to be his world. It is no coincidence that Gerry and Sophie quarreled over how Don should spend his time during the family vacation: They were struggling for ownership.

It seemed that Don's primary attachment in childhood was to Sophie and that she encouraged an infantile dependence that met his need of relatedness but did not promote maturation, which is frequently the effect of siblings serving as surrogate parents— attachment sans development. If Sophie were at all like Gerry, then standing up to Sophie's wishes when they differed from his own would have been a formidable task. In addition, the threat of losing his primary attachment would have been unbearable.

Now, in adulthood, Don remained in infantile-dependent relationship to both Gerry and Sophie. Interestingly, in Gerry he had married someone who was willing to stand up to his family. This helped him to separate from them, but without personally entering the conflict that this entailed. Gerry took the brunt of their anger while Don maintained the role of golden boy, dutiful husband, son, and brother.

Finally, Don obtained a sense of being recognized in his relationship with Gerry. In divided relationship to himself, only Gerry recognized his underlying sense of himself as a bad boy, and yet did not leave him. She saw the "sensitive side" of him, as well as his faults. By confronting him with these split-off and disavowed aspects of himself, Gerry challenged Don to grow and to enter relationship that was more real to himself and to her—a challenge he has yet to meet. Nonetheless, Gerry helped him "think about things," which seemed more of a "bringing things up," and offered a countervailing relationship to the one of being "there but not there."

SUMMATION

We may sum up the problem in the relationship as follows: As Gerry
was unable to locate Don and detect her own loveableness in his
eyes, so Don was unable to locate a substantial sense of himself
through Gerry's attentions. Each looked to the other to fill the
deficiency in his/her sense of self, while the conflict in their
relationship protected each from the dangers associated with intimacy. Don and Gerry unconsciously recognized each other as an
available repository for their respective projections and as a willing
participant in the reenactment of their respective intrapsychic issues
in the theater of the marriage. Each interpersonalized the intrapsychic in the futile attempt to resolve their individual issues in the
interpersonal, that is, by mastering, controlling, and changing the
other.

The marriage of Gerry and Don thus constituted a single
psychic entity. The relationship was a vehicle through which each
could continuously defend against the return of the repressed while
trying to omnipotently master it through interpersonal relationship.
The irony was that through the marriage, each spouse continued to
recreate the traumas and excessive frustrations of childhood, in
which needs for secure attachment went unmet.

Of course, it must be kept in mind that these are only
hypotheses, merely the therapist's attempts to think about the
couple's situation. Tentative interpretations may be given in the
service of informing the spouses of what the therapist is thinking,
not what he "knows." In turn, the spouses are encouraged to modify
and refine his understanding, and to develop their own capacity to
think about their experience. For cognitive *and* affective change, it
is necessary that the understanding that results is personally meaningful to each partner. It is through the couple's collaborative
investment in the treatment process that the therapy acquires its
modifying capacity. Until an interpretation "feels right" to the
couple, it is without mutative value, and until the holding environment of treatment is established, the spouses will limit their
investment in the collaborative process.

Parenthetically, this vignette illustrates how so much of what goes on in a session is in latent, but near-manifest, form and how any given session may contain many, if not all, of the elements of the couple's total situation—if we can only identify and decipher them. The capacity to identify and think about our thoughts and feelings, rather than remaining in reactive relationship to them, is the topic of the next chapter.

13

Containment:
Ego Support versus
Impingement or Neglect

A holding environment is not enough. Although a secure treatment framework (Laing 1960, Winnicott 1961, 1970) is necessary for the emergence of the self, it is not sufficient to its development. The capacity to think about and process experience is essential.

Given the unpredictable stresses and strains of life, even mature individuals can become overwhelmed. For personality-disordered individuals this is a day-to-day occurrence, triggering paranoid anxieties and narcissistic injuries. To manage the situation the personality-disordered individual resorts to primitive defenses to reactively deny and discharge their experience of that which is threatening, in the attempt to maintain psychic equilibrium. As long as denial is occurring resolution is not possible. The goal of the therapy is to help the spouses reintegrate their experience in manageable form. While the holding environment promotes the emergence and elaboration of experience, the containing environment promotes the processing and integration of experience.

Winnicott (1960a, 1960b, 1965) distinguished ego-supportive

actions, which support the integration of the self, from ego-impinging actions, which overwhelm the self, fostering fragmentation and disintegration. Such, for example, is the difference between weaning and deprivation. Both are initiated from outside the child, but differ in their impact. In weaning, the mother makes gradual the loss of the breast, while providing alternate forms of succor, which expand nurturing possibilities and support independence. Weaning enhances autonomy and the capacity to enter the broader world. In contrast, deprivation is abrupt and overwhelming, without consideration of, and consequently beyond, the child's capacity to manage. Overwhelmed by instinctual needs (separation anxiety) and lacking environmental support, the child's psychic equilibrium is disrupted, breaking the continuity of the thread of the self. Baldly thrust into the unmediated "outside" and unbuffered against a backdrop of survival concerns, the child's introduction to the broader world is brutal. Basic insecurity, mistrust, and pessimism prevail, rather than basic trust and optimism (Erikson 1968). The therapist's capacity to help the spouses contain and process their experience serves a similar function to that of the good-enough parent. The therapist strives to bring the spouses into relationship with a manageable reality.

The advocated therapy is a collaborative effort in which the therapist enlists the spouses in the telling of their stories. Because of splitting and denial, the stories will contain gaps and incongruities, missing pieces of the puzzle, which impede understanding. Treatment entails the unfolding of a mystery, the developing of the story of the living history of each spouse, which makes sense of their way of perceiving and organizing experience, including the marital relationship. In service of developing the mystery, the therapist struggles to identify with the spouses' experience and to identify with what the spouses are consciously and unconsciously communicating. As the therapist introjectively identifies with their experience it becomes subject to his own self-organizing and secondary process (thinking) capacities until he is able to make sense of it. That which can be understood can be borne and subsequently becomes available for integration.

This process takes various forms. For example, many times the therapist may not be able to make sense of his experience of the couple, no matter how hard he tries. In this event, he may acknowledge confusion and enlist the spouses in helping him to make sense of his experience. As the therapist's tentative understandings and puzzlement are explored with the couple, the ongoing development of their story is fostered. Satisfaction is achieved when what was previously experienced as not-understandable becomes understood. With understanding, each spouse's way of perceiving and relating becomes normalized in the historical perspective.

Normalizing is the opposite of pathologizing. It involves the recognition that symptoms are signals of underlying needs, fears, and conflicts that have not yet been understood and resolved. With "cogni-affective" (Lewin 1995, personal communication) understanding, symptoms diminish and the "craziness" of the situation, which is the vehicle through which the unconscious is brought to awareness, abates. Subsequently that which is understood is available for re-introjection and integration. As each spouse is increasingly able to identify that which is constructive in themselves and in the other, and that that which they saw as destructive or "bad" in themselves or in the other is not necessarily so, the sense of self becomes more separate, individuated, and differentiated. As their sense of self continues to grow, they may more fully consider that which is damaging in themselves and make genuine amends.

TREATMENT ON TWO LEVELS

The processing of the spouses' relationship occurs on two levels: **the intrapsychic (intrapersonal)** and **the interpersonal.** The level of intervention constitutes an expansion or contraction of the holding environment in conjunction with the changing needs of the spouses and the therapist's identification of issues.

In respect to interpersonal interactions, the importance of the therapist's separating the spouses when they begin to rely on primitive defenses is paramount. Indiscriminate interaction between two undifferentiated spouses stimulates the use of primitive defenses, resulting in fight-or-flight interactions, a loss of observing ego, and the inability to learn from experience. The holding environment of treatment can be maintained via the therapist's shifting between supporting direct spousal interaction, which provide grist for the therapeutic mill, and intervening between the spouses to process that which has been talked about. In addition, the therapist intervenes between the spouses whenever they begin to rely on primitive defenses, which signal that the sense of self of one or both spouses is threatened.

The therapist shifts the level of interaction from the interpersonal to the intrapsychic by engaging the spouses in separate dyadic interactions. This alteration decreases transferential relating in that the spouses are no longer in direct relationship and thereby helps the therapist create time, space, and boundary in which to help each spouse "be with" and process the experience that occurred in the spousal interaction. By alternating between the interpersonal and intrapsychic dimensions, the therapist is able to manage the treatment situation, titrating periods of transference relating with periods of working through.

The day-to-day process of therapy becomes a back-and-forth movement between the intrapsychic and the interpersonal. However, in that relationship to self and relationship to other develop reciprocally (Giovacchini 1976), work on both levels is occurring simultaneously. With the development of the self, each spouse's sense of security increases and reliance on primitive defenses decreases. As this occurs, more time may be spent exploring spouse-to-spouse interactions on the interpersonal level. Indeed, the spouses' capacity to maintain spousal interaction in the service of sorting through their experience on an interpersonal level, without the need to resort to primitive defenses, would be an indication of substantial progress in that it entails a decrease in primitive splitting and projection and an increase in self-observation and self-reflection.

The Process of Separate Dyadic Interactions

There are three basic functions of the therapist's engaging the spouses in separate dyadic relationships. First, as soon as the spouses enter blaming and shaming relationship, reactivity substitutes for reflectivity. There is a loss of observing ego, and, therefore, the capacity to learn from experience is impeded. This speaks to personality-disordered individuals' infamous refractoriness to treatment efforts. Separate dyadic interactions help reestablish a safe holding environment, which supports the maintenance of an observing ego and fosters the emergence of the self of each spouse.

Second, separate dyadic interactions create a space for the observing spouse to abide with his experience while the therapist and the mate are interacting. It may appear that one spouse at a time is getting treatment, but this is not the case. Treatment for both is ongoing, even when the therapist is interacting with only one. The therapist is simultaneously creating space for going-on-being and for going-on-being-with for both spouses. There are several advantages to the observing spouse. First, she is not on the "hot seat." As the therapist strives to understand the internal experience of the participating spouse, the observing spouse's defensiveness can ebb. This frees her to witness the therapist's empathic attunement and responsiveness to the mate and to begin hearing things she has not understood about her mate and the mate's vulnerabilities. Often the observing spouse will comment, "I didn't know that about her," or "He never talks to me the way he does with you." In addition, the observing spouse is able to witness struggles in the therapist and participating spouse dyad that are similar to those in her own relationship to the mate. This facilitates differentiation between what is relatively variant (not particular to her) and what is relatively invariant (particular to her) in the problems she has with the mate. Moreover, the observing spouse is free to go-on-being-with the therapist (identify with him) as he speaks to the mate, or to go-on-being-with the mate as she identifies with his struggles in relationship with the therapist, or to go-on-being-with herself in that she is not required to interact. When the therapist engages the observing spouse in relationship, he continues to foster the observing spouse's relationship to self. He doesn't ask, "What do you think about what your spouse has been saying?" which would imply that the therapist expected the observing spouse to be organized around the mate's utterances. Instead, he asks, "What has been on your mind while your partner and I have been talking?" The latter question supports the observing spouse's right to simply "be" in the session.

Third, the process of separate dyadic interactions establishes an oscillating experience of togetherness and separateness, which is a part of normal relatedness and of the oedipal level of development in which the capacity for "thirdness" is achieved—the very process with which the spouses struggle. The therapist's separate interactions with each spouse, along with his speaking to them jointly as a couple, recreates oedipal phenomena in which a child must learn to move from dyadic to triadic interactions, and to be included at times and to be excluded at other times. This experience helps establish each spouse's separateness and the awareness of relationship as a "thirdness" that is not of one or the other spouse but borders upon, separates, and connects them.

The therapist's exploration of each spouse's intrapsychic dynamics while the mate remains in the consulting room is similar to, but not the same as, individual therapy. First, it occurs in the context of a marital therapy and the particular issues explored arise in response to the marital interaction. Second, since both spouses are in the room, what each spouse discusses is influenced by the modifying presence of the other. Third, the observing spouse may interject, which at times can be impinging, but also may provide valuable information that the participating spouse has denied. For example, Chloe described at length a "normal" and "healthy" family upbringing. It was not until Mat revealed that Chloe's mother hadn't spoken to him for the first four years of their marriage, and that they had thrown her father out of their home on numerous occasions due to his verbal abusiveness, that Chloe's upbringing was revealed to be less than ideal.

Fourth, in that the therapist is in relationship to both spouses, his internal image of the spouses and their relationship is not shaped solely by one spouse's view of the other, but by his experience of the marital interaction and his separate relationship to each spouse.

Throughout the treatment process, the therapist endeavors to be attuned to the experiences of each spouse and to help each enter relationship with his or her own experience. As critical moments in the therapy are "freeze-framed" for processing, the spouses benefit from the experience of making time and space to examine and work through the relationship to self and other. Via the repeated examination of their interactions, the spouses become increasingly reflective and evolve a more continuous sense of self across time and circumstance. They have a growing sense of holding the string to the yo-yo of their feelings, rather than being yo-yoed by them. A mutuality of shared experiences, rather than disconnection and deepening alienation, becomes possible.

Useful work along the interpersonal dimension becomes feasible as each spouse develops a more differentiated, autonomous, and less defensive sense of self. The spouses become better able to contain their thoughts and feelings instead of impulsively acting them out. Through direct experience, they come to recognize the importance of containment to developing an increasing sense of mastery and competence. As this occurs, the therapist is gradually relieved of the necessity of maintaining boundaries as a primary focus of therapy, and is able to shift his attention to supporting the spouses in the pursuit of understanding. Such gains are won, lost, and won again, but with progress the therapist is increasingly able to address the couple's interpersonal process and interlocking dynamics more along the lines of treatment of the normal/neurotic couple.

Progress on either level of intervention is not a "once and for all" achievement but a "to and fro" process. Progress leads to the emergence of new issues and areas of regression. For example, as one spouse's resistance to real relationship is worked through, the other spouse's defense against intimacy often comes to the fore. Each regression results in the return of primitive defenses, although customarily with less intensity. These must then be worked through again and again, as the different facets of each spouse's resistance to relationship emerge and demand attention. This is the process of working through the various part-self and part-object relationships that make up the dynamic unconscious in the service of integration, and toward whole-object relationship. The holding environment of treatment must thus be capable of forming and reforming, of expansion and contraction, in response to the fluctuating needs of the spouses' psychological situations.

Following is a vignette of a family session that illustrates these concepts. As the therapist moves between individually oriented explorations and their interpersonal impact, an increasing identification and mutuality of experience is achieved.

CONTAINMENT AND THE DEVELOPMENT OF MUTUAL IDENTIFICATIONS

At the time of referral, the Lovells had numerous problems. The children still in the home, Jackie (age 14) and Suzie (age 11), had been truant from school for a year. Jackie was highly oppositional. Her favorite words were "Fuck you," and her major ambition was to get pregnant. Suzie suffered from panic disorder and followed in Jackie's footsteps. Mrs. Lovell had a twenty-year history of agoraphobia, panic disorder, and bulimia, with two inpatient hospitalizations. Mr. Lovell suffered from depression, for which he was being treated with medication alone, in that he and his therapist agreed that individual therapy was not useful to him. A similar fate befell Mrs. Lovell's individual therapy soon after entering family therapy. In that her psychiatrist had recommended me to the insurance company, I felt somewhat abandoned and imagined all the preceding therapists to be letting out a collective sigh of relief because of their no longer being part of the case.

The Lovells lived in a two-story house, the upper floor occupied by Mrs. Lovell's father and mother, who were intrusive, demanding, and incessantly critical of everyone. Mrs. Lovell reported that since her childhood her parents had continuously demanded her assistance, which they then inevitably criticized and devalued. To add to Mrs. Lovell's woes, she was unable to drive due to panic attacks and was reliant on Mr. Lovell, who worked shift work, for her transportation.

As treatment began, the profound chaos, aggression, and dependency that permeated the family's existence and interfered with its capacity to support the developmental needs of its members was apparent. The Lovells' three adult children, who generally lived outside the home, were in constant crises, demanding Mrs. Lovell's involvement and helping her to perpetuate her lifelong role as helper. Both of her adult daughters were pregnant and in physically abusive relationships. Mrs. Lovell was the primary caregiver to their children as well. Mrs. Lovell's persecutory world of manipulation and control was evident in her view that her daughters had intentionally become pregnant to trap their boyfriends into marriage, as if one child each was not already enough.

Michael (age 24), the oldest child and only son, was living in the Lovells' home with his girlfriend. He worked episodically, used cocaine extensively, and was intermittently violent, particularly when drunk and with his girlfriend. He refused treatment. His chaotic and frightening influence on the children was so great that the first six weeks of treatment were focused on exploring with Mr. and Mrs. Lovell the importance in setting limits on him. It was clear to me that the fear and chaos he engendered in the family greatly diverted attention from the needs of Suzie and Jackie and the grandchildren in the home. Suzie and Jackie were typically ignored and could claim attention only through acting out. Six weeks into treatment the Lovells were able to take a stand with Michael and remove him from their home. This occurred after he beat up his girlfriend and knocked Mrs. Lovell down. He subsequently rammed his car into his girlfriend's car several times, before departing in response to Mrs. Lovell's calling the police over the objections of Mr. Lovell.

Finally, to add to my bucolic introduction to the Lovells, Mr. and Mrs. Lovell deemed me ready to hear that Mrs. Lovell had been refusing sex with Mr. Lovell for over a year because she felt he treated her like a "whore." In addition, the entire family was convinced that Mrs. Lovell was having an affair with, of all people, her oldest daughter's boyfriend. Mrs. Lovell acknowledged spending time with other men, but she claimed they were simply friends whose company helped her fend off the panic attacks that occurred when she was alone. For his part, Mr. Lovell did not deny Mrs. Lovell's charge that he spoke to her like a "whore," but was seemingly so angry with her that he did not care. Bitter and cynical, he asserted, "the world is full of assholes and I am one."

Given this beginning, I had little confidence that I would be of any more use to the Lovells than were my predecessors. I prepared myself to be a huge disappointment to both the Lovells and the insurance company. I set out to treat the family without ambition beyond that of satisfying my curiosity about what governed their miserable existence. Nonetheless, my hope for therapeutic benefit was enhanced when Mrs. Lovell expressed pride in the progress she had made in developing a clearer sense of self in previous therapies. She was particularly pleased with her increased ability to spend time alone and her control of her bulimia. In addition Mr. Lovell, although angry most of the time and reluctant to speak, responded well to prodding and humor. He seemed to guardedly enjoy my being interested in understanding him without any ambition to change him.

Aside from these glimmers of hope, the family sessions were reflective of their lives: chaotic and characterized by a near absence of boundaries. Nonetheless, true to chaos theory, the sessions themselves took on a pattern. For example, everyone—except Mr. Lovell—talked at the same time, but about different subjects, so that fragments of many conversations were constantly going on simultaneously. To add to my confusion and sense of frustration, the family frequently arrived late or on the wrong day for their session. Mr. Lovell always looked grim and stood aloof from the rest of the family, a position that mirrored his involvement at home. Mrs. Lovell dominated the sessions with her feelings, perceptions, and insights, but was easily diverted whenever Jackie or Suzie interjected to claim her attention with a complete change in subject. Her centrality in the family was reflected in the family sessions.

Mrs. Lovell recurrently complained of Mr. Lovell's noninvolvement and his undermining of her authority. He countered that nothing they did ever helped and that the kids would "get theirs" when they failed later in life. He also complained that Mrs. Lovell was "always helping someone when we can't even help ourselves," and thereby added to the chaos of their lives. He would also gripe that he was not even at the bottom of the list of his wife's concerns. Mrs. Lovell countered that when she was available he sabotaged their being together by responding catastrophically to any indication of her anxiety attacks. Neither felt able to set effective limits with the children, who simply refused to go to school and cursed their parents without consequence. Jackie and Suzie talked in simultaneous spurts to their mother, who would immediately enter conversation with them, or sat in sulking silence interspersed with occasional impossible-to-hear comments that they refused to repeat. My overall sense of the family was of a whirlpool of needs, unrecognized and unmet, out of which aggressive and depressive affects exploded with as much predictability as water from a boiling pot.

In the midst of this situation, I felt strongly that all I had to offer was my own curiosity and interest in continuing to think about things, which occasionally resulted in momentary spaces in which the family actually considered what was being said or enacted. One day I raised a question I generally never ask, for it can be interpreted by the patient as a disguised directive to leave treatment. I wondered why they continued coming when everyone agreed that, to quote them, "Things did not seem to be getting better." Mr. Lovell responded, "A lot of times I hate the idea of coming here. I don't think anything is getting better, but I always feel better by the time we leave." Jackie and Suzie stated they were forced to come and Mrs. Lovell commented that they all liked and trusted me. Despite an absence of behaviorally measurable progress, these comments, and a subtly developing quality of play in the sessions, suggested that there was a germination of the holding environment.

The session to be described began with Mr. and Mrs. Lovell entering the room uncharacteristically silent and grim, while Jackie and Suzie appeared amused, seemingly impervious to their parents' dark mood. The disparity in demeanor between the children and their parents was so striking that I wondered if the girls were being passive-aggressive in their gross lack of rapport with their parents' mental state. I wondered what was going on. I had not seen the girls for several weeks and their concerns were often lost to those of their parents, so I chose to begin the session with them.

T	(to Jackie and Suzie): "Good to see you girls. How are you?" Suzie is occupied with a school notebook and doesn't respond. Jackie looks at me blankly and shrugs without speaking. She has refused to speak with me for several sessions, having accused me indignantly of "acting as if you know what's in my head," when I tentatively interpreted what might be going on with her. Her rejection of me, originally quite angry, now had a playful and seductive quality, as if she were intent on seeing how I would handle her refusal to speak. In fact, I respected it, believing that if you cannot hate your therapist, whom can you hate?
T	(to Jackie): "You're still not talking to me?" I use a playfully hurt voice and she smiled and nodded her head.
Mrs. L:	"They have been going to school and they met with Ms. X yesterday for the first time." Ms. X is the child therapist to whom I had referred Jackie and Suzie two months earlier. Until now, they had refused to see her. When I had suggested the referral, Jackie had provocatively stated, "Ms. X is a hick," although they had never met. I had responded, "Well, I don't know if she is a hick or not, but if she is, she is a smart hick and has a feel for teenagers and the problems they face." Jackie had laughed.

	Recalling this interaction I asked Jackie, "Is Ms. X a hick?" She laughed delightedly.
Mrs. L:	"She liked her."
T	(to Suzie): "Did you like her too?"
Suzie:	"She was okay."
T:	"Is that a school book you have there?" (By the time of this session, Jackie and Suzie were attending school intermittently.) Suzie nodded affirmatively.
T:	"Making any friends at school?"
Suzie:	"Yeah." Then looking at Jackie instead of me (I feel dismissed), she told some school gossip. Jackie responded and they briefly discussed their feelings about some other kids at school. I feel like I have landed in a scene from the TV program *90210*, but am pleased that they are getting involved in school.
T:	"Wow. It sounds like a lot is going on." The girls ignored me and soon returned to their state of silence.
T	(to Mr. L): "What's cooking with you? You look pretty grim."
Mr. L	(looking at Mrs. L): "Let her tell you."
T:	"You think that Mrs. Lovell knows what's happening inside of you better than you do?"
Mr. L:	Having worked with me for six months, Mr. Lovell knows that I am not about to shift to his wife in order to hear about him. After a grudging silence, he remarks, "How I feel doesn't matter. Last week I made my feelings clear that I didn't want to be a part of putting the dog to sleep. But that didn't matter. Mrs. Lovell still pushed me to do it and got angry with me when I told her that I didn't want to. I still did it, but I didn't want to." Mr. Lovell continues in the vein of how useless it is to express his feelings because they don't matter to anyone. The previous session Mrs. Lovell had spoken about the impending need to put their aged dog to sleep and Mr. Lovell had been clear that he could not handle dealing with the dog's death. He had been unwilling to go into

detail about his feelings. The issue came up at the end of the hour and there was no opportunity to pursue it.

T: "Yes. I do remember you being very clear about that." In this family, attention given to one member is soon experienced as a slight by the other members. In that Mr. Lovell had been speaking for several minutes, I turned to Mrs. Lovell who had remained uncharacteristically silent and withdrawn.

T: "You look grim as well. What's going on with you?"

Mrs. L (in a low and depressed voice): "I'm surviving."

T (after a pause to register the melody of her words, I responded in a low and quiet voice, instinctively ratcheting my tone in the direction of her own): "What do you mean?"

Mrs. L: After a few moments of silence she responded in stuttering form, pushing the words out through her emotions-constricted throat. "I mean . . . it's hard . . . to even draw . . . a breath . . . I'm getting worse . . . I am eating . . . and throwing up . . . several times a day . . . It scares me . . . It's the only thing that gives me any pleasure. It's the only thing I feel I have any control over." After a long pause, she continued while I noticed that the girls were feigning inattention, unconvincingly preoccupied with their school notebooks. "He doesn't care about me . . . and my kids don't care about me." Her voice is devoid of energy, conveying profound hopelessness. It was clear she equated her feelings with a reality that she had no choice but to accept.

I sat for awhile, my mood darkened by the blackness of her own. She was more hopeless and despairing than I had ever seen her. I recognized that her regression to bulimic activity was a terrible loss and profound blow to her self-esteem. I felt sad. She had been so proud, in the past months, of her capacity to manage her urges. All this now seemed lost and she appeared to feel so alone.

	In the effort to identify more fully with her experience, I commented, "You sound completely hopeless, like you know you must continue to plow a field but without hope that anything will ever come of it."
Mrs. L	(correcting my image with her own): "It's like I'm dog paddling in the ocean, just trying not to drown and no one else is around." Through this image, she conveyed her fear, futility, and "all aloneness."
T	(in a gentle voice): "All alone. All alone," to "be with" her in her aloneness. Tears began rolling down her cheeks as her nose ran. I sat quietly, realizing that for the first time in my experience of this family everyone was quiet. Jackie was looking at her mother with concern and Mr. Lovell was staring stoically, straight ahead, avoiding eye contact. I had the impression he felt both angry and guilty, both wrongly blamed and partially responsible, while also upset that he himself has gone unheard by Mrs. Lovell. Suzie's head was turned to the side, her face buried in her shoulder in a posture of grieving.
T:	"Jackie, could you reach around and hand that box of Kleenex to your mom?" Jackie complied without a word.
T	(to Jackie, in an attempt to begin examining Mrs. L's assumptions): "Do you agree with your mom? Is it true that you don't care about her?"
Jackie:	"Yes. It's true. I told her that just this morning. It doesn't mean I don't love her; I just don't care about her."
	I was baffled by this response, but recognized that Jackie was attempting to differentiate feelings. Her response was qualified, drawing a distinction between love and caring. I explored this with her, but her distinction eluded me. I shifted my focus back to Mrs. Lovell, trying to understand her feelings in the context of contemporary events.
T	(to Mrs. L): "Does some of what you're feeling have to do with putting your dog to sleep?"

Mrs. L: "Yes. . . . Rue was my dog. He was special to me. I had made plans for one of my friends to take me with Rue to the vet's, but his condition worsened suddenly and I couldn't reach my friend for a ride. I explained that to Mr. L. He realized that I needed his help and he was just angry. He doesn't care about me. (pause) And the girls, they didn't have a chance to say goodbye to Rue. Jackie did, because she was outside. But Suzie was inside when we were leaving, so she didn't get to say goodbye."

I thought about the stream of losses Mrs. Lovell was describing and then wondered about the dog's name: Was it "Rue," as in "Rue the day," or the French word for "street"? I suspected that these considerations were my effort to get away from the feelings in the room. I did not understand why Suzie had no opportunity to say goodbye to the dog simply because she was in the house. But I decided that pursuing these questions would distract from whatever Mrs. L was experiencing, and, consequently, my efforts to bring it more fully to consciousness. Then, thinking of Suzie's not having had the opportunity to say goodbye to the dog and of Mrs. L's loss, I felt sad. With all this in mind, I said, "That's too bad," which seemed to encompass Mrs. Lovell's feelings about the death of the dog and Suzie's not having had an opportunity to say goodbye. We were all quiet again and after a few moments, Mr. Lovell spoke.

Mr. L: "It's not true that I don't care. Mrs. Lovell just doesn't understand. I told her what my feelings were and they didn't matter." Mr. L seemed worried that no one would believe him.

T: "I do remember your being very clear about not wanting to have anything to do with Rue's being put to sleep. What I don't understand is that Mrs. Lovell explained the circumstances and she needed your help."

Mr. L   (eyes flooding with tears and face contorted with emotion): "I helped her. Even though it was really hard for me, I helped her. She doesn't understand."

T   (very quietly): "What is it she doesn't understand?"

Mr. L   (his voice choked with emotion, beginning to cry): "I was in Vietnam. I saw a lot of death there. It was all around me."

T: Having heard that only one of five people were in combat positions in Vietnam and wondering if Mr. Lovell might be using this as an excuse, I asked, "What was your job there?"

Mr. L: "It was like everybody else's job there . . . infantry." Mr. Lovell begins sobbing and having difficulty getting his words out. "There were dead bodies all around me. My foxhole buddy was shot in the head. I had his brains all over me. (sobbing) I had to push his body out of the hole . . . where it got shot some more, so I could have room to move." He broke down crying, unable to continue. Everyone was silent. After several minutes, I turned to Mrs. Lovell.

T: "Had you heard about this before?"

Mrs. L   (after a long pause, responding in a flat and unmoved tone): "No."

T   (struck by her absence of compassion and trying to make sense of it in my own mind, associating her apparent lack of caring to that of her children for her at the beginning of the session): "Does what Mr. Lovell shared with us help you understand why he had difficulty helping you put Rue to sleep?"

Mrs. L   (after a long silence): "No. To tell you the truth I think he is just saying this to have a reason for not helping me."

I was both stunned and informed by Mrs. Lovell's response. Although I had had a similar suspicion, I had checked it out to my satisfaction. If an acting job, his emotions, particularly out of a person that usually

suppressed any feeling but anger, had me completely
fooled. I noticed that Jackie was paying close attention
with a serious look upon her face. Suzie still buried her
head in her shoulder but was now crying. Mr. Lovell was
wiping tears from his eyes and avoiding looking at
anyone. Believing that family members typically understand what's going on better than the therapist, I turned
to Jackie.

T: "Jackie. What are your thoughts? Do you think your dad
          is faking it?"

Jackie: "I'm fourteen years old and I've never ever seen my dad
          cry. I know he's not faking it."

In considering this information I reviewed the
session in my mind, remembering the incongruity of
demeanors of the various family members when the
session began. Mr. and Mrs. Lovell had been morose
while the girls had appeared amused and unconcerned,
almost as if to highlight their resentment of their
parents. Jackie had struggled to make a distinction
between "loving" and "caring" about her mother. The
bits and pieces of data that had emerged during the
session were now coming together and I verbalized my
thinking in the form of a tentative interpretation to Mrs.
Lovell.

T: "Mrs. Lovell I just had an imagining. I don't know if it's
          true or not, because I can't read Jackie or Suzie's minds.
          And, I hope they will correct my fantasy where it's not
          accurate. My fantasy is that if I was in your girls' shoes,
          with all the problems you've had, after a while I would
          feel like your problems are just another excuse to not
          take care of me. I'd be very tired of hearing about your
          problems. I could understand that they are real but after
          a while that wouldn't do much for making up for all that
          I have lost and continue to lose. Perhaps that was what
          Jackie was trying to explain earlier. She loves you but she

	can't afford to care because it doesn't change anything. She also feels loved, but not cared about, by you and Mr. Lovell, for her needs and feelings continue to go unrecognized and unmet."

Mrs. L (after a long silence, responding in a regret-filled tone): "I can see that. I would probably feel the same way." Recognizing her regret and wanting her to elaborate further, I prompted her.

T: "I think you are in their shoes. I think you all are in the same shoes, everyone feeling 'alone, alone.' How does that make you feel?"

Mrs. L: "It makes me feel bad. I know they've lost a lot and I know Mr. Lovell and I haven't been the best of parents. I've been trying really hard to make things better."

T: "You don't feel like you've made any progress?" My comment is of particular interest because it is misattuned. After the fact, I realized that my comment had nothing to do with the process, but everything to do with me in the process. I was momentarily caught up in the intensity and my personal experience of reaction to the "terrible truth" of loving but not caring, of retaining love but having accumulated losses of care. My attunement skipped here, like a scratch in a vinyl record. It records my "scar," now surfaced.

Mrs. L: "No. When I think about it, I know we have. Michael's out of the house and we can pay more attention to Jackie and Suzie. I guess I just felt so bad this week. I've regressed. My bulimia's back and my agoraphobia is worse. And when I'm in trouble no one's helping me. I feel if they loved me they would help me." The beauty of Mrs. L's comment was that she continued undaunted by my misattunement. She was so used to everyone being in that state that my lapse went unnoticed, even partly by *me*.

T: "I think I can understand your feeling. It's terrible to be in real need and to feel that no one is there to help. I think that's the way everyone is feeling. In fact, it seems to me that you are treating Mr. Lovell's feelings in the same way you feel your feelings are treated. And, Mr. Lovell, you treat Mrs. Lovell's feelings and those of Jackie and Suzie as you feel your own are treated." I recovered quickly from my misattunement. In essence, I invited *my* internal parents, who had barged in, to sit to the side while I got back to work. This worked because I was good-enough and not perfect. My comment to Mrs. Lovell may be read: "Everyone in this room has been treated this way. I have learned something about being more caring, even to those from whom my experiences of loss of care have been generated. It is important, if not to love less, to *care* more. Let me *show* you something of what I mean, since it is so hard to tell. . . ." In this moment, the family's coming to health met my own.

After a long and thoughtful silence, I continued. "Mr. Lovell couldn't help you the way you would have liked with ready acceptance. And, I can understand that was hurtful when you were feeling so torn up inside. Mr. Lovell can see that. Nevertheless, at the same time, Mr. Lovell tried to let you know last week that confronting death posed a very real problem for him. And, this week he tried to help you understand that his resistance wasn't because he doesn't care about you, but because of his own very disturbing memories about death, sharing them in a way he's never shared anything before. Yet, you feel that he is just making an excuse. I think that's the same way the girls feel about you when you are having a very real problem. They love you but can't afford to care about you because their needs go unrecognized. You all end up doing this to each other."

Mrs. L   (after another long pause and in a quiet voice): "I see what you mean. It's true what you're saying. I am treating Mr. Lovell the way I feel treated by the girls and by him. It's a vicious circle."

T   (to Mr. L): "And, Mr. Lovell, you tend to treat Mrs. Lovell in similar ways. If your feelings can't be taken into account due to changing circumstances, you react as if Mrs. Lovell is trying to manipulate you and doesn't care about your feelings, even though she explained to you the circumstances."

Mr. L: "Yeah. I can see that. I didn't want to be that way. I just couldn't help it. I couldn't believe that I was in that spot of having to put Rue to sleep when I had tried so hard to make it clear that I couldn't handle that."

T: "Like having to push your buddy out of the foxhole."

Mr. L   (sobbing): "Yeah. I never realized that till you just said it. I pushed my buddy out of the foxhole. I felt like I betrayed him. Like I killed him. I know I didn't, but I felt like it. I just couldn't do that to Rue."

T: The session was nearing the end and I wanted to synthesize what had been explored in terms that related to the family's overall functioning. "You know what impresses me about you all today? I'm looking around the room and I see tears in everybody's eyes. Till now all I've seen is a very angry family. I think that maybe all this fighting and all this anger has been to not feel how much sadness there is and how much feeling there is."

Jackie: "It's a lot easier to feel angry than to feel sad. I don't like feeling sad."

T: "I understand that. It is easier to feel angry rather than sad, but it ends up leaving you feeling isolated and alone, as if you're a dog paddling in an empty sea, just trying not to drown. Don't you feel more connected now with each other, less alone? And, I wonder, if we can't allow ourselves to feel what we feel aren't we isolated from ourselves? And, then how do we let anything mean much to us, because if we lose it won't we feel sad again?"

T   (after a pause in which Jackie looked less than con-
            vinced and no one spoke): "We are out of time for
            today." The family got up to leave in a sober mood, so
            much in contrast with past sessions. As Mrs. Lovell was
            leaving, she said two words as she gently touched my
            arm: "Thank you." I read this as: "Thank you for the
            work and the sharing of your own experience."

CONCLUSION

It is worth noting that one of the "magic" moments of this session
arose from the therapist's recovery from a misattunement. It
brought into the session the affective component of the therapist's
own experiences of loss, affirming for the whole family the humanity of their grief and sacrifice. It illustrates the importance of the
therapist's self-work to be able to do this type of work. The therapist
needs a "hold" and provides his own "hold," creating a powerful
hold for the family. In turn the family held the therapist, not feeling
persecuted and attacked by him (the paranoid-schizoid mode), as
they easily could have, but tolerating his misstep with a basic faith in
him and allowing the session to proceed.

The therapist's misattunement also points out the intensity of
regressive pressure when the family's issues strike the bulls-eye of the
therapist's experiences of love and loss, and that the holding
environment the therapist creates for himself is the only one he can
extend to the family. All gaps in the therapist's attunement and
responsiveness are related to the therapist's capacity to hold and
contain his own experience. The therapist who is not providing his
own holding environment and containment can only extend the
very same gaps in what he offers the patient/couple/family. Some of
this self-holding and containment can be repaired with input from
the therapist's therapist. But it is only the therapist—all alone, all
alone in the session—who can mind his own matters while extend-
ing caring to the others in the room, which may occasionally
representationally include the therapist's own parents and children.

In this sense, the therapist cannot simply learn theory, for he or she is the tool.

This chapter illustrates the concepts of holding and containing, and of how the therapy takes place on two levels: the intrapsychic and the interpersonal. In this vignette, the concept of working separately with each member of the family, and how these individual explorations are woven into interpersonal understanding, is depicted. In addition, the therapist's use of self, his attempts to form trial identifications, to follow affect, and to remain curious about the incongruities that arise during the session, in the service of deepening understanding, is portrayed. Finally, the evolution of the family members' ability to form mutual identifications through the therapist's own capacity to identify is described.

The therapist creates a space for each family member to feel feelings and to think thoughts. With the development of understanding, the therapist helps normalize the spouses' behaviors by developing their meaning. As each family member struggles with thoughts, feelings, and perceptions, the therapist lends his own observing capacities, both direct and countertransferential, and his secondary process thinking, to help the couple consider and think through their experience. In this way the therapist fosters both identification with and differentiation of each family member in relationship to the others on the interpersonal level, *and* differentiates internal self and object representations on the intrapsychic level, so that the world of the past does not continue to be unconsciously recreated in the reality of the present.

As the work proceeds, the spouses gradually develop the capacity for "thirdness," that is, the ability to enter triadic as opposed to dyadic relationship to self and other. This, in turn, involves the development of an "I" who can think about the experience that accrues to the "me" of the paranoid-schizoid mode. With the development of "thirdness," the all-or-nothing, this-or-that, binary way of organizing and perceiving becomes "triadic." The two alternatives, this or that, become modified by the possibility of a third alternative. With the development of "thirdness" the possibility of many alternatives ensues. The manifestation of this process in therapy is the topic of the next chapter.

14

Thirdness

Personality disorder is a pre-oedipal condition: The child's need of attachment was not satisfactorily met in the mother/infant relationship, and so a secure platform from which to separate and to securely add further relationships, including self-relationship, was not provided. The father also failed in his function in that he was frequently a peripheral or harsh figure in the child's upbringing and so failed to provide a viable alternative to the mother/infant relationship. Consequently, the child did not separate from the mother to add a relationship to the father, but simply substituted the relationship with the father for that with the mother. In other words, the addition of the father to the child's world did not lead to the evolution from the mother/infant dyad to the father/mother/child triad (the experience of thirdness and the resolution of the oedipal conflict) and the separation and differentiation it entails. Instead, the mother, father, and subsequent "others" merely become inter-changeable objects with whom the child continues to pursue infantile attachment in what becomes an ongoing series of relatively undifferentiated dyadic relationships. In that there is no alternative to the "two-ness" of the mother and infant dyad, the child never learns that something might be other than "this or that." Subsequently the child's, and later adult's, relationships remain precarious and insecure, similar to the stability of a stool with only two, rather than three, legs.

It is in the realization of "thirdness," of being both a "part of" and "apart from," that the "I" and the capacity to think of three-role relationships, which opens the door to many-role relationships, emerges. No more all-or-nothing, or this-or-that, two-role relating: not saint versus sinner, victim versus victimizer, or hero versus villain. Life and relationship are now seen in more complex form. The "I" stands as a third that is capable of thinking about, bridging, and separating opposites; and of identifying all that stands between. The binary two-dimensional relatedness of the paranoid-schizoid mode is then replaced by the three-dimensional multivariant relatedness of the depressive mode.

The depressive mode capacity to tolerate complexity leads to integration (integrity), while the paranoid-schizoid mode reliance on primitive defenses fractures and fragments experience, leading to disintegration (dis-integrity). To the degree the spouses engage in splitting and denial (dis-integrity), integration is impeded and disintegrative anxieties prevail. "Dis-integrities" are revealed in skewed, incongruous, or discordant perceptions and whenever sensation, feelings, words, thoughts, and actions do not go together. Dis-integrities manifest the presence of underlying conflict of a "this or that" binary nature and constitute an obstacle to the development of multiroled, multifaceted real relationship to self and other.

Dis-integrities provide a doorway into the unconscious world of the spouses that the therapist must endeavor to enter and work to expand in the effort to make the unconscious conscious, so that conscious choice is available. This is a particularly difficult task with personality-disordered spouses who, unable to abide with and process painful experiences, rely on primitive splitting and denial to defend the doorway against admission. It is these split-off and denied experiences, the existence of which are manifested in dis-integrities, that must be uncovered and brought to consciousness.

Integrity both arises from and leads to integration. It is an important part of the process of uncovering to confront each spouse and the couple with their dis-integrities in order to bring them into consciousness and foster integration.

Because of dis-integrities, the focus of insight-oriented couples therapy is not restricted to the mechanics or structure of the contemporary relationship—or, for that matter, to linear thinking, logic, or reason. Where logic and reason are sufficient, common-sense thinking, advice from friends, or counseling will do. It is when reason and logic do not resolve the problem that "psycho-logic" is required. Psycho-logic is the logic of the unconscious.

When dis-integrities or incongruities resist understanding through reason, the therapist realizes that the past is overshadowing the present (transference and primitive projective identificatory processes). The value of reason or logic is in its capacity to bring us to and help us identify that which is "ill-logical." Typically, that which is "ill-logical" marks the border of the subterranean unconscious world of pathologic self and object relationships. Here the therapist must leave logic behind in favor of psycho-logic. In practice, the therapist alternates between logic and psycho-logic, using logic to work from the outside in, from that which is understood to that which is not understandable, and psycho-logic to work from the inside out, to make the not yet understood understandable.

The complexities, nuances, and defensive motivations of each spouse's relationship to the other are often not transparent. It is often extremely difficult to distinguish whether perceptions of a spouse are founded in present-day reality or in the past. In this differentiating process, the therapist must struggle to identify and bring to cognitive and affective awareness the internal world of pathological self and object relationships of each spouse and how they may be re-created in the couple's relationship. This is often an extremely trying task, for the spouses relate in two-dimensional, this-or-that fashion, perhaps with width and breadth but without depth. For example, typically concrete and literal-minded, they converse in headline fashion, making statements or charges without supporting information. In addition, each remains resistant to identifying with the experience of the other in that the other often functions as a respository for the split off and denied aspects of his or her own self.

For these reasons, from the moment the spouses enter the consulting room, the therapist strives to have each identify and elaborate upon their experience in relationship to his or her self and to each other. A creative process begins, for each spouse believes that what he or she experiences and the reasons behind it are self-evident (the perfect knowledge of the internal world imposed upon external reality). It is when they have to elaborate upon their perception that the gaps or incongruities in their experience are exposed. This leads to heightened uncertainty and the potential for further defensiveness and conflict, as well as to the identification of further areas for exploration and potential under-standing. As with any creative project, the course is sometimes easy and sometimes difficult. All the while, the project shapes the creator(s) as much as the creator(s) shape the project. In therapy, the process of storytelling shapes the storyteller as the storyteller shapes the story.

Vignette: The Development of Thirdness

One of the complaints of Mrs. Lovell was that Mr. Lovell under-mined her attempts to set limits on their children. Although Mr. Lovell denied the charges, he acknowledged opposing her calling the police when their son was violently out of control; that he could not set limits upon the children; and that he did blame Mrs. Lovell, in front of the children, for the problems in the family. Mr. Lovell's undermining of authority became most evident following a court hearing in which he and Mrs. Lovell were threatened with legal action if Jackie and Suzie continued to be truant from school. In a session several weeks after the hearing, Mr. Lovell criticized the school and the courts as "stupid bureaucrats." Specifically, he complained that the school had made errors in keeping attendance records (as if this were the problem), and had advised the children, to the point of encouragement, that if they were sick they should stay home. Rather than creating space for contemplation, in which things are neither "this nor that," Mr. Lovell collapsed space and supported reactivity and acting out. He fumed about being treated like a criminal for his children's behavior, indignantly pointing out that *he* maintained steady employment and kept the law: "I actually produce something, while those bureaucrats steal a living by snooping into other peoples' lives and telling them how to live."

As Mr. Lovell raged, I thought about how I had supported the school in taking a hard-line stance. I realized that I too could be described as spending my life snooping into other peoples' lives and, perhaps, telling them how to live. I was also acutely aware that I had not been remarkably useful to the Lovells thus far and perhaps never would be, and so I certainly wasn't producing anything. I realized that I felt useless and shamed by Mr. Lovell. I thought, "How dare he blame me for the lack of progress in therapy when he has been so resistant to change" (therapist's "I" attending to the thoughts and feelings of the "me," using his countertransference as part of the data of the session).

During his tirade, Mrs. Lovell sat in stoic silence, unmoved. The difference in their manner reminded me of how difficult it was for them to identify with one another. I realized that I also felt no compassion for Mr. Lovell and then wondered if I might be defending against my own feelings of helplessness and uselessness with my anger toward him. I also wondered if the curious mix of my feelings—anger, uselessness, and shame—might reflect an aspect of Mr. Lovell's self-experience that he was projecting into me. Perhaps he felt useless and ashamed and suffered from such self-hatred that that he was unable to acknowledge, much less think about, the harm he had done and the motivations underlying his destructive parenting (therapist's attending to his countertransference experience from which he formulates hypotheses and considers harsh, superego-dominated compulsions by Mr. Lovell that may impair his ability to look at the motivations that underlie his behavior).

T: "You seem to feel criminalized and humiliated by the courts?"

Mr. L: "I do. Those bastards looking down their noses at me and treating me like I'm less than they are. I work hard and I don't get any recognition for all the things I do." This struck me as a transference manifestation in that Mr. Lovell is speaking about his relationship to others in general. "How am I supposed to control the behavior of my kids? That's not fair." This comment represented Mr. Lovell's search for compassion and a dis-integrity or ill-logic in that he disregards the fact that since the court intervention he and Mrs. Lovell have been successful in getting the kids to school, where they are involved and doing well.

T: "You seem very angry that you should be held responsible for your kids behavior and, yet, since the court hearing your kids are going to school and doing well. How do you account for that?" I confronted him with the dis-integrity between his view that he has no influence over and should not be held accountable for his children's behavior and the fact that since the hearing the children have been going to school.

Mr. L: "I guess they just got scared they would lose me and their mom and have to stay in a foster home."

            Mr. Lovell denied any influence, thereby relieving himself from personal responsibility and any sense of his own power. I again wondered if his disavowing position is unconsciously motivated by the need to avoid the impact of harsh superego functioning and/or the awareness of his own importance.

T: "It's curious that your thinking takes away any credit you and Mrs. Lovell may be due, as if there is nothing you or Mrs. Lovell could do that would make any difference" (therapist functioning in role of intrapsychic third, confronting Mr. Lovell with the personal implications of his statements and asking him to think about them). I pursue the line of Mr. Lovell's thinking while pointing out that he himself does not affirm his own capacity for doing anything right, the very sin of which he is accusing the school and court. This last incongruity may reflect Mr. Lovell's projecting his own harsh and devaluing judgements onto the school and the court, so that he is in conflict with them rather than with himself.

Mr. L: "That's right. The kids do what they want and never listen to me." Mr. Lovell continued to deny his own influence. Quite the opposite, he portrayed himself as victimized by the kids, thus emptying himself of any substantial sense of himself in relationship to his children.

Mrs. L: "That's not true. You're doing a lot different and you've let them know you're serious about their going to school. You don't get in the way of my calling the police if they refuse to go and when you're home in the morning you've been waking them up and driving them when they miss the bus. And, when you're not at home, you call in the morning to make sure we're all up and getting ready for school." Mrs. Lovell confronted Mr. Lovell with another dis-integrity, the denial of his influence when in fact his substantial efforts to get the kids to comply have met with success. She was now functioning as an interpersonal third, pointing out discrepancies between his description of reality and actual behavior, while requiring nothing of him.

Mr. L: "Hell. I don't know. Yeah. That's true. But they still wouldn't be going if they weren't scared of having to go to a foster home." Mr. Lovell acknowledged Mrs. Lovell's observations, but continued to minimize his influence and importance.

Mrs. L   (turning to me): "He just doesn't get it. He doesn't realize how important he is to the kids. Since he's been doing these things they have been more loving to him and he has been more patient with them."

I wondered why Mrs. Lovell was able to see Mr. Lovell's contributions while he remained devoted to denying them. I was also impressed by her support of his efforts. Mrs. Lovell appeared to carry the warmth and hope in the relationship (libidinal ego strivings).

T: "Mr. Lovell, your wife is suggesting that it's hard for you to acknowledge your importance in the family. What do you make of that?" (therapist functioning in the role of intrapsychic third, asking Mr. Lovell to think about his wife's observation of how he relates to himself).

Mr. L: "I don't know. She always says that crap. It leaves me cold." Mr. Lovell responded in a counteridentifying way, denigrating the value of Mrs. Lovell's observations. His obstinacy and cynicism was impressive. I again wondered what made it so hard for him to acknowledge his own value and importance. His defensiveness suggested that to acknowledge his importance would somehow threaten him.

T: "That's interesting because when the kids are here they always talk about their feeling that you don't love them. Now with your greater involvement, which Mrs. Lovell is describing, they are more loving toward you and you are more patient with them. I'm confused. It would seem that you would be warmed by your value to them, but you're left feeling cold." (The therapist is not forcing these observations to make sense, nor assuming a position of professional certainty, but expressing confusion and inviting Mr. Lovell to function in the role of intrapsychic third, that is, to become the focus of his own curiosity and to examine the incongruities in his own thoughts and feelings.)

Mr. L: "I don't feel important. I think what she's saying is just bullshit. If the kids loved me they would stop giving me crap and listen to me. And, for that matter, if my wife loved me she would want to spend time with me." Mr. Lovell associated the love of his kids and the love of his wife. This suggested that he may have been displacing anger toward his wife onto his children, and acting his anger out by not being available to them in a supportive way. Also, he equated love with blindly doing what he says.

Mrs. L: "It's true that I spend a lot of time involved with other people. But, when I try to do something with you it's not okay if it's not exactly the way you want it. If I get anxious in the car, you won't just let me ride it out. You immediately turn the car around and end the trip, as if it's my fault. If you want to go out you pick a place you know I don't like. It's not just me."

Mrs. Lovell described the lack of thirdness, of alternatives other than "this or that." In addition, Mrs. Lovell described her own experience of not being taken into account, of being criticized and put down, and of not being able to get anything right in relationship to Mr. Lovell. It was either his way or no way. I also knew from past sessions that for Mrs. Lovell the feeling of being sabotaged and blamed dated from childhood. She had spoken often of devoting her life to her parents and yet never feeling appreciated by them. Accordingly, I wondered how much of her description of Mr. Lovell's sabotage was projection or unconsciously invited by her, and how much related to Mr. Lovell's narcissistic vulnerability and envious attacks upon his kids, who he saw as getting what he wanted.

T: "Mrs. Lovell, that feeling has long roots, not only in your marriage, but with your parents, which continue to this day" (therapist functioning in the role of intrapsychic third to Mrs. Lovell, creating a space for Mrs. Lovell to consider her internal world of self and object relationships, and in the role of interpersonal third, associating her past relationships to the interpersonal world of the contemporary relationship).

Mrs. L   (becoming tearful): "I know. I'm so sick of it. Why can't we be happy?" There was a long pause as I waited to see if either Mr. or Mrs. Lovell came up with any answers to that question.

T: "That's an important question. What binds each of you to such an unhappy way of being together?"

Both Mr. and Mrs. Lovell were silent, lost in their thoughts, but tears began to run down Mrs. Lovell's cheeks. Here, the therapist was highlighting a question that has both intrapsychic and interpersonal ramifications for each spouse.

Mr. L   (obviously moved by Mrs. Lovell's crying): "I don't know. Really, I just feel crummy about myself. Like I'm a bad person inside. I think I'm pretty black on the inside. Pretty stupid really."

For the first time, Mr. Lovell became self-reflective and more personally revealing. His words reflected his awareness of an extremely poor self-image and low self-worth. His general nastiness toward others was now making more sense. He tears other people down to make himself feel better and more powerful. If he can't have what they have he can make sure they don't have it either. On the other hand, when they are injured by his activities, he then alternates to having concern for them. His behavior thus alternates between attacking, when in "bad" self and object relationship, to repairing, when the other as a "good" object that can be injured or destroyed emerges into his awareness.

T: "I guess that feeling about yourself translates into the feeling you don't have much to offer and that you will never have much. You seem to feel that way no matter how much other people tell you otherwise or show you that it's not the case."

Mr. L: "I've always felt that way. It's just the way I am. It's a part of me." Mr. Lovell described his experience of himself as an object to which things just happen, and exhibited symbolic equivalence: The way he feels is the way he is.

T: "Tell me about that" (therapist encourages Mr. Lovell to abide with and elaborate upon his self-experience, pursuing depth of experience).

Mr. L: "I don't know what to say."

T   (after a short pause that allowed Mr. Lovell to flounder with his experience): "Anything that comes to mind." (therapist in the role of intrapsychic third, encouraging Mr. Lovell's free associations instead of binary, this-or-that thinking). The therapist is also supporting Mr. Lovell's abiding and floundering with his experience to enable the inherent organizing tendency of the self to come into play.

Mr. L   (after a period of silence): "All I can think of is that I was much younger than my siblings. I grew up by myself. I didn't have any friends. I felt like I didn't fit in. Like I was a dork. I was always alone." Mr. Lovell was functioning collaboratively in the treatment effort, trying to make sense of his feeling of "badness." He described a sense of never fitting in and of being inadequate.

T   (after a pause to allow for further comments or spontaneous utterances): "You felt that something was wrong with you?" (tentative interpretation of what Mr. Lovell was saying).

Mr. L: "No. I thought I was all right. Just a loner." Mr. Lovell seemed to contradict himself. He appeared to describe the experience of never fitting in, which he had internalized as "Something is wrong with me," yet he refuted my translation. Perhaps my translation was incorrect, or he was defending against a thought that he found difficult to bear. I didn't try to force any of this to make sense. We each sat quietly.

        In considering what had been talked about I realized (although I didn't know why it came to mind) that Mr. Lovell had not mentioned anything about his parents, the primary caregivers in his early life, from whom self-esteem would initially flow. I made this process observation.

T: "I noticed that you haven't mentioned your parents?"

Mr. L: "My parents were great. Mrs. Lovell and my siblings say they were abusive, but I just don't remember that. For me, as long as I behaved myself they left me alone, and I always behaved myself."

His parents having left him alone may account for his absence of associations to them, as well as his inherent sense of having never fit in and of having something wrong with him. I found his highlighting of the importance of behaving himself and of his reward of "being left alone" interesting. It was as if the alternative to being left alone was that something bad would happen. Mr. Lovell was continuing to collaborate by freely associating and by thinking about underlying reasons for his sense of "badness" without having to form rapid or premature conclusions. Self-relation was being fostered.

Mrs. L: "Your father was generally easygoing, but he would go into rages and drive the car fast, just like you when you're angry. My God, he even nailed the windows to the house shut when he got angry at your mom for leaving them open. (Talk about the collapse of the consideration of other possibilities!) And your mom's very critical and aggressive. You always avoid her. If she comes downstairs, you go upstairs. If she goes upstairs, you go downstairs. You never stay in the same room with her." Mrs. Lovell brought in information that Mr. L had denied. She confronted him with an incongruity in his description of his parents as "great."

Mr. L: "I'm that way with everybody." Mr. Lovell failed to consider the meaning of Mrs. Lovell's observations. He immediately minimized them in a manner to obstruct more serious contemplation of her observations and his relationship to his parents, particularly that with his mother.

T (after a silence): "What I don't get is that you say you always felt bad about yourself even though you always behaved yourself." I pointed out another incongruity in

Mr. Lovell's story to encourage his becoming curious about the gaps and contradictions in his story.

Mr. L: "Yeah. That doesn't make sense." For the first time, the tone of his response suggested genuine puzzlement. I also noted what when Mrs. Lovell told him "how things are" he became defensive. Perhaps he felt that it needed to be her way or his way. However, when I expressed puzzlement and pointed out the incongruity of his statements, without coming across as all-knowing, his own curiosity was aroused. He was not being consciously dishonest in recounting the myth of his childhood; he had not thought deeply about it.

T: "I imagine it makes sense. We just haven't figured out what sense it makes." I did not portray professional certainty, but opened the potential space—the possibility of bringing internal world and external reality into understandable, if not yet understood, relationship. The puzzle of how he felt so "bad," when his behavior was always so "good" became a transitional thought-object, allowing him to travel beyond his being defined by the immediacy of his experience. Now, intra- and inter-entered potentially mutually-enriching relationship.

Mr. L: "I don't know what to say about it."

T: "Take your time." I again supported Mr. Lovell's floundering, encouraging his use of free associations and the operation of the natural organizing tendency of his self.

Mr. L: "The only thing I remember is that I could never please my mother. No matter what I did, it wasn't good enough." Mr. Lovell's tone conveyed a feeling of despair masked by an overlay of anger.

Mrs. L: "What are you talking about? You could never do any wrong with your mother." Although Mr. Lovell was speaking sincerely and in a vulnerable way, Mrs. L reacted dissonantly, in an affectively misattuned manner that suggested that Mr. Lovell was a fool, even though she herself had spoken of how critical Mr. Lovell's mother was. In so doing, she suddenly enacted the role of his mother, whom Mr. Lovell felt he could never please.

It is interesting that Mrs. L became attacking at this moment. On a surface level, I would have thought that she could identify with the experience of never being able to please a mother. Yet, she acted just the opposite. Mrs. Lovell's critical and belittling manner collided with the fragile possibilities of the potential space. Nonetheless, Mr. Lovell considered her observation for a moment, apparently not registering the tone of her voice.

Mr. L: "That's true. But all she had to do was give one of those looks and I felt awful." Mr. Lovell described his mother in harsh superego terms.

T: "What kind of look was it?"

Mr. L: "You know. One of those looks that there is only one way to do something right. If you don't do it that way then you're really stupid." Mr. Lovell's mother was becoming known as given to idealizing and devaluing projections, further evidence of "this or that" thinking. She maintained an idealized "My son can never do any wrong" relationship to him as long as he didn't go against what she wanted. However, if Mr. Lovell differed from his mother's way of doing things she could be powerfully spurning (hostile rejection) with just a look. Mr. Lovell appeared unaware that his description of how his mother treated him paralleled Mrs. Lovell's description of how he treated her and the children.

T: "Kind of a disgusted look?" I tried to clarify and elaborate Mr. Lovell's experience and search for the source of the shame that seemed to underlie his anger and much of his self-experience.

Mr. L: "Yeah. That was it. It never occurred to me that there was any other way. For my mom there was the right way or no way. It took me years to realize that there was more than one way to do something. Like at work, I would get really impatient if one of my guys would do something differently than I would. But, I told myself to keep quiet and sometimes their way was better than mine. (He chuckles.) Even if it wasn't, it usually got the job done." Mr. Lovell described a diminishment in his narcissistic vulnerability over the years, and the development of thinking that was at odds with and differentiated from his mother's.

T: "That must have been an eye-opener for you. Was your dad that way too?"

Mr. L   (thoughtful pause): "No. He was a machinist and later ran a store with my mom. He knew how to get along with people." This statement suggested that his mother did not get along with others, or at least not as well as his father did. "The basement was full of machines and I would go down there with him and he would let me take things apart and put them back together again. He wasn't critical." Mr. Lovell again implicitly underscored his mother's criticizing character. "If I couldn't get something back together he would do it. He never made me feel bad." Again, by implication, he suggested that his mother did make him feel bad. (In a quieter voice.) "But, he never was one to say I did a good job either." Mr. Lovell again underlined his experience that his parents were never proud of *him* as a person. He never received affirmation. The best he could do was to avoid his mother's disgusted look by fitting in with her expectations.

T: "You know when I listen to you now your voice is softer as you speak of your dad. But usually it's much harder and harsher. I wonder if that's when I'm hearing a lot of your mom in you. You're kind of grumpy and critical and you talk of how you were like her at work. And, it seems you're maybe like her with your kids. But I don't hear much of your Dad in you. What do you make of that?" (therapist in role of intrapsychic third).

Mr. L   (tearing): "My dad died when I was fifteen. At that moment, I decided not to let anyone close to me. I guess

I pushed my dad out of my life when he died. I never wanted to be hurt like that again." This explanation alone does not fully account for the extent of Mr. Lovell's isolation and poor self-esteem. However, when combined with his earlier statement that he was alone growing up, that he never misbehaved and tried to do everything to avoid displeasing his mother and to win his father's approval, it is more compelling. Again, I followed the line of his thinking to encourage his continued elaboration.

T: "By not remembering him you didn't hurt anymore?" (tentative interpretation put in question form, fostering further reflection).

Mr. L: "I guess that's it. When I think about him I miss him a lot." Mr. Lovell began crying. He had a difficult time speaking, obviously trying to fight off his emotions.

T   (after giving him some time to settle): "You made a conscious decision at that time?"

Mr. L: "No. That was when I was eight. A car killed my dog and I was so torn up I decided not to feel that close to anyone again. I guess when my dad died I felt the same thing and reminded myself not to let anyone close." Mr. Lovell was becoming increasingly spontaneous in his recall and offering information that was deepening the telling of his story.

T: "So you have a history of pushing things away—people, thoughts, feelings—that are painful to remember?" (therapist's offering a tentative interpretation).

Mr. L: "I never thought about it like that, but I think that's true."

T: "So you felt alone growing up. Your closest companion, your dog, was killed when you were eight. Your Dad, the parent you felt most comfortable with, died when you were fifteen and your Mom took care of you. But, in your heart of hearts you didn't feel like you could ever please her or your dad." Mr. Lovell began crying again. After several minutes pass, I commented, "Trying to be someone who could do no wrong is a pretty tall order. You must have felt like you were failing or at least at risk of failing all the time?" (therapist functioning with empathic attunement and responsiveness, and fostering the space [intrapsychic third] in which various affect-laden aspects of Mr. Lovell's childhood experience may coexist, stimulating cogni-affective awareness).

Mr. L   (crying): "I really did. I really did."

T   (after several minutes of silence to allow room for Mr. Lovell's sadness and experience of loss): "There are many things to think about in what you've said. You're the boy who could do no wrong, who, in his loneliness, feels that he could do no right. I guess this helps make sense of your hostility toward the school and court authorities who you felt were telling you, you could do no right." I return to the opening theme of the session: Mr. Lovell's angry and counteridentifying relationship to authority. "Your antagonism toward authority of any kind is expressed in your fury at the courts and in your inability to identify with your own authority in relationship to your kids. As you felt looked-down-on by your parents, unable to please them, you felt looked-down-on by the judge who seemed to ignore the good you have done. I suspect your fury toward the courts contains much of the fury toward your parents." Mr. Lovell continued to cry quietly, but was looking at me intently as tears rolled down his face. "In addition, you treat your children as you were treated in childhood. You avoid them and have become the king of the 'disgusted look.' As you felt you could do no right in your parents' eyes, so your kids feel they can do no right in your eyes. Now, they have also become masters of the 'disgusted look.' I didn't make the connection before, but that's what they convey when they curse you and roll their eyes when you speak, as if to suggest that you're crazy and that what you have to say isn't important. I guess this keeps you in the kind of relationship you had with your parents?" The reciprocal relationship between the intrapsychic and the interpersonal was verbalized and highlighted.

Mr. L: "Yeah. I guess it does. I haven't been that angry in a long time [referring to the courts]."

T: "I think what makes it particularly hard for you is that deep down you really don't believe you can do anything right (self-rejecting internal world). When authority figures were talking to you, you felt they were looking down their noses at you, maybe somewhat similar to your mom's look of disgust? And, when they didn't acknowledge anything right that you've done, maybe that was similar to never getting approval from your dad?"

Mr. L: "I guess it was all in there. I'm not sure about the dad part, but the mom part sure was." Mr. Lovell continued to exhibit his own thinking, confirming part of my interpretation of events and differing from another.

T: "Which also happens to be how you feel about yourself in your heart of hearts." I highlighted the unconscious dynamics of the internal world of self and object relationships.

Mr. L: "Yeah. That's true. I feel like a loser."

T: "Something that still puzzles me is the hard time you have setting limits on your kids, having serious expectations of them. Instead you just get angry and disgusted with them and gloat that 'they'll get theirs when they grow up.' It's like you're willing to let them blow their lives so that you can prove yourself right, but don't really do anything in an ongoing way to help them straighten their lives out. Instead, you experience their obstinacy as a personal attack against you, rather than a challenge for you to show them you really care enough about them to struggle with them."

Mr. L: "I don't know." The tone of his response seemed to represent both emotional fatigue and resistance, his wish to get away from his experience (therapist attending to interpersonal interaction).

T: "You know, Mr. Lovell, I'm beginning to think that when you say 'I don't know,' you're not giving yourself the time to think at all. Or, maybe, it's that you don't like what we're thinking about. Or, you're afraid to be wrong, as if that would be a terrible thing. Yet, every time I've heard what you think, you really have something to say. I think you're taking away your own authority right here as we speak. I think you're afraid to be wrong and afraid to be involved, and that screws up the relationship with your wife and with your kids." (Mr. Lovell remained quiet.) "You know, now that I think about it, your kids repeatedly give you a look of disgust in family sessions when you say what's on your mind, and that stops you dead in your tracks. I think you have the relationship with your parents confused with that of your wife and children" (therapist making a more direct interpretation, weaving together the intrapsychic and the interpersonal). Mr. Lovell resumed crying.

Mrs. L: "He never sets a limit on them and when things aren't going well he always blames me if the kids get upset."

Mrs. Lovell came in with a critical, rather than compassionate, voice. I felt annoyed with her, protective of Mr. Lovell, and wondered about the timing of her attack, again seemingly linked to moments when Mr. Lovell was obviously vulnerable. At the same time, she piled on top of my confrontation of Mr. Lovell, which gave the impression that we were allied against him. Accordingly, I opted to ignore her to remain focused on Mr. Lovell, attending to interpersonal interactions and process and choosing to remain on the level of the intrapsychic, rather than shift to the level of the interpersonal, so that Mr. Lovell could continue in relationship to the meat, rather than the scraps, of his experience. However, I filed my observations away, to address them with Mrs. Lovell later.

T: "What do you think, Mr. Lovell?"

Mr. L: "I hate to admit it. I hate the idea of it, but you might be right. I've never been able to say 'no' to them or to set limits with them. I hate the feeling of displeasing them, but at the same time I'm angry at them most of the time." Mr. Lovell also ignored Mrs. Lovell's agenda, showing that he too was gripped by the unfolding of his intrapsychic and interpersonal relationships in a way that had meaning for him.

T: "And so you walk around angry all the time with a look of disgust on your face and you convey to them how you felt in relationship to your own parents: that they're losers, while it's you who feels like a loser."

Mr. L   (continuing to cry): "I feel I'm damned if I do and damned if I don't. What I generally do is stay to myself."

T: "And then you're all alone again, feeling like a loser."

Mr. L: "Yes . . . I've never thought about it like this. I want to be important to them, but I just can't believe I am." Mr. Lovell was grappling with his sense of self as irrefutably unimportant versus a vision of who he could be.

T: "Well. Maybe part of the problem is that if you had your own authority, you might have to go about things a different way than your mother did. I guess you'd have to make up your mind if your way of thinking was okay or if you should continue thinking in your mother's way" (therapist as intrapsychic third, intervening between Mr. Lovell and his internal representation of his mother; fostering separation, individuation, and differentiation). A half a minute passed as Mr. Lovell cried silently.

Mrs. L: "He doesn't act like a parent. He is more like one of the kids and adds to my troubles."

Mrs. Lovell was again beating the drum of her own agenda, belittling and shaming Mr. Lovell while failing to identify with and have compassion for the pain he was in. She was completely out of tune with the moment. Again, I felt resentment for her piling her invectives on top of my statements, as if they were the same and we were allied against Mr. Lovell. I wondered what motivated this ruthlessness in her (therapist attending as the interpersonal third to the relationship, and the intrapsychic third to Mrs. Lovell, while attending to his countertransference).

T: "Mrs. Lovell, to tell you the truth, I think that's old news. I think Mr. L has acknowledged that. It's interesting that in your marriage and family, each of you seem to repeat so much of what happened in your original families. Neither of you felt like you could do anything right and I think you're repeating that right now. Although I really did hear how affirming you are of Mr. Lovell's importance to the family earlier in the session, right now he could use some empathy and understanding for what he has revealed here today, rather than a continuing pointing out what he has done wrong in the past. I'm puzzled by the pattern of your relatedness. I've noticed that when Mr. Lovell becomes open and vulnerable you seem to attack him, and yet when he is closed and resistant you are more empathic. I guess my question is what allows you to feel for him when he doesn't show his feelings to you and what gets in your way of feeling for him when he shows his feelings to you?" (therapist as interpersonal third: setting boundaries between the spouses, managing spousal aggression, and making interpersonal process observations. Therapist as intrapsychic third; encouraging Mrs. Lovell to think about the internal motivations of her behavior in terms of the interpersonal process he has commented on).

Mrs. Lovell was silent for a few moments and I worried that I was too confrontational. I knew I was overinvolved at this point. However, one of her strengths was that she was able to learn from such confrontations, which seem to strengthen her trust in the therapy.

Mrs. L: "I see what you mean. It's hard to catch myself." (To Mr. Lovell.) "I'm sorry. I think you've done a lot today in this meeting. I do love you." (Turning to me.) "I don't know what happens to me. I don't know if it's my anger toward him or what."

T: "What I've noticed is that when Mr. Lovell resists your acknowledgments of the good he has done you are very supportive of him, and, yet, when he is hurting and vulnerable you become cold and critical. What do you make of that?" I ignored Mrs. Lovell's statement of confusion, repeated the earlier description of the pattern between them, and again asked Mrs. Lovell to comment, continuing to encourage the development of her thinking. I also refused to accept Mrs. Lovell's compliance and half-hearted, agreeable guessing, which would cast a patina of closeness or connection on what she just leaped over.

Mrs. L: "I don't know. I guess I shouldn't say I don't know. It's a cop out. (She has the idea now.) I just feel angry. He acts like a kid and puts more weight on me." Mrs. Lovell's disparaging use of the word "kid" suggested internal attacks upon any kidlike feelings in others or in herself.

T: "I can understand that part, but still it's interesting that when he's hurting you pile on top. I wonder if that's what you do with your own feelings when you are hurting? I wonder if that's how your feelings were handled when you were growing up, when you were a kid" (tentative interpretation of anti-libidinal ego attacks upon the libidinal ego).

Mrs. L: "Oh, my God, yes. Anytime I was upset my parents told me I was selfish. I always had to keep things going and do things for my parents."

T: "So, when you were upset they were critical of you?"

Mrs. L: "Yes."

T: "And, as you were made to feel selfish for having your own feelings, you feel Mr. Lovell is being selfish when he has his?"

Mrs. L: "Yes. I can see that."

T: "This still seems kind of intellectual to me. That suggests
            we really haven't gotten to it yet. What other thoughts do
            you have?" I was paying attention to experience in
            gauging the depth of the work. Mrs. Lovell said "I can see
            that," but didn't actually identify with it. I was pushing
            Mrs. Lovell deeper into her own experience.

Mrs. L   (a long silence; Mrs. Lovell seemed lost in thought):
            "What comes to my mind is that whenever I was sad it
            wasn't important. My parents' feelings would always be
            bigger than my feelings. I think that when Mr. Lovell gets
            sad, I feel angry with him because I can feel for his
            feelings but he never feels for mine." Mrs. Lovell was
            tearful.

T: "Never is a big word, but I understand what you're saying
            and what you're saying feels sad."

Mr. L: "It's not true that I don't care. I think I'm just so angry
            most of the time that it's hard for you to tell." With
            this spontaneous and unsolicited utterance, Mr. Lovell
            showed his capacity for compassion. He was challenging
            Mrs. Lovell's equating him with her parents.

T: "You know, Mrs. Lovell, I think Mr. Lovell is telling the
            truth. I've noticed in here that when you get sad it clearly
            affects him. I think we'll need to look at why it takes you
            getting sad before he responds to you. But that will have
            to be a subject for another day, for we are out of time for
            now" (therapist as interpersonal third and suggesting
            areas of further exploration for intrapsychic consider-
            ation).

By paying attention to and following the incongruities (dis-
integrities) between words, thoughts, feelings, and actions of each
spouse individually and between the spouses as a couple, the issue of
authority in one form or another arose repeatedly. Mr. Lovell
became increasingly reflective about his own behavior and recalled
childhood experiences that influenced his relationship to self and

others. The genesis of his out-of-proportion angry response to the courts and his hostile and rejecting relationship to his kids became clear. The discussion did not remain on an intellectual level, limited to the pointing out of dis-integrities, but led to the uncovering of affective memories. Mrs. Lovell also became more aware of the spiteful things she did to upset Mr. Lovell. She both recognized her angry response to feeling unloved by him and was able to feel more compassion and concern for him as she identified that she was treating his feelings of distress as her own had been treated in childhood. Interestingly, Mr. Lovell was different than her parents in this regard. He was often compassionate when she was upset, but unfortunately not until she became upset.

This session supported each spouse in observing and reflecting upon their interpersonal interactions and in abiding with, elaborating, and thinking through their self-experiences and perceptions of the other. Repeatedly, a space was created, the thirdness of the potential space, in which the intrapsychic and the interpersonal could enter mutually enriching relationship. In this process, memories of childhood were recovered that helped make sense of and gave meaning to each spouse's ways of perceiving and relating, fostering individuation and differentiation. The family members' internal worlds of fused self and object relationships were partially modified, as past was partially differentiated from present. Blaming and shaming diminished.

CONCLUSION

This chapter describes the importance of the development of the capacity for "thirdness" that is achieved as the individual develops from pre-oedipal dyadic forms of relationship of mother and infant, to oedipal triadic forms of relationship of father, mother, and infant. The therapist, recognizing that the couple's devotion to action kills contemplation, fosters development by representing and maintaining an area of thirdness, a moment of hesitancy, the space for contemplation, between thought and action, on both intrapsychic and interpersonal levels, all the while interrelating the two. With the development of thirdness the couple moves from binary, this-or-that, all-or-nothing ways of perceiving and relating to affiliative forms in which "this and that *and* all that stands between" can be taken into account.

The importance of the development of the capacity for thirdness is correlated with the development of subjectivity and the potential space. With the awareness of thirdness a dialectic is created between two points of view, which leads to alternatives that might not have been imaginable by either spouse singly. The possibility of establishing a third and thereby a fourth or fifth or more points of view leads to the development of genuine relationship in which the various aspects of the two spouses as whole individuals can exist simultaneously with one another. With the awareness that "some other thing" is possible, many other possibilities become imaginable.

The movement from binary relatedness, based on the projection of two-dimensional images, to genuine relationship involving the feelings and needs of both spouses, however many and contradictory they may be, leads to personally meaningful relationship, in which surface and depth, and past and present, are distinguished. The therapist assists the spouses in discovering personal meaning in self and other, by representing and creating space for thirdness: the interpersonalized third at the interpersonal level, and the intrapsychic third at the intrapersonal level. Essentially, thirdness allows for observation and reflection on both levels.

In this treatment effort, the therapist is concerned about the self and other relations of each spouse, while not needing or requiring anything of the spouses or the couple. The therapist's generally (therapists are human too) nondemanding, nonjudgmental, and nonexpectant stance facilitates space for contemplation and learning, which was previously collapsed or never developed in the face of activity and reactivity.

In addition, the therapist, as a full-contact participant in the process, attends not only to spousal interactions, or therapist/ spouse interactions, but also to the details of his countertransference experience (self-relations) that arise in relationship to the spouses. All the while, the therapist makes no effort to force things to make sense and forgoes the illusory harbor of professional certainty in favor of his own capacity for floundering, befuddlement, and tentativeness.

It cannot be stressed enough that relationship between two people is contingent upon the development of the self-relations of each. Accordingly, the therapist struggles to understand the evolving experience and perceptions of each spouse—not only cognitively, "from the outside in," but affectively, "from the inside out." The therapist fosters the spouses' entering full relationship to self and other, appreciating that genuine understanding is a cogniaffective experience. To this end, he does not settle for intellectual insight to the relative exclusion of affect, or for affect to the relative exclusion of insight. As one patient said, "Logic without feeling is as crazy as feeling without logic."

Containment, the therapist's holding and processing of experience, is also illustrated. The therapist functions as a "third" in both the intrapsychic and interpersonal realms, processing the spouses' interpersonal and intrapsychic experiences in the service of reality-testing, synthesis, and integration. In this effort, the therapist functions like the mother bird. He tastes without swallowing, chews without deriving nourishment, and delivers a pasty mash to the baby bird for swallowing and sustenance. In this approach to treatment, containment introduces but does not proscribe thirdness. Thirdness emerges naturally through the therapist's efforts to reflect upon experience. As the therapeutic triad that is marital therapy works together, thirdness develops and becomes available for internalization. With the spouses' internalization of the therapist's containing function, they enter relationship to themselves not as fixed and brittle objects, but as ongoing and evolving subjects who are able to construct the meaning of their own lives.

As the therapist creates multiple thirds in working with the couple, his experience becomes interlaced with their own, generating wide-ranging countertransference responses that can be used to help the spouses process their own experience. Sometimes he is nurturing, other times he is confrontational, most of the time he is both thinking and feeling. In these ways, he introduces the thirdness of the good-enough mother *and* father, establishing time, space, and boundary for the processing of experience.

15

Transference and Countertransference

Sooner or later in every therapy, impasse occurs. This is the time when the therapist shifts from a reliance on logic to a reliance on "psycho-logic." In part, this entails encouraging the use of the couple's free-associative processes. The therapist urges the partners to say whatever comes to mind without censor. The therapist also models this behavior, for example, by commenting that a particular association came to mind although she might not know why. In this way, the therapist engages the couple in a fluid and collaborative process of thinking, valuing the inherent organizing tendency of the self, the gaps in knowledge, and the "not-yet-known" as much as the "known."

Psycho-logic also entails the therapist's use of the transference relationship. Transference is manifested in perceptions, images, thoughts, feelings, attitudes, and actions that involve relating to another in present-day reality as if he or she was an object from the past. The transference relationship includes the transference between the spouses, between each spouse and the therapist, and between the therapist and each spouse. The therapist's use of her transference, that is countertransference, to therapeutic ends is based on the assumption that the therapist has sufficiently worked through her own conflicts to examine her thoughts, feelings, and reactions in a thoughtful way in the service of better understanding the spouses.

The process works something like this: The spouses present a puzzle, the conflict in their relationship, that they are unable to sort through and resolve. Due to the difficulty in understanding the problem and its refractoriness to treatment efforts, the problem becomes akin to a puzzle in which essential pieces are missing. These have been denied or have never achieved recognition. In an attempt to uncover the missing pieces, the therapist attends to the total situation of the therapy, including dis-integrities, the latent content of the spouses' thinking, *and* her countertransference reactions that arise in relationship to the spouses. Her attention to her countertransference allows her to recruit her own at least partially-unconscious reactions in service of trying to better access and understand the unconscious communications of the spouses. In essence, the therapist uses her unconscious, manifested in her countertransference reactions to the spouses, to be in contact with the spouses' unconscious. Once aware of countertransference reactions, the therapist struggles to tease out an understanding of them and may even use the spouses to help her make sense of her experience. Typically, this process provides further information, gleaned from the unconscious, concerning the missing pieces of the puzzle.

The therapist's returning of her countertransference experiences to the field of the relationship in which they have arisen is critical for many reasons. **First**, it furthers the integrity of the treatment. If the therapist chronically avoids addressing uncomfortable subjects or feelings in relationship to the couple, she must function with dis-integrity, that is, feeling one thing while trying to convey another. This is iatrogenic in that it runs counter to the development of real relationship, and, in fact, corrupts it.

Second, convictions are conveyed. The therapist's perceptions, including her thoughts and feelings, are inevitably conveyed, in myriad ways, both in and out of awareness. This is evident, for example, in that most therapists are not successful treating people they dislike.

Third, unexamined transference phenomena become felt as taboo subjects or unspeakable secrets, held in a "bastion" (Laing 1960) and denied by all. For the therapist to deny or avoid working through her positive or negative feelings toward the spouses is to collude with transference projections. To avoid working through uncomfortable feelings is to implicitly confirm frightening inner realities. Treatment is then iatrogenic in that it implicitly supports existing structures of perception. Conversely, transference working-through is counterprojective; it fosters real relationship and understanding.

Fourth, denied experience creates gaps, dis-integrities, or incongruities that generate anxiety, insecurity, and "false self" functioning. If the therapist denies his experience, he implicitly or explicitly throws into question the reality base of the spouses' perceptions, which is "crazy making."

Fifth, the therapist's failure to help the spouses identify and process their projections, particularly when they are directed toward him, is a breach of the explicit, implicit, and unconscious treatment contract between the couple and the therapist. It is a failure of both attunement and/or responsiveness and impedes the therapist's capacity as a healer.

Sixth, the therapist's willingness to explore thoughts and feelings, including her own, develops the culture of processing experience as it arises in relationship, making it available for internalization. In that the therapist is not blaming or shaming but striving for understanding, the couple has the opportunity to experience the possibility of healthy conflict, that is, of conflict leading to resolution and a deepening of relationship, rather than as inevitably destructive.

Seventh, the therapist's willingness to explore the transference in the therapist/spouse dyad paves the way for the subsequent working-through of the more intense parallel transference distortions in the marital dyad. The working through of the former facilitates the working through of the latter (Sonne and Swirsky 1981).

The willingness of the therapist to use the data of her self-experience in the service of developing relationship is a practicing of what she preaches. As she struggles to understand herself in relationship to the couple, the process is made available for internalization by the couple. Again, lip service is not enough. In popular terms, the therapist must not only "talk the talk." First, she must "walk the walk," then "walk the talk," then "talk the walk," before the spouses will begin to trust what she has to say, even if she can "talk the talk."

Identifying and understanding countertransference experience is by its nature difficult. Often it is an impossible task to make sense of an experience in the moment, or even after the fact, through reliance on one's internal processing alone. Fortunately, the therapist does not have to go it alone. As long as he has a will toward vulnerability, is not shaming or blaming, is genuinely curious, and can report his experience along with his confusion about it, he can enjoin the spouses to help him make sense of it.

Nonetheless, the raising of countertransference issues, particularly with personality-disordered individuals, often takes courage because it involves the spouses' primitive projective identifications, which, by definition, involve thoughts and feelings that threaten the spouses and that therefore they are driven to deny. Because they threaten the spouses, the therapist's attempts to bring them to their awareness may result in her being perceived as persecutory and becoming the target of their aggression.

Vignette: Countertransference

The following vignette from individual therapy offers a dramatic illustration of the outlined principles. Karen was thirty-one years old and unmarried. She entered therapy with me following an eighteen-month course of therapy that included individual, couples (with her boyfriend of seven years), and group therapy, all with the same therapist. She had initially sought treatment with her previous therapist for depression and had been on antidepressant and antianxiety medications following the death of her mother. In addition, she was unhappy in her seven-year relationship to her boyfriend, fearing that the problems in the relationship were all her own. However, she was afraid of breaking up and of being alone. Karen had terminated treatment with her former therapist when she felt that he and her boyfriend had become "fed up" with her continued grieving of the loss of her mother, which had been going on for about a year. She reported that they both felt she had to get on with her life. Unable to follow these admonitions, Karen was angry with both men for "their unfeeling and uncaring attitude." According to Karen, they confirmed her view that men were hard and unfeeling objects, "like nuts, bolts, and springs." Finally, other behaviors on the therapist's part, such as not calling when he had found that she had left her purse in his office and some seductive-ness, had resulted in her feeling that he did not have her welfare foremost in mind.

After a year of hiatus from treatment, and having made no headway in resolving her depression with medications, Karen sought treatment with me. During the ensuing eighteen months of therapy, a series of medication changes not only offered scant relief, but left Karen with substantial complaints about side effects, to which she felt I was less than sensitive. In addition, although some progress had been made in identifying the genesis of Karen's depression and underlying self-hatred, there had been little lessening of her pain. Throughout the course in therapy, she would alternate between idealizing and devaluing transference reactions toward me. How-ever, at best, she felt I was "less than caring, but empathic enough for a man." Karen alternated between states of vegetative depression and demands for medication changes. She berated me for my referral to a psychiatrist who was "incompetent and uncaring" and who prescribed medications to which she had side effects, and furious for my not helping her to feel better. She complained about the time my incompetence was costing her, ventured that I just saw her for the money, compared me unfavorably to her brother's analyst, and episodically demanded a referral to another therapist.

Under this continuous onslaught, my own feelings of hopelessness and inadequacy (countertransference) paralleled her own for herself and about me. Although I sometimes wondered if another, more empathic, therapist might be more effective and offered to make the referral, I also advised against it, seeing it as her attempt to determine if I cared enough about her to continue. On some level, I felt she was really gauging whether or not I could stand her any more than she could stand herself. After processing each such demand, her condition would improve for a few weeks, only for the cycle to begin anew.

At this point, eighteen months into treatment, Karen's aged father died after a long illness. Karen, being the only local relative, had spent much of her free time attending to his needs. For the last two years, she had visited him on a daily basis in the nursing home and responded to his numerous phone calls to her home and office. During the last months of his life, she occasionally wished he would die. These feelings were followed by intense feelings of guilt and flagellating self-hatred. The impossibility of meeting her own perfect expectations of herself as a daughter, of what she should do, how she should behave, and how she should feel and think about her father, eroded her physically and emotionally. Only with great difficulty and considerable treatment efforts was Karen able to moderate the frequency of her visits to him, so she could begin to attend to her own needs and have a life of her own.

During our work together, Karen had described her father as passive and dependent. From her description, he appeared to suffer from dependent personality disorder. Throughout her childhood, he had largely kept to himself. Although they lived in a wealthy neighborhood in a house his father had left to him, his income was not sufficient to support their lifestyle and they sold belongings in piecemeal fashion to make ends meet. Consequently, they had a house that was glorious on the outside but a hovel inside. Karen remembered her mother placing a clothesbasket on the couch to cover a hole—the basket remaining there for years. She also tearfully recalled looking out her bedroom window to see her piano being carted away. Her parents had sold it without telling her. Even her father's employment was an embarrassment. He had obtained his job through his father's connections, and after his father's death he was given a desk in what previously had been a storage room, with nothing to do.

Although her father had not been available in a substantial way, he was the idealized parent, for Karen's mother suffered from bipolar disorder, alternating between bouts of intoxicating excitement at one moment and dark and frightening rages the next. She demanded the constant attention of her children and concocted endless chores so that they could not go out to play.

Her father's death, like her mother's, affected Karen deeply. Her depression worsened and she mourned him each session, often in the voice of a little girl, between episodes of sobbing and wailing. She condemned me for encouraging her to reduce the number of visits to him and she felt that because of me she had abandoned him in the waning moments of his life. She felt she was an awful person in relationship to an equally awful therapist.

Six weeks after his death Karen continued to engage in an intense display of grieving. She sobbed uncontrollably, flagellated herself repeatedly for having wished her father dead, cursed me for not supporting her role as a good daughter, and was generally engaged in a destruction of her total situation. Despite this, I realized that I felt strangely unmoved; if anything I was bored and impatient. Puzzled by my reaction, I also realized that for the most part I had not had much feeling for Karen's loss of her father from the beginning. I wondered about my lack of empathy. *Was I burnt out with Karen or perhaps less available due to events in my own life?* Disturbingly detached, I observed her across the room, thrashing in grief on the couch. I imagined her engaged in an ancient ritual of self-flagellation, gnashing of teeth, and rending of clothes. Ashamed, I realized that I wished she would just shut up. As I sat with these thoughts and feelings, I recalled that my reaction was akin to that which she had described of her boyfriend and previous therapist. That made me feel even more inadequate. I had fallen far short of what they had endured: They had lasted almost a year, whereas I had lasted less than two months. I wondered if there was something to be learned from this.

As I continued in my reverie, I questioned my own humanity. *What kind of monster am I, that I cannot feel genuine compassion for such a legitimate loss? Perhaps Karen, with all her talk of how men lack empathy, has seen into my soul and detected what I had not realized; that I am comprised of springs and bolts without genuine human feeling.* To offset these disturbing feelings, I tried valiantly to look into my heart and summon feelings of compassion, but failed miserably. I still felt apart from Karen's grief and wished she would stop her wailing.

In continuing to consider my thoughts and feelings, I wondered if Karen's display of grief was unconsciously designed to distance me. The unkindness of this thought then struck me. *Was this not just an attempt on my part to rationalize my monstrous callousness?* I then felt anger toward Karen's father. To my astonishment, as she grieved him, I hated him and his inability to have been there for her in any substantial way. I then realized that this was true of me as well.

Thirty minutes into the session, continuing to be bombarded by Karen's wailing and unable to make any further sense of my feelings, I realized that given the part-object nature of my thinking and feeling I was in the throes of countertransference. In addition, I felt that it was important to make sense of my countertransference in that it offered hope of a new way of thinking about what was going on with Karen. At the same time, I knew that Karen would experience my making even tentative interpretations from my countertransference as a direct assault. For example, if I hypothesized that her feelings might be covering up her anger toward her father, she would certainly experience this as an intellectualized rejection of her experience. I knew that I would feel completely let down if I was feeling what she appeared to feel and someone said that to me. Nonetheless, I reasoned that my lack of compassion was not typical of me but had arisen in relationship with Karen. In addition, to pretend a compassion that I did not feel would be dishonest and "crazy making" for Karen, whom I felt on some level would be aware of my disingenuousness.

The prospect of saying anything filled me with intense anxiety.

I knew that Karen was sure to experience me as she had her boyfriend and her previous therapist. I also knew, from our history together, that she would respond with very personal attacks upon me. I felt that Karen's abrupt termination of treatment was a real possibility and that if that occurred I would feel that I had been incredibly damaging without the opportunity to make repair. At the same time, I cared about Karen and I felt that such a radical incongruency between her feelings and mine had to indicate the presence of a crucial dynamic that must be explored if I was to be of help to her. Thus conflicted, I spoke.

T: "Karen, as you've been grieving I've been struggling with my own experience. As you know, I believe in putting back into the session my own experiences that puzzle me. Right now I'm having one of those experiences that I don't understand and was hoping that you may be able to help me cast some light on it."

Karen (wiping her tears): "Go ahead. I'll try."

T: "To my surprise, I'm having difficulty identifying with your grief." Before I could get another word out, Karen reacted.

Karen: "I can't believe this! My father has only been dead six weeks and you're already telling me to stop grieving. You shit! How can you be such monster? You're just a machine. At least my boyfriend and George (the previous therapist) let me grieve for a year. I can't believe it. My father has only been dead six weeks. Jesus, what kind of therapist are you?" Although my worst fears were coming true, I couldn't help but marvel at how her thinking about my feelings had so accurately paralleled my own. I persisted.

T: "Karen, I can understand why you would take what I've said the way you have. I had those very same thoughts and feelings before I spoke. I also want you to understand that I don't think you should stop grieving. You should grieve as long as you need to. All I'm saying is that I'm experiencing something that I don't understand and I feel it's my responsibility to share that with you in the hope of trying to understand it. It may be just me, but I don't think so. I don't typically feel this way when someone has had a loss. I'm really puzzled."

Karen (shouting): "Yeah! You want to make it my fault. You're such a shit. (After a long pause) You should apologize to me. What you've said is awful and if you don't apologize I'll never be able to trust you again." Karen's demand left me in a risky position. Although I felt for her distress, to apologize would be a "dis-integrity" on my part, for I felt that it was my responsibility to explore the incongruity of our experience. On the other hand, if I didn't apologize she was likely to end therapy immediately. I landed on the side of integrity.

T: "Karen, I would apologize if I could do so genuinely, but I can't. I really am sorry that you are upset and I can understand it. But, I believe that my experience has to do with you and your relationship with your father and I think it is important."

Karen (aghast): "You won't apologize to me when you're being so awful. Christ. You're just like them, just springs and bolts. You're a monster. You just can't stand to feel. If you don't apologize to me, I can't work with you any longer."

T: "Karen, I like working with you and I think I can be of help. But, to apologize to you when I feel I'm doing what I need to do wouldn't be sincere and then you really couldn't trust me and should find another therapist. Lip service is not enough, and it shouldn't be enough for you. I can't apologize because I think I'm doing what I need to do to try to be of use to you. Now, do you think you can step back from it all for a minute to at least consider what I am saying?" After several minutes of silence in which Karen appeared to be wavering between staying or leaving, she finally responded in a small voice.

Karen: "Okay, I'll try. I think there may be something to what
you're saying. I can't stand it, but I don't think I'm really
feeling anything either." She begins crying, but somehow
differently, in a way with which I could empathize. "I'm
not feeling what I know I should be feeling and I feel like
a monster. I feel like I must be really sick, far more
damaged than I can bear to think. I think I'm trying so
hard to act the way I think I would be acting if I were
feeling what I think I should be feeling if I were healthy.
I was hoping that by acting the way I should be feeling that
I would begin to feel those feelings and be normal. But, I
can't. I'm afraid that I'm beyond help, a monster."

I was struck by how Karen's feelings and struggles paralleled my
own and I felt great empathy for her. I admired her ability to
collaborate with me in making sense of what I was feeling, and
thereby to make sense of her own feelings. It had been important
that I shared my feelings with her, and that I had refused to
apologize for them, while still managing to convey my caring for her.
It was in my being able to acknowledge the incongruity between my
feelings and hers, and to open my feelings to exploration with her,
that she was able to identify and acknowledge the incongruity within
herself, the absence of her own feelings, which she had felt to be
unspeakable.

In this and subsequent sessions Karen and I explored our
shared experience in more detail, including my feeling angry
toward her father. She was able to identify her own angry feelings
toward her father, listing numerous instances of his passive, nonprotective, self-absorbed presence. Moreover, she remembered how she
and her siblings had felt the need to buttress his sense of self,
providing him company over the years, while he showed little
interest in them. She spoke of being the audience for his timeworn
stories and of forcing herself to laugh to protect his feelings, while
silently feeling awful for resenting his stories and her time with him.
She recalled how he had been unavailable to her in any substantial

way, failing to protect her from her mother's rages, and told of his
once leaving her at a store, having forgotten her. She spoke of her
terror of abandonment, her shame over their home to which she felt
too embarrassed to bring her friends, and the pain that she was
unable to express over the abrupt loss of her piano. Finally, she
spoke of the years of her adult life that she had devoted to his care,
at the expense of the development of her own life. She described
living her life as a lie, just as she had lived in a house that appeared
glorious on the outside but was really a hovel on the inside.

Only after acknowledging and exploring her anger toward her
father was she able to recall moments of feeling loved by him. She
reminisced about his gentleness and his comforting her after one of
her mother's particularly horrendous rages. Now when she cried,
her tears and her feelings of loss evoked feelings of compassion
within me. Rather than feeling disengaged, I felt sad for her and
empathized with her frightened sense of being on her own in the
world. Through her grieving, she recognized her inherent sense of
shame, her fear of exposure, and her defensive need to act as if
everything was fine when it was not. As she processed myriad
thoughts and feelings about her parents over the next year, she
came to put both her father and her mother into perspective, seeing
their failings and their strengths. She wondered at the lives they had
defensively created for themselves. She was now able to evolve from
her internal part-object relationship to them to a more mature and
differentiated whole-object relationship.

Karen separated from her boyfriend following an effort at
couples therapy from which he withdrew. She experienced that
relationship as a lie. Although she cared about him, she recognized
that he was unable to identify with her needs. Like her parents, he
insisted that she live her life in accordance with his needs, without
regard for her own. Subsequently, she had a series of relationships,
each healthier than the next and each contributing to her ongoing
development and growing independence. Eventually, she formed a
relationship with an extremely compassionate man who was capable
of identifying with her needs as well as his own.

CONCLUSION

The therapist's use of countertransference in relationship to the individual or to the couple is an essential part of the treatment process of making the unconscious conscious. Via the use of countertransference reactions, the therapist can return denied and projected aspects of the patient's self to the patient in more manageable form. In this process, the therapist lends her developmental capacities for containing and processing to the patient, so that that which previously felt unbearable can be borne and understood.

However, the capacity to make conscious that which is unconscious and to re-integrate denied and projected aspects of the self is not enough. There is also the issue of damage done in relationships and the importance and complexity of the effort to make repair. This is the topic of the next chapter.

16

The Capacity for Reparation

Speaking generally, the long-term goal in working with personality-disordered couples is to help the spouses evolve from the reactivity, persecutory anxieties, and ruthless aggression of the paranoid-schizoid mode to the ability for self-observation, self-reflection, and empathy of the depressive mode. Klein (Klein 1935, Klein and Riviere 1937) suggested that such development was fostered from the individual's meeting with "a preponderance of good results" in the pursuit of object relationship. Bion (1962a, 1963, 1967) asserted that the depressive position was attained through the child's participation with a containing other who was able to help the child process experience. Winnicott (1948) noted that the attainment of the depressive position came about from a decrease in primitive splitting, so that the "good" need-satisfying object and the "bad" need-frustrating object were understood to be the same. With this whole-object "real-ization," the wish to destroy the need-frustrating object becomes tempered by the awareness that the need-satisfying object would be injured as well; genuine concern ensues.

It seems quite plausible that all of these explanations apply. However, at least one more element is required for the attainment of depressive-mode capacities and is particularly important in the treatment of couples, in that one or both spouses feels injured by the other. This is the capacity for reparation. In that injury, from disappointment to grievous insult, is inevitable in relationship, the capacity for reparation is paramount.

Winnicott asserted (Winnicott 1958b, 1967b) that an important part of development included the planned and unplanned failures of mothers. Not only did failures introduce the child to reality, but they also offered the child the lived experience of the mother's caring as it was manifested in her efforts to soothe (Winnicott 1954, 1960a). In addition, Winnicott noted that the child's own sense of value was contingent upon her (the child's) experience of being able to make repair for damage done to the mother. Such damage could arise from the child's voracious neediness, which can test the patience of any parent. An example of repair would be the child's successful revitalizing of the exhausted parent with cooing and smiling.

Alternately, without the possibility of reparation, the child is left in a world in which every misstep and every wound, no matter how grievous or slight, is forever lasting. In this circumstance, the only way to deal with injuries is to deny them. The individual is then left in fragmented and polarized relationship to self and other. He either strives to maintain the precarious illusion that he never injures or makes mistakes, or becomes enveloped in the never-ending injuriousness of his own aggression. When the child is not able to reach the hole in the mother, the child, and later adult, feels the hole within herself, in the form of an inherent sense of "badness" or basic fault. This is not only a function of the inability to internalize a nurturing breast, but is also the internalization of a damaged breast that is felt to be beyond repair.

Indeed, this is the fate of personality-disordered individuals. They have no way of dealing constructively with disappointment or injury. Consequently, they never feel "disappointed." Instead, every misstep is catastrophic, and guilt and shame are rampant, defended against with ruthless aggression. Their relationships are blaming and shaming as they engage in behaviors that elicit or inflict punishment as a form of redress or atonement, but not repair.

Acts of repair have much in common with gift giving. Both require the cooperation of two people. With gift giving, as with reparation, one person must give the gift and the other must accept it. Similarly, for a reparative act to be reparative, one partner must make the act of repair and the other partner must allow the gesture to reach the hole within, thereby giving it meaning.

For personality-disordered individuals to engage in acts of repair is a developmental achievement. Consider, for example, that one person must acknowledge that he has been harmful. To make such an acknowledgement requires at least a glimpse of whole relationship to self. Without this glimpse, the sense of one's own "badness" for the wound given would obliterate any sense of "goodness." Of course, acts of genuine repair must be distinguished from mea culpa-like acts that may only serve guilt alleviation through self-punishment or magical undoing, noted in the words "I've said I'm sorry. What else do you want?"

Taking in an act of repair is at least as difficult as making one. Just as a wide receiver in football must reach for an almost-accurate pass, sometimes even diving and falling to the ground to work for the reception, to take in a gesture of repair is to risk injury and betrayal. This act suggests that the receiver of the gift feels "good enough" about herself that she can risk such a betrayal and still survive, that is, she experiences a relative state of autonomy. The courage entailed is most evident when we consider that in personality-disordered couples gestures of repair have been in part-object form, as witnessed in the classic cycling of abusive relationships. The abuser, after having ruthlessly attacked the other as a "bad object," apologizes in the face of the threatened loss of the other. The abuser then becomes charming and apologetic. Of course, the victim also relates in part-object form, maintaining the cycle of abuse by withdrawing from the other as a "bad object," when the other is attacking, and then reentering relationship to the other as a "good object" when sounds of remorse are made. In that each partner is in ahistorical relationship to the other, the slate is wiped clean and the cycle can begin anew.

Conversely in whole-object relationships, the words "I am sorry" are not enough, nor is the bestowal of flowers and gifts. What is required is the genuine recognition of the damage done to the whole of one person from the whole of the other. The damage becomes part of their history, under the right circumstances for-given but not forgotten. Genuine repair is reflected in learning from experience, not repeating it. When both partners are capable of acts of reparation an ongoing knitting of the wounds results. In adulthood, only repeated experiences of reparation can overcome the damage caused by early deficits in trust. In this sense, integrity is the suture to attachment wounds and permits the malignant circle of love, hate, and aggression to be transformed into the benign circle of love, hate, and reparation. For these reasons, the appear-ance of even seemingly minor acts of genuine repair in the treat-ment situation heralds a huge developmental leap—perhaps only short-lasting, but breaking new ground nonetheless.

The treatment of personality-disordered marriages is a high-risk endeavor for the therapist. The therapist is inevitably bom-barded and even battered by the spouses' transference, projections, persecutory anxieties, and hostility, which may leave her disorga-nized, disoriented, and vulnerable. To avoid or defend against this danger, therapists often work hard at looking smart and acting healthy. Hopefully, if we and our patients are lucky, this does not get too much in the way of the work. We are able to tolerate our vulnerabilities and the experience of the "hole" within, thereby giving ourselves the chance to identify and meet it within our patients and, just as important, our patients the chance to identify and meet it within us.

Given the intensity and the tumultuous nature of the work there are repeated instances of the need of repair. Clinically, acts of repair often begin in the therapist/spouse dyad rather than in the marital dyad. Therapists, like mothers, are only human, and make mistakes. It is in the therapist's genuine concern and ability to acknowledge mistakes and to repair that the capacity to repair first becomes available for internalization by the spouses.

Moreover, it is when the therapist is able to take in the spouses' acts of repair and allow them to reach the hole within that the spouses may experience a way out of their inherent sense of "badness" and internalize the ability to accept repair.

Vignette: The Gift

Rosalie and Sam were in their early thirties. Rosalie had stabilized on an outpatient basis following eighteen months of psychiatric hospitalization after an overdose on psychotropic medication. Over the course of her fifteen-year psychiatric history she also self-mutilated via cutting and burning and had been diagnosed with major depression, bipolar disorder, borderline personality disorder, and multiple personality disorder.

For his part, Sam held a high-ranking position with an aerospace company. Although he had no history of psychiatric treatment, he fully met the criteria of schizoid personality disorder. He was devoted to the logical and the concrete and almost completely divorced from his own feelings and incapable of identifying with anyone else's. What little Sam portrayed of his family life suggested an atmosphere of psychological isolation and relationships devoid of meaning. This atmosphere was re-created in the marriage via his massive aloofness and withholding. His only acknowledged anxiety was of "making a mistake," which referred to anything that included the remotest possibility of leaving him open to ridicule and humiliation.

The first months of couples therapy focused on stabilizing Rosalie on an outpatient basis. As she developed a routine and maintained a more continuous sense of self, her focus began to shift to her feeling that she and Sam had little genuine connection. She worried that it was a relationship of convenience for Sam and that she held no special importance to him. She was describing the experience of an object-to-object relationship and wanting a subject-to-subject relationship in which each of them had personal meaning for the other. This shift to issues concerning the quality of the relationship and the pursuit of gratification, as opposed to the previous focus on issues of survival, reflected Rosalie's growing consolidation of a sense of self and movement toward depressive-position capacities. However, Sam responded in his usual aloof and intellectualized way. He explained, "I'm attending the sessions as a part of Rosalie's therapy, and as she continues to improve things will improve between us."

Rosalie refuted Sam's implication that all the problems in the relationship were of her making. She persisted in trying to determine whether or not she had personal meaning for him, questioning if he really loved her or only used her as a part-time wage earner, housekeeper, cook, sexual object, and generic companion. Rosalie repeatedly broached these issues with great courage, but eventually began to regress in the face of Sam's continued refusal or inability to affirm her value to him. She gradually withdrew, sitting in either volcanic silence ready to erupt at any moment, or in vegetative depression, unreachable by any means.

As summer turned to fall, Rosalie began attending sessions in bulky turtleneck sweaters, the necks of which she pulled over her head, so that she appeared like a child hiding under a cover. Sam also withdrew, stretching his legs out and closing his eyes. Thus on one side of me sat Rosalie, inside the protective confines of her sweater, and on the other sat Sam, slouched with his eyes closed. In the ensuing weeks, my efforts to understand and process their experience were repeatedly rebuffed and I also began to withdraw as the therapy took on the atmosphere of a nuclear winter: gray.

For a while I thought confidently, *This is a lesson for me of the depressive position. The therapy is not in my control and its outcome is not completely up to me. Eventually we will understand what is being acted out here.* However, as the weeks passed into months my every effort at exploration and interpretation was met with disparagement or indifference.

In the silence that took over the sessions, I slowly became immersed in a quagmire of despair. I felt that my therapeutic convictions, the sextants by which I navigated, were useless, relegated to the level of delusions designed only to give false hope to naïve therapists. I thought, *The lessons of the depressive position be damned. Not only is the treatment not completely up to me, but I am not up to the treatment.* My inadequacy and worthlessness were tangible. I was exposed for the charlatan I was, to them and, even worse, to me.

My mood alternated between indifference, vulnerability, and anger. I drifted in reverie, wondering such things as, *For what am I being paid? What's for dinner tonight?* or wishing for a good book to read, anything to distance me from the cold and unremitting isolation of this couple. However, most of all I prayed for the interminable hour to end.

My focus of attention often narrowed to the struggle to keep my eyes open, as my eyelids became increasingly heavy with a determination of their own. My eyelids became my enemy and I imagined ways to defeat them—for example, inventing "eyelid jacks" that, like tiny car jacks, could be used to prop them open. My eyelids were now permanently at half-mast, a compromise position maintained with considerable effort.

Reduced to the narrow world of my own sensations, I was defeated, speechless, struck dumb. Thinking was beyond me. Intermittently, I tried to break out of my morass, but the couple stymied me at every turn. Eventually, whenever a wish to establish human contact with them arose within me, I attacked the wish with the specter of the pain of rejection that would surely follow. Increasingly my reveries excluded the couple.

Thinking was now episodic. In one such moment, when I could summon the care and concern to ponder my experience, I realized I had no sense of space of any kind: no surrounding space, no space between, and little sense of space within myself in the presence of this couple. Certainly no potential space, in which play could occur and things could be thought about. Instead, deadness and isolation were all that existed. Magically, my fatigue, along with my benumbed and claustrophobic self-experience, would evaporate as soon the couple left my office.

As the months passed, I contemplated ending the therapy. Yet,

I couldn't. I thought, *There is something to be understood here. For instance, how do I account for Sam and Rosalie's continuing to come to the sessions at considerable expense of time and money? Sam had to leave work early and each of them traveled seventy-five minutes each way to attend the sessions. Isn't this evidence that they are in search of something and that the torment isn't only my own? Wouldn't my ending therapy simply be letting them down, my own distancing from that which they cannot bear?* I could not bring myself to fire them. At the same time, I wanted to shout, "You must get better so I can tolerate being with you!" It's what I felt but could not say.

As Christmas approached, gray indoors matched the weather outdoors, and hope, for me, died. My only ambition was of sleeping through the next hour and then being free of them over the Christmas holidays. Only fifty more endless minutes to go and I would be free for two wonderful weeks.

However, as Rosalie entered the room with a ribboned box, leaving it on the coffee table where it could not be ignored, I realized with a sinking feeling that my plan to sleep through the session was not to be. It was obviously a gift for me and I felt angry that I would be put in a position of having to interact with her. I noticed that she seemed hesitant, strangely vulnerable, an experience of her I had long forgotten. As usual, the session began in silence.

After some moments Rosalie said, "I've brought something for you." I nodded in response, struggling with the sense of languor that had taken over me in anticipation of the session. I imagined the box as a Trojan horse, just another way to get inside my defenses to degrade and humiliate me. I fantasized that it was a bomb and would blow up. I hoped it would. At least that would be something different happening and put us all out of our misery. I waited in silence. I did not know what to say, had little energy to say anything, and nothing seemed required. I hoped nothing would be required. Above all, I feared having to make a gracious response that I did not feel for a gift I did not want.

With a twinge of horror, and despite my every effort, I recognized a tattered vestige of curiosity arising within me, a Judas betraying the protective confines of my protective lethargy. It was not curiosity about the box or what it contained, but something about Rosalie's attitude. What was it? As I considered this question, I again noticed the sense of vulnerability that surrounded her, a qualitatively different experience of her than I had had over the months of isolation and rejection. I also noticed that Sam was different. He sat silently in his usual slouch and seemed to be trying to convey the impression that this session was an everyday event, but his vigilant attitude, in addition to his open eyes, gave him away. I suspected, *He's interested because I'm being set up for the kill. He wants to see how I'll handle this attempt to get inside my defenses. He doesn't realize that I'm no longer defended. I just don't care anymore. Damn them. Isn't it just like them to expect something of me right at the moment that all I want is to get away and to have them go away.*

At this point, Rosalie, to my annoyance, intruded into my thoughts, saying, "I've baked you a cake." My instantaneous association was that the cake was poisoned and they wanted the pleasure of watching me die in front of them. However, Rosalie seemed embarrassed, almost apologetic, and then I knew that the cake was not poisoned for she would not be that way if she were trying to kill me. Still enshrouded in a sense of stupor, I reluctantly asked myself, *What's going on? What does she want of me?* I had no answer. I nodded and ordered my mouth into what I hoped was the shape of a smile, relieved that I did not feel required to speak. I then realized, to my own surprise, that my silence was in tune with Rosalie. She was trying to express something and was not finished. There was a beseeching quality about her. I recognized, to my amazement, that she was struggling with something. I had not noticed such a will toward expression, and vulnerability, on her part in months.

Despite or perhaps in defense against the novelty of these experiences, I became aware of how depressed I felt in the company of this couple, an experience not quite unbearable, but despairing nonetheless. I thought of their inadequacy and mine, of what a pathetic threesome we made, occasionally feebly struggling to defend against the fact that we were locked together in failure, only refusing to give it voice. Rosalie then said, "I baked this cake from scratch. I've been thinking for some time about opening a bake shop." Sam abruptly chimed in enthusiastically, "It's a gourmet cake! It's very good!" I feared I was having auditory hallucinations. But this fear was set aside as I sensed that Sam took genuine pleasure in Rosalie's giving of the gift.

Rosalie continued. "I know the last months of therapy have been very hard. I wanted you to know that, even though we haven't been making much progress." I thought, "That's the understatement of the decade," but she continued despite my rudeness, "I really do appreciate your efforts although I don't always keep that in my mind. I know that you are trying to help us."

At this point, I thought, suddenly ashamed, *Not for a long time now. I've just been trying to get through. You're the one taking the risk and doing the work.* Then I felt a strange sensation, unlike anything I recall feeling ever before. It was a sense of collapse, like a huge sigh, a letting out of air, a relaxing simultaneously with a poignant feeling of inexpressible gratitude. It was only at that moment that I realized how thoroughly I had been stuck in the mire of the work, to a degree that I hadn't fully appreciated, although I thought I had.

I then wondered, *What is this feeling of gratitude? Why am I feeling it?* Almost instantaneously, I understood that my feeling of gratitude had to do with Rosalie's reaching into the hole that was within me to make contact and rescue me. The hole in them and their relationship had swallowed me and become the whole of our relationship. Even though I was depleted and had internalized the badness of the situation, Rosalie had still seen the good in me.

I still had not spoken. I did not feel impelled to make a comment or to struggle to find something to say. I was content to let whatever I would say come to me. As I waited, I thought about the gift of the cake made from scratch, which itself nurtured, but far more so in the way in which the gift was given. Rosalie had risked vulnerability—the giving of a gift that, given the persecutory world of the sessions, could well have been rejected, an outcome Rosalie had every right to fear. The giving of the gift also acknowledged me as an individual. It was a giving that required a taking. Rosalie had risked feeling care and concern for me and acknowledged their role in my difficulties.

I was with my thoughts for some time, enjoying the space to think and feel. Although I was comfortable with the silence, I was aware that Rosalie seemed tense and Sam vigilant, both waiting to see what I would do. How was I to handle the situation? Should I interpret it? Should I refuse it? Should I simply accept it? I discarded these options as technical considerations untrue to the moment. They were not in tune with how I was feeling and would diminish the gift. I realized that what struck me most was that Rosalie had made emotional contact, not only *from* the core of her but *with* the core of me, and that Sam was vicariously participating in the exchange. More than anything I wanted to acknowledge and accept this contact and to return it in kind.

I decided to simply verbalize my experience. I described my feeling of being rescued from an abyss and of being replenished by Rosalie's taking the risk of giving a gift and of recognizing me. I expressed my respect for her courage in caring enough to risk rejection.

I asked Sam if he had been involved with the making of the gift. Predictably, he demurred but Rosalie related that he had gone to the store to pick up the ingredients and discussed the kind of cake to make. I recalled his enthusiastic comment about it being a gourmet cake. I thanked him as well.

Rosalie was silent for several moments and then said, "I was so worried about giving you a gift. I was afraid that you would not accept it or would analyze it. I just wanted to give you a gift and for you to accept it. I am glad this turned out this way. You did not analyze it and I can tell it meant a lot to you. I can't believe how good I feel about that. I can't believe how much it meant to you."

The various aspects of the gift giving and the reason for the onset of the nuclear winter were explored in further sessions. Rosalie, feeling rejected and humiliated by Sam, had decided to reject and humiliate Sam. As starved for human validation as she had been, I had come to be rejected and humiliated as well by default. Eventually I had come to despair as Rosalie despaired.

In allowing the gift to reach the hole within me, I had been able to give Rosalie the gift of the experience of being able to make reparation. In the subjective experience of the gift giving, that most important of human experiences—personal meaning—was achieved. The cake was not just a cake; its importance was in how it was given and how it was received.

It is with the decrease in primitive splitting and denial, and the resultant capacity for concern, along with the willingness to engage in the give-and-take of reparation that the destructive circle of love, hate, and aggression gives way to the benign circle of love, hate, and reparation. In this instance, it occurred between a spouse and the therapist; in other instances it can occur between the spouses themselves.

17

Treatment as a Recurring Process

In workshops, after much of the material has been presented I am sometimes asked, to my own bewilderment, "What do you do then?" It's as if the questioner is still thinking that therapy is a linear process involving a step-by-step formula that empowers the therapist to omnipotently treat everyone and every circumstance, if she can just get it right. Upon hearing this question I know that I have failed in making my point, at least to the questioner. Somehow I haven't conveyed to him that treatment is a living process, comprised far more of eddies, ebbs, and flows than straight lines. Typically, I can't think of anything new to say, except what seems self-evident to me: "You just do it all over again, and then again and again."

The couple's problem is inevitably comprised of a group of interrelated problems. In turn, each problem is multifaceted, and, just as we may rotate a diamond to grasp its entirety, so in therapy we look at the couple's problem(s) from many facets until the problem itself becomes adequately defined and understood, including the couple's resistance to change. Consequently, sometimes it appears to our patients that we are addressing the same problems over and over again. They might even complain, "We've already talked about this. Why are we here again?" In fact, we're not "here again"; we're in a new place looking at the same problem from a different perspective and we'll probably continue to return to look at it, hopefully from fresh perspectives, until the problem is resolved or the couple decides to end therapy.

Treatment is like a wheel. Sometimes progress is evident in that we actually come to grips with a problem, achieve traction, and move along—evolution via revolution. At other times, when impasse exists, therapy is just a spinning of wheels. Impasse inevitably claims the focus of therapy in that we are unable to move ahead until it is resolved. Even when progress has occurred, later in therapy it may be revisited as subsequent discoveries help us to see the problem or the motives behind it from new perspectives.

Treatment is a recurring process not only throughout the course of therapy, but also within the course of a given session. Each session is constructed by the couple in a way that manifests the different aspects of the internal world of each spouse in relationship to the other, even though the issues and themes may change. As the spouses' ways of perceiving and relating form and reform through-out the session, so too do the therapist's. He experiences the shifting pressures of his own life, changing countertransference experiences in relationship to the couple, over- and underinvolvement, and an oscillating ability to make use of his experience in relationship to the couple. The whole process is organic, with a life of its own, which lives itself out in repeated and different ways within and between sessions and in subsequent sessions until progress is made. To confuse things even more, progress is often followed by regress, which, in turn, may lead to further progress.

The following vignette illustrates the to-and-fro movement of the ever-shifting relationships of therapy. As the issues—either verbalized or acted out—change, so too does the therapist's approach. The therapist is not dancing by the numbers but is in dynamic relationship to the spouses. All the while, the therapist recurrently relies on the basic skills stressed repeatedly in this book. He identifies and addresses incongruities between the spouses and between himself and each spouse. He uses reason and logic to define areas of ill-logic. He struggles to discern his countertransference and its relationship to the couple. He oscillates and fluctuates between over- and underinvolvement, moving closer in relationship to the couple, using fuller contact to gather data and to intervene; and distancing himself from the couple in order to create the space to think about his experience in relationship to them and to provide them the space to work directly with each other until primitive defenses arise. He offers deniable interpretations.

This is far from a precise interaction. The therapist stumbles toward understanding, at times focused on the interactions between the spouses and at times occupied with his own reveries to the extent he is barely able to hear the partners speak as they persevere in constricted ways of perceiving and relating. Foremost, he labors to remain true to himself and to value his capacity to feel and to think, even though this may bring him into conflict with the couple's assumptions about what may be felt, thought, and talked about.

In this vignette, you will note mistakes by the therapist. In truth, I'm not too concerned about these. I believe that it is more important for the therapist to be genuinely involved with the couple and to bring his self into play, than to function too carefully or in too role-bound a way such that it interferes with spontaneity, play, and genuine connection. Winnicott (1971) wrote, "Psychotherapy is done in the overlap of the two play areas, that of the patient and that of the therapist. If the therapist cannot play, then he is not suitable for the work. If the patient cannot play, then something needs to be done to enable the patient to become able to play, after which psychotherapy may begin" (p. 65). There is no right or wrong way to play. All play is perfect. Above all else, couples are interested in genuine connection and suspicious of the overly careful, overly directive, or guarded therapist.

Indeed, the therapist's failings are often reassuring to the couple,[4] particularly if the therapist is willing to acknowledge

---

4. Of course, some patients are so caught up in the internal world of persecutory object relationships that they are unable to tolerate any mistakes at all. The problem here is that for the couples therapist to strive to be mistake-free, from the

mistakes and make repair when they occur. Mistakes humanize the therapist, provide an opportunity to manifest caring in his willingness to make repair, and deepen the therapist's understanding of and relationship to the couple. Conversely, the "perfect" therapist is responded to with waves of attack and retreat from the therapist *and* the therapy—a hyperbolic distortion of the typically strenuous ebb and flow of work with the personality-disordered couple.

Vignette: Therapy as a Recurring Process

Ellen and Edward were referred for marital therapy by Ellen's therapist, who was concerned with Ellen's reports of verbal and physical abuse within the marriage. Ellen was an obese woman with a long history of psychiatric disability, including multiple personality disorder and years of inpatient and outpatient therapies. She possessed such an impressive sense of entitlement and was so long-suffering that she fell short of being likeable. Typically, she felt victimized in the face of less-than-perfect agreement with her views and perceived any kind of exploration as invasive or attacking. Her tendency to experience herself as victimized was made apparent when a detailed exploration of her complaints of verbal and physical abuse led to her acknowledgement that although she felt abused this feeling was not related to any observable event, other than Edward's sometimes raising his voice.

Edward, equally obese, was a banker and in his third marriage. He played guitar during church services and spent much time in church and community activities. While Ellen presented as eternally suffering, with an uncanny ability to make others suffer right along with her, Edward presented as a saint, often martyred, who would patiently stand by Ellen through thick and thicker in the expressed

point of view of these patients, would require that the therapist forgo acknowledging and valuing the mates' concerns. Such egocentric and narcissistically vulnerable patients may do well in individual therapy but not in couples therapy, at least until they are able to tolerate different views without experiencing difference as attack.

conviction that one day she would be well. Armed with these convictions, Edward was well able to avoid reflecting upon his own contributions to the problems in this relationship as well as in his earlier marriages.

Developing the Space to Think and Feel

Six months into once-weekly couples therapy, Edward and Ellen arrived fifteen minutes late for the session. Ellen swept into the room without greeting, took a single chair as far as possible from the group setting, turned off the lamp next to her, closed her eyes, and put her head in her hands. Edward trudged in behind her, completely ignoring Ellen's dramatic entrance, and greeted me with hollow enthusiasm. I was curious and felt anxious, wondering what was going on with Ellen and how it was going to be divulged in the session. Given their entrance, I anticipated the session with foreboding. Ellen did not appear to be in a mood receptive to the work and Edward was his usual bonhomie self, all of which promised a tedious evening. It was late, and I was tired and hungry. The prospect of negotiating Ellen's sensibilities and Edward's false enthusiasm held no appeal. Yet the thought of sitting through an hour ignoring the obvious with this couple bespoke an even less palatable future, marked, as it would be, by my having to participate in and be corrupted by this couple's pathogenic form of relating.

Edward began the session by launching into a report on the week's events. He spoke at length in a monotone, devoid of affect or vitality, each unpunctuated word flowing into the next. It was difficult to pay attention and soon I felt annoyed by the effort of trying to piece together the underlying theme to what he was saying. Eventually, stymied in my efforts, I gave up and instead began attending to the numbing power of his droning monologue. I wondered, "Why does he speak in such a way?" As he moved from one topic to another, without transitional statements, I could detect no rhyme, reason, or unifying thread to what he was talking about. All the while, I was increasingly aware of Ellen's obvious withdrawal and Edward's complete ignoring of it. Finally I concluded, with irritation over the energy I had spent, that Edward was just talking nonsense. The point of his words was not to lay the groundwork for a problem he wished to address but to fill time, distract, and avoid confronting the issues in the session. The interesting aspect of his presentation, as I struggled to salvage one, was that his demeanor was in total contrast to Ellen's. He was speaking as if nothing were wrong in their lives. Indeed, he seemed defiantly upbeat.

When Edward finally paused to draw breath, I commented to him that Ellen seemed to be distressed, and that while he had discussed the length and breadth of their week, he had somehow failed to mention this unmistakable fact. Edward responded with annoyance, stating irately that he had no idea what Ellen was distressed about, and that his every effort to find out had been rebuffed. Figuring that Edward had not tried too hard, probably suspecting the root of the problem but not wanting to address it, I turned to Ellen.

T: "You seem upset. What's going on with you?" Ellen did not give any inkling that she heard me. After a long silence, I realized she wasn't going to respond and was irked with her passivity, as well as the inexorable demand this couple's avoidance was placing upon me.

Ellen   (suddenly indignant): "I resent your focusing upon me."

I was taken aback by this unexpected attack, so completely out of tune with the spirit of my initial inquiry. With my indignation, I reasoned that I had asked a reasonable question and I had been patient in waiting for her response. I did not deserve to be rudely treated. Furthermore, with total objectivity, I recalled her dramatic entrance and subsequent one-person play entitled *Human Misery Is Alive and Well*, which had been impossible to ignore. I felt angry to be so unfairly put in the role of abuser, victimizer, or wrongdoer. Furthermore, I reasoned, I could not afford to be intimidated by her hostility or stymied by her aggressive behavior. In short, her unexpected attack became the lightning rod for my pent-up frustrations.

T: "I guess it's difficult for you to see what part you play in becoming the center of my attention?"

It was only as these scornful words escaped my lips that I realized, despite my self-serving rationalizations, how impatient and angry I was, and how I was being as provocative to Ellen as she was being to me. Belatedly, I wondered whether Edward's blatant ignoring of Ellen's distress was actually an expression of his own well-founded anger toward her for being rebuffed in similar fashion before the session had begun. As I stewed, Ellen remained silent. I became increasingly annoyed that my earlier prediction that the session would be a demanding one had so quickly materialized and that, despite such foreknowledge, I had been unable to alter its course. I knew we would have a session in name only if she continued with this behavior. What could I do? Would Edward continue to "report in" while Ellen remained a silently rebuking presence? Could I pretend that this was an okay way to proceed? I could not tolerate these options. I again spoke to Ellen with a conscious effort to bridle my negative feelings by struggling to affect a quiet and reasonable tone.

T: "Ellen. I'm wondering why you chose to come to the session and then not speak?"

Again, in hearing my own words, I realized that I had deluded myself into thinking that I had sufficiently processed my frustration and anger. Although I had thought about my reactions, I had not worked toward understanding their countertransference implications. In word and tone, I conveyed an invitation for her to leave—or worse, a suggestion to stay and be demeaned. Aware of my mistake, I hunkered down to await retaliation. I did not have long to wait. Her answer was coldly efficient and emphatic, as if speaking to the village idiot.

Ellen: "Because we had an appointment."

I felt checked and checkmated. Shut out by Ellen's refusal to be drawn out and Edward's monotone ramblings, I accepted defeat and began focusing internally on my own feelings without further regard to making anything happen in the session.

After a few moments, Edward renewed his dry, factual reporting of events, filling the silence and cloaking us all with the cadence of his voice. With Edward's voice droning in the background and with the certainty that he required no response from me, I entered a twilight state of reverie, without ambition or desire. I felt unburdened by any need to force understanding and was content to allow whatever formed in my consciousness to emerge. After some minutes, an image arose in my mind that depicted the experience I was having of the couple. I thought about it and then interrupted Edward. I told him that I found it hard to listen to what he was saying, knowing that there was a dispute going on that I did not understand. I told them that I wanted to share an image of them that I found troubling.

T: "While I was sitting here, I imagined a lake in which two people were in separate rowboats paddling in opposite directions, passing each other without sign or recognition. With that image, I realized I felt not in the presence of a couple, but of two people on different tracks going in different directions, never acknowledging each other and never intersecting."

Edward   (feelingly): "That's exactly how I feel. It's so frustrating."
Ellen   (jumping): "I don't matter to Edward. Only his needs are important. If I disagree with him, he becomes furious. You don't realize what a price I pay when I speak in here. Edward exacts his revenge."

With this, Edward took issue. Edward and Ellen began discussing their anger, each perceiving the other as unreachable and uncaring. The previous angry-but-sterile feel of the session was replaced by a feeling of investment and energy. Each felt genuinely hurt by the other, and yet unable to identify with the other's feelings.

My initial effort to enter meaningful discussion with this couple had been rebuffed, both by Edward's tedious reporting of the week and by Ellen's withholding refusal to speak. Their anger and their sense of helplessness and alienation were captured in the image of my reverie, which articulated their situation without blame. A space for reflection had been created that held the potential for sorting through. Of course, the sharing of my reverie could just as easily have been met with silence. The outcome wasn't up to me; all I could do was to put my experience back into the relationship in which it had arisen.

The Therapist as the Container of Experience

Despite this progress, Edward and Ellen's discussion soon regressed to a mutually blaming and shaming interaction. I commented, "Each of you is talking but no one is listening. Each of you is more concerned with blaming than with understanding." They became quiet. This was a more settled quiet, in that Edward was no longer filling the silence with noise and Ellen was no longer hiding her head in her hands.

As the silence lengthened, I looked at Ellen and felt empathy. Her facial expression seemed both sad and afraid. I made an effort to confirm my experience and to follow her affect.

T: "You seem both sad and afraid."
E   (quiet for some moments before answering): "You confuse me with those words. I don't know if they're your feelings or mine. I feel pushed."

Though her words were similar to those of her earlier rejection of my attempts to understand her situation, her tone was markedly different. I did not feel attacked or rejected. I felt she was stating what for her was a genuine problem. She did not know whether I was trying to push my feelings into her. I also wondered about her experience of human contact as always threatening of invasion. I responded in recognition of the poignancy of her dilemma and the genuineness of her confusion, as well as my own limited ability to help,

T: "I'm not expressing my sense of you to push you or to say that you are feeling what I sense, but to say that this is what I was feeling about you. That way you can correct me, so that you can let me know what I don't understand. This is the only way I know of getting to know you."

E   (after a period of reflection, in halting voice): "I've never talked with anyone like this before. I've never done this before, but I can see what you mean. I am feeling afraid and I guess sad. Edward and I keep at this but seem to go nowhere. I don't know if it's going to work." Edward sat quietly, listening intently.

Such moments of vulnerable contact, so different from the previous defensiveness, are like nuggets of gold in their poignancy and aliveness. As Ellen was able to consider that she might be sad and afraid, she was able to locate the genesis of her feelings in the frightening thoughts of separation and loss that stood like foreboding shadows behind them. A moment of intimacy had occurred, and I found myself liking Ellen for her humanness and Edward for his obvious interest in and concern for her feelings.

From Present to Past and Past to Present

Progress was again followed by regress as the dialogue between them eventually came to an abrupt halt. Edward had become more animated and Ellen had demanded in sudden outrage that he lower his voice. Although Ellen perceived Edward as shouting and trying to bully her, this was not at all my perception. Equally curious was the fact that Edward did not contest Ellen's depiction of him. Instead, he immediately complied and returned steadfastly to his previous monotone and lifeless manner of relating, sometimes with a fleeting glimmer of irritation. It seemed to me that Edward's ready compliance suggested that some part of him agreed with Ellen's depiction of him, that is, that he experienced his own spontaneity and aliveness as potentially dangerous.

In thinking about how to address this curious interplay between Edward and Ellen, I felt anxious. Ellen seemed supremely confident in the reality of her perception and I feared she would perceive my questioning of her perception as attacking and respond to me accordingly. At the same time, I could easily imagine Edward disavowing the importance of my inquiry and responding as if I were making a mountain out of a molehill. Despite my concerns I could not help but pursue the incongruity between their perceptions and mine. Such incongruities, particularly when recurrent, are invariably important to understanding each spouse and their relationship. I knew that I could not allow the taboos this couple had against thinking about experience govern the sessions, or the therapy would become as barren as the marriage itself.

I explained that I was interested in incongruities between people's perceptions and that at that moment my perception was at odds with theirs. I clarified that I did not view myself as the arbiter of reality, that my perception could well be incorrect, but that I felt it was important to share perceptions in a relationship, including the treatment relationship, so that we could understand each other better. I expressed the hope that they would share their perceptions with me. I then went on to describe my view that Edward was not being very loud or intimidating, while at the same time Ellen appeared certain of it and Edward did not contest it; so I was confused.

To my relief, Ellen was open to thinking about the discordance in our perceptions. As the session continued, Ellen finally associated Edward's increased intensity with being sexually abused by her maternal uncle when she was a child. When he babysat for her, she would hide. After her parents left, he would hunt for her, calling out to her, the increasing intensity and excitement of his voice foreshadowing the abuse to come.

As we spoke together, I recognized that my anxiety about speaking to this subject may have been related to the fear that Ellen would experience my questioning of her perceptions as a questioning of what had happened to her, even though I had not known what it was. I thought back on my earlier foreboding and wondered whether she had spoken of her abuse and been discounted. I asked if she had told anyone and she revealed that she had gone to her mother, who had angrily demanded that she never make up such stories again.

Having clarified the underpinnings of Ellen's intense response to the animation in Edward's voice, I turned to him to explore his readiness to concur with a delineation of himself as intimidating and bullying. What was even more surprising about his readiness to implicitly accept her delineation of him was that it was so at odds with his delineation of himself and his public persona as a saint. As usual, he was not psychologically minded, and although he conceded the logic that on some level he concurred with Ellen's perception of him, he claimed to have no idea as to why he was so ready to accede to her reality. I encouraged him: "Value whatever comes to mind, even if it doesn't seem related to this topic." After a few moments, Edward volunteered that he was his parents' favorite and strove to meet their wishes. In contrast, his only sibling, a younger sister, caused his parents much grief. He was angry with her for this, although he acknowledged secretly concurring with many of her complaints. Still, he insisted, family life would have been far more tranquil "if she had just been willing to go along."

Although Edward typically held an unassailably idealized view of his parents, he briefly mentioned that his father was stern and would not tolerate disrespect, which appeared to be defined as someone voicing a view different from his own. In turn, he described his mother, a devout churchgoing woman, as totally in support of her husband. Edward affirmed that he had been fearful of his parents' displeasure, noting that "a glance from them" was all that was required for him to behave. He strove diligently to meet their expectations in counterpoint to his sister's troubling rebellion. To this day, he viewed his sister as demanding and selfish.

From Edward's commentary, it appeared that he maintained the status of the "good" child, and thereby the love of his parents, via repression of his needs and spontaneity. It also appeared that Edward maintained a precarious sense of their love as conditional and of himself as worthwhile. Accordingly, Edward's self-esteem was not internally derived but contingent upon the reaction of others.

From earlier sessions, I knew that Edward had taken the role of rescuer with his two previous wives. A similar dynamic had influenced his attraction to Ellen, whom he knew had problems when they met. I marveled at how, despite this seeming imbalance in relationship, he inevitably came to be derided and scorned by his wives. As I thought about this, I realized that Edward seemed compelled to establish relationships with women whom he perceived as acting in ways similar to those he detested in his sister. I thought about the splitting of himself and his sister into good child and bad child, and about his parents' contribution to the formation of a harsh, self-attacking superego. I speculated that Edward was in divided relationship to himself, overidentified with those aspects of himself that he equated with goodness and in counteridentifying and disavowing relationship to the more aggressive and need-pursuing aspects of himself that he equated with badness. I thought Edward interpersonalized his intrapsychic dynamics, maintaining his identification to his internal parents by continuing in the role of good child, while he selected wives who were predisposed to be respositories for his aggression and neediness. Thus his marriages were actually at least a foursome: the recreation of his family of origin, in which he could variously relate to his wives as his sister, seeing them as selfish and needy, or as his parents, such as when Ellen would criticize him when he became animated. In this way, Edward used the interpersonal conflicts within the marriage to sustain his sense of self.

As I explored these thoughts with Edward, I realized that the discussion was purely cognitive, without affect, and that it was as depersonalizing an experience as listening to him drone on monotonously at the beginning of the session. I felt he was being a good child, relating to me as if I were in the role of his parent. Again, I felt frustrated in my efforts to form a substantial connection. Extrapolating from this experience, I wondered whether Edward's readiness to identify with Ellen's view of his spontaneity and excitement as bad reflected his compliance with his internal parents, now transferentially projected upon Ellen, who frowned on difference and spontaneity. If so, the marital interaction reconfirmed Edward's unconsciously held belief that investing himself in relationship in a personally meaningful way risked the loss of the loved object. Consequently, he repressed his aliveness, living his life in a dull monotone.

I was aware that without personal investment and affect the entire discussion would be fruitless, merely another re-creation of his going along with his parents' point of view without substantial human connection or development. I also recognized that my sense of frustration and helplessness in respect to achieving a sense of connection with him may have paralleled his own in relationship to his parents. I shared my experience and asked him about this. He was silent for some time and I was feeling that my effort to make genuine contact would be unsuccessful, when it became apparent to me that Edward was struggling with emotion, trying to master it and choke it down. I said, "If you continue to swallow your feelings, you'll always be isolated and never obtain the feeling of love you so desire." His eyes welled with tears that soon left trails down his cheeks. However, he did not speak.

Ellen, who had been sitting quietly, appeared concerned. In an apparent effort to make amends for her accusations that he was abusive, she offered that in the heat of the moment she had difficulty distinguishing between his excitement and that of her uncle. She went on to say that she knew that Edward had never abused her and had tried in many ways to meet her needs. Finally, in a gentle voice, she said, "I would like to meet your needs. I would like to feel that I could, but often you won't let me."

Edward, in a voice constricted with emotion, responded, "What do you mean?" As an example, Ellen recalled that in the preceding week, she had agreed to go to the state fair with him, but he had delayed so long that they could not, because of previously made plans. She noted, "I felt so frustrated and angry. You're always on me about my not caring about you, and yet when I try you won't let me." Edward refuted Ellen's example, rationalizing that she was taking a nap and that he did not want to wake her. Ellen sensitively confronted him with the fact that she had specifically asked him to wake her and now felt he was holding her responsible for their not going. Edward was silent.

Given Edward's fear of his own needs and spontaneity, I asked him whether he might not have a problem allowing Ellen to meet his needs, in that he might begin to feel more need-full, alive, and threatened. Edward responded quickly that this was possible, but his response again had more of the flavor of a good child trying to please, rather than of a serious consideration of the question. I pointed this out to him. He was again quiet, then turned to Ellen, saying, "I know you try to be there for me, but when you are it's like I can't let you." He started crying again. I commented, "It's hard to allow yourself to drink the milk when it's given to you." Ellen and I waited in silence while Edward gathered himself. The hour was up.

THE EFFECT OF THERAPY AS A RECURRING PROCESS

Repeatedly, throughout the course of each session and across the course of the therapy, the therapist is in dynamic and evolving relationship to the couple. Over time, in a good outcome, we would hear something along the following lines, if we were to listen to the internal dialogue of the observing spouse. (Assume that Ellen is the observing spouse.)

"Not only am I unable to relate to Edward, but I can't imagine him relating to anybody else. But here I sit, listening to him in conversation with Charles, who appears genuinely interested in what Edward is talking about. In fact, Charles seems, from time to time, even to understand Edward. This is puzzling. The words Edward is saying are words I've heard before. What's the big deal? Why is Charles so interested?"

Ellen's line of thinking might later evolve to other thoughts such as: "What is Charles' problem? He doesn't really believe Edward, does he? Why is Charles wasting my time? How can he think this is relevant to me? Charles seems to be genuinely interested and to care about me, so why is he spending all this time with Edward? Why does he seem to be moved by what Edward is saying? I've heard Edward say these things time and again, though admittedly there are some new words that I have not heard before. Something must be important because every time I interrupt this nonsense, Charles, sooner or later, gets back to Edward as if preoccupied by what he is saying. You know, something is happening. Charles can be kind of weird, but the funny thing is that Edward feels free to say things that he's never said before—at least, not to me and not in this way."

Gradually Ellen might come to the following discovery: "Funny, I don't feel attacked by Edward. I don't feel so accused or on the spot. He is talking about me, but he's talking more about himself. I don't sense Edward trying to push his feelings into me, or running away from me. Nor does Charles superimpose Edward's perceptions on me. He may ask me what my thoughts about Edward's perceptions are, but he never places them above my own. Charles is more questioning and curious than sure of anything. In fact, Charles seems less concerned with the reality of Edward's perceptions than with the perceptions themselves. Edward is speaking of his experience in a way that doesn't attack me or change Charles' view of me. This is clear because Charles always comes back to me for my point of view with equal, if not more, concern and interest. What's this? Edward is crying. I've never seen him do that. I know how that feels. He seems sad. He's always trying so hard to be so good. It's infuriating. But, now I understand. He's so afraid that people won't love him. I never knew he felt that way. I never knew so much of it didn't have to do with me."

18

Conclusion: What If?

by Ron Zuskin

Treatment of the personality-disordered couple begins far away from the strategic, structural, and communicative-interactive approaches that focus on doing, doing better, and doing differently. Treatment begins with intervention focused not on doing, but on *being*. The challenge to the therapist is not what to do but how to be—or, more difficult at times—just to be with the couple. Personality-disordered couples challenge the very self of the therapist.

The therapist of personality-disordered couples is subject to intense personal experiences (countertransference), partially manifested in internal dialogues that grow out of the work with the couple. Many therapists, from a deep desire to help, feel the urge to *"do something, anything"* in response to the pressure created directly, indirectly, or transferentially in working with the couple. Such a dialogue may go something like this:

Oh God, not this again. There, I've done it. I'm exposed. Helpless. Futile. I am at a loss.

I want to say: "Snap out of it! Get a self! Get a life! Leave me alone! Stop making demands!" I can't solve this. Lord knows, I cannot let you know that I don't know. Maybe a word of advice—something that worked for a friend of mine. For my brother. For me. Dare I offer anything?! I'm a fool and this is a charade. . . . No. I'll sit quietly. I'll nod. I'll repeat what the patient says. I know: I'll reframe it! Yes, a reframe! I haven't tried that yet! Today.

What an internal dialogue! But what if we brought our appreciation for "thirdness," our understanding of potential space, our wonder at the modes of experience and expression, our view that these people are a couple (if only in the mind of the therapist), and a relaxed readiness to *turn our thinking down a notch?* Our internal dialogue, in response to the work with Edward and Ellen in the last chapter, might be more like this:

Oh God, not this again. There, I've done it. I feel stuck and stupid. I wonder whether this is coming from her, or me? If it's coming from me, it might be like being a third grader again. But what if it's coming from her? Stuck. Stupid. Stuck in place; trapped with that uncle. Stuck. Mom won't help. Dad won't help. I feel tight. Tight in the chest. Hard to get a breath, if I'm not in control. Relax. I'm all balled up, like a fist. Clenched up. In defense or offense? Maybe both? What if this is her? Tense. Taut. Offense as defense. Defense as offense. Maybe her blasting me, as she does him, is a way of creating breathing room. She is saying things that make me think she is comfortable with the distance. The deadness. I wonder what she will say if I say to her, "You know, I might be way off base here. Please let me know where I miss the boat. I thought that my attempt to identify your feeling might have led you to feel trapped, unable to breathe. When you told me how wrong I was, I wonder whether you were making some breathing room for yourself. Maybe it feels better to you with me sitting with my thoughts, than with me closing in on yours. . . ."

What if clinical expertise were rooted in uncertainty? What if uncertainty led to our paying attention to our cognitive/sensory/affective experience, noting the complementary extremes of our thoughts/wishes/fears and considering our associations to our experience, given whatever conceptual ideas grow out of that experience? What if this led to our offering a deniable interpretation, to be rejected, revised, or refined by our patients? What if we were tuning our therapeutic instrument by allowing the modes of human experience to inform us mutually in a space much like that of free, exploratory play? What if by tuning ourselves we could tune into the experienced life of our patients, allowing the meaning of their expression to reshape our "sense and sensibility" about their selfhood and couplehood? What if this skilled clumsiness, this naïve intelligence, were repeated over and over, and then over again? *That* might begin to explain the ineffable feel of work with personality-disordered couples: the sense that treatment, in the deepest *and* broadest sense of the word, is a recurring dynamic process.

Epilogue

The writing of this book over the last seven years has been a personal and professional journey, both humbling and rewarding. If anything, it has recurrently brought home to me the experience-near value of object relations theory. The effort to "get something out," to translate the *sense* of something in my gut into thoughts and feelings and then to articulate and think about them, was a central element in the creative process. The Book wrote me as I wrote it. The Book and I had a love/hate relationship. Many times The Book was a black cloud of obligation hanging over my head. At other times, it was a lover that provided me with a relationship in which to express an overpowering "something," if I could only determine what it was. Friends and colleagues would say, "It's ready. Just finish it. Send it in. Give it to me for a week and it will be done." I could not. I was not happy with it. I had not gotten out that which I needed to get out. If I could only figure out what it was.

During this seven-plus years, I went through major upheavals in my professional and personal life. Mental illness struck down a family member, and for several years (or was that lifetimes?) caused terrible anguish and injury. In this context and through my earlier, but interrupted, analysis, I too had the humbling opportunity to be a "patient," to observe my own denial and acting out, and to be a "family member of the patient." To ride elevators in hospitals in which staff goes quiet because "patients are aboard," to see the curious glances of staff members and to visit "the patient" on the unit, directly experiencing staff members wielding their power in both wise uncertainty and all-knowing ignorance. I was reminded that therapists are people too, as foibled and flawed as any other group of people.

I had the fortunate and unfortunate opportunity to participate in family therapy with several different therapists. To derive great benefit from some and little from others—the latter, at least from my perspective, becoming imbued with disabling anxiety, resulting in their bombarding the patient with questions in the frantic effort to "ensure the safety of the patient," all the while defending against their own anxiety and collapsing the space to think about the "patient's" thoughts and feelings and the patient's space in which thoughts and feelings could emerge. Such experiences led me to a healthy appreciation and compassion for my human foibles and to know what it feels like to be the "patient" in a variety of contexts. It also led me to the conviction that getting a "good" therapist is a crapshoot, unless the therapist is highly recommended, and can easily result in an iatrogenic treatment experience.

On the other hand, I was also fortunate to encounter therapists who taught much, not only in word but in deed, about the importance of "being a human being" as a therapist. The latter therapists were individuals who had failed a lot and knew it. They had been around the block many times in their own lives and walked the walk, not only talked the talk. Humbled by life and wiser, they accepted their limits, looked into the heart of their sadness and the sadness in their heart, and thereby could unflinchingly identify with the sadness in mine, and help me feel.

While all this was going on, long-term inpatient treatment was being torn asunder; the Goths were at the gates. The B-2 treatment team, the equivalent of a Stradivarius violin, was being turned into a toy banjo. For me, it was too painful to see this unthinking destruction of a source of human wisdom to further corporate profit motives. It also became unbearable to meet with a family entering inpatient treatment with hope for their loved ones when I knew that what they needed was no longer available. Struggling with the insecurities of leaving, but knowing that I would feel like a tick on an ugly dog if I stayed, I entered full-time private practice in 1992, not knowing if I could make ends meet but all the while knowing that it did not matter. I could not continue to be associated with a "treatment" program that no longer provided treatment. My world felt like it had been torn apart—not in an orderly fashion at the seams, but between the seams, a shredding the like of which I had not experienced since being sent to boarding school in France for two years when I was 11 years old.

From these experiences—all of which I would have gladly forgone for the illusion of invulnerability provided by ignorance—the basic assumptions in my life, which had provided me with the illusion of knowing, were exposed to a harsh reality that was beyond my control and shattered completely. I learned that wisdom and a sense of internal security is obtained through the willingness to look into, rather than deny, our own suffering. It is through "the window of our losses" (Lewin 1996) that we begin to truly discover ourselves. Rather than feeling empowered, I was led to a recognition of my own limits that was both sad and freeing. I am not responsible for everything. I cannot make everything right. I cannot "cure" anyone. I can only help people in the process of learning how to heal themselves.

I do this by trying to provide all that goes into forming a genuine relationship, including mistakes and failures, and analyzing with the individual or the couple that within themselves that obstructs this goal. I discovered I can cajole, advise, interpret, encourage, educate, confront, and so on, but ultimately it is up to the patient to make the autonomous act of seeking help, taking help in, or diving to receive the help that is offered when it is less than perfect.

Now, in my practice, I no longer accept responsibility for the

progress a patient makes. If I am helpful, I am glad, but I feel that
what I contribute is the willingness to be real, to feel and think with
them, and, if they do not know how to think, to teach them. Some
are able and willing to learn. Others, too wounded by early
experience and wedded to the destructive internal world of self and
object relationships, are not. Many fall somewhere between these
two poles. Generally, it is not for me to say which is which or who is
who. If patients are willing to attend reliably and to pay their bill
(one aspect of my dependency on them), I am willing to try.

I listen for the echoes of movement within the isolated core of
the patient that is protected within the cave of their defenses against
genuine human contact. If I believe that a patient or couple is
simply using treatment to sustain a pathological form of relating I
will tell them so and end therapy. However, this is difficult to know
and my fear is that I could be countertransferentially acting out. So,
I never make such pronouncements without carefully thinking them
through, both by myself and with the patient. Indeed, in my years of
practice, this has been the case in only two or three instances. What
I have discovered is that such patients withdraw from treatment
when I am unwilling to sacrifice my integrity to be in relationship to
them. This was illustrated in several vignettes.

In addition to the processing of my experience during the
writing of this book, I came to the realization, helped by my friends,
of the fear of ending it. The black cloud of the book, the love/hate
relationship to it, was a companion and an organizer of my life—a
working-through and a transitional object, eventually becoming the
medium through which I grieved all that I had lost and learned to
value and enjoy what I had gained. It is now time for me to move on,
to see what is around the bend in the river and to enjoy knowing
that I have no idea what is there, but with faith that I will make the
journey a personally meaningful one. I wish the same for you as well.

References

Adler, G. (1980). Transference, real relationship, and alliance. *International Journal of Psycho-analysis* 61:547–558.

Andolfi, M. (1983). *Behind the Family Mask: Therapeutic Change in Rigid Family Systems.* New York: Brunner/Mazel.

Balint, M. (1968). *The Basic Fault: Therapeutic Aspects of Regression.* London: Tavistock.

Bion, W. R. (1962a). *Learning from Experience.* New York: Basic Books.

——— (1962b). The psycho-analytic study of thinking: a theory of thinking. *International Journal of Psycho-analysis* 43:306–314.

——— (1963). *Elements of Psycho-Analysis.* London: Heinemann.

——— (1967). *Second Thoughts.* London: Heinemann.

Bollas, C. (1987). *The Shadow of the Object: Psychoanalysis of the Unthought Known.* New York: Columbia University Press.

Casement, P. (1985). *On Learning from the Patient.* London: Tavistock.

Davis, M., and Walbridge, D. (1981). *Boundary and Space: An Introduction to the Work of D. W. Winnicott.* New York: Brunner/Mazel.

Erikson, E. H. (1968). *Identity, Youth, and Crisis.* New York: Norton.

Fairbairn, W. R. D. (1940). Schizoid factors in the personality. In *Psychoanalytic Studies of the Personality*, pp. 3–27. New York: Routledge, 1952.

———— (1944). Endopsychic structure considered in terms of object-relationships. In *Psychoanalytic Studies of the Personality*, pp. 82–136. New York: Routledge, 1952.

———— (1946). Object-relationships and dynamic structure. In *Psychoanalytic Studies of the Personality*, pp. 137–151. New York: Routledge, 1952.

———— (1949). Steps in the development of an object-relations theory of the personality. In *Psychoanalytic Studies of the Personality*, pp. 152–161. New York: Routledge, 1952.

———— (1951). A synopsis of the development of the author's views regarding the structure of the personality. In *Psychoanalytic Studies of the Personality*, pp. 162–179. New York: Routledge, 1952.

———— (1952). *An Object Relations Theory of the Personality*. New York: Basic Books.

Fraiberg, S. H., Adelson, E., and Shapiro, V. (1975). Ghosts in the nursery: a psychoanalytic approach to the problems of impaired infant–mother relationships. *Journal of American Academy of Child Psychiatry* 14:387–422.

Giovacchini, P. L. (1976). Symbiosis and intimacy. *International Journal of Psychoanalytic Psychotherapy* 5:413–436.

———— (1981). Developmental vicissitudes, object relationships, and psychopathology. *Contemporary Psychoanalysis* 17:258–275.

———— (1986). *The Transitional Space in Mental Breakdown and Creative Integration*. Northvale, NJ: Jason Aronson.

Guntrip, H. (1961). The schizoid problem, regression, and the struggle to preserve an ego. *British Journal of Medical Psychology* 34:223–244.

———— (1962). The schizoid compromise and psychotherapeutic stalemate. *British Journal of Medical Psychology* 35:273–287.

Joseph, B. (1984). Projective identification: some clinical aspects. In *Psychic Equilibrium and Psychic Change*, ed. M. Feldman and E. B. Spillius, pp. 168–180. New York: Routledge, 1989.

———— (1985). Transference: the total situation. In *Psychic Equilibrium and Psychic Change: Selected Papers of Betty Joseph*, ed. M. Feldman and E. B. Spillius, pp. 151–167. New York: Routledge, 1989.

Kernberg, O. (1967). Borderline personality organization. *Journal of the American Psychoanalytic Association* 15:641–685.

———— (1975). *Borderline Conditions and Pathological Narcissism*. New York: Jason Aronson.

Kipling, R. (1910). If. In *Rudyard Kipling: The Complete Verse*. London: Kyle Cuthie, 1990.

Klein, M. (1935). A contribution to the psychogenesis of manic-depressive states. In *Love, Guilt, and Reparation and Other Works, 1921–1945*, pp. 262–289. London: Hogarth, 1975.

Klein, M., and Riviere, J. (1937). *Love, Hate, and Reparation*. London: Hogarth.

Kohut, H. (1984). *How Does Analysis Cure?*, ed. A. Goldberg. Chicago: University of Chicago Press.

Lacan, J. (1964). *The Four Fundamental Concepts of Psycho-Analysis*, ed. J. A. Miller, trans. D. Macey. New York: Norton, 1978.

——— (1977). *Ecrits: A Selection*. New York: Norton.

Laing, R. D. (1960). *The Divided Self: A Study of Sanity and Madness*. Chicago: Quadrangle.

Lewin, R. A., and Schulz, C. G. (1992). *Losing and Fusing*. Northvale, NJ: Jason Aronson.

——— (1996). *New Wrinkles*. Evanston, IL: Chicago Spectrum.

Mahler, M. (1968). *On Human Symbiosis and the Vicissitudes of Individuation*. New York: International Universities Press.

Mahler, M., Pine, F., and Bergman, A. (1975). *The Psychological Birth of the Human Infant*. New York: Basic Books.

Maltas, C. (1992). Trouble in paradise: marital crises of midlife. *Psychiatry* 55:122–131.

Masterson, J. (1981). *The Narcissistic and Borderline Disorders: An Integrated Developmental Approach*. New York: Brunner/Mazel.

McCormack, C. C. (1989). The borderline/schizoid marriage: the holding environment as an essential treatment construct. *Journal of Marital and Family Therapy* 15 (3):299–309.

McDougall, J. (1989). *Theaters of the Body: A Psychoanalytic Approach to Psychosomatic Illness*. New York: Norton.

Meissner, W. W. (1987). Projection and projective identification. In *Projection, Identification, Projective Identification*, ed. J. Sandler, pp. 27–49. Madison, CT: International Universities Press.

Meltzer, D., Bremner, J., Hoxter, S., et al. (1975). *Explorations in Autism*. Perthshire, Scotland: Clunie.

Ogden, T. H. (1986). *The Matrix of the Mind: Object Relations and the Psychoanalytic Dialogue*. Northvale, NJ: Jason Aronson.

——— (1989). *The Primitive Edge of Experience*. Northvale, NJ: Jason Aronson.

Phillips, A. (1988). *Winnicott*. Cambridge, MA: Harvard University Press.

Sandler, J., and Perlow, M. (1987). Internalization and externalization. In

Projection, Identification, Projective Identification, ed. J. Sandler, pp. 1–11. Madison, CT: International Universities Press.

Scharff, J. S., and Scharff, D. E. (1992). *Scharff Notes: A Primer of Object Relations Therapy*. Northvale, NJ: Jason Aronson.

Searles, H. F. (1975). The patient as therapist to his analyst. In *Tactics and Techniques in Psychoanalytic Therapy, Volume II: Countertransference*, ed. P. L. Giovacchini, pp. 95–151. New York: Jason Aronson.

Segal, H. (1957). Notes on symbol formation. *International Journal of Psycho-Analysis* 38:391–397.

Shapiro, R. S., and Carr, A. W. (1991). *Lost in Familiar Places: Creating New Connections between the Individual and Society*. New Haven: Yale University Press.

Shengold, L. (1989). *Soul Murder: The Effects of Childhood Abuse and Deprivation*. New York: Fawcett Columbine.

Sonne, J. C., and Swirsky, D. (1981). Self-object considerations in marriage and marital therapy. In *The Handbook of Marriage and Marital Therapy*, ed. G. Piroosholevar, pp. 77–102. New York: Spectrum.

Stern, D. N. (1985). *The Interpersonal World of the Infant: A View from Psychoanalysis and Developmental Psychology*. New York: Basic Books.

Stolorow, R. D., Brandchaft, B., and Atwood, G. E. (1987). *Psychoanalytic Treatment: An Intersubjective Approach*. Hillsdale, NJ: Analytic Press.

Sutherland, J. (1989). *Fairbairn's Journey into the Interior*. London: Free Association Books.

Tustin, F. (1984). Autistic shapes. *International Review of Psycho-Analysis* 11(3):279–290.

Winnicott, D. W. (1948). Reparation in respect of mother's organized defense against depression. In *Through Paediatrics to Psycho-Analysis*, pp. 91–100. New York: Basic Books, 1958.

——— (1951). Transitional objects and transitional phenonmena. In *Through Paediatrics to Psycho-Analysis*, pp. 229–242. New York: Basic Books, 1975.

——— (1954). The depressive position in normal development. In *Through Paediatrics to Psycho-Analysis*, pp. 262–277. New York: Basic Books, 1975.

——— (1956). Primary maternal preoccupation. In *Through Paediatrics to Psycho-Ananlysis*, pp. 300–305. New York: Basic Books, 1975.

——— (1957). The child in the family group. In *Home Is Where We Start From: Essays by a Psychoanalyst*, ed. C. Winnicott, R. Shepherd, and M. Davis, pp. 128–141. New York: Norton, 1986.

———— (1958a). *Collected Papers.* London: Tavistock.

———— (1958b). The first year of life: modern views on emotional development. In *The Family and Individual Development,* pp. 3–14. New York: Basic Books, 1965.

———— (1958c). The capacity to be alone. In *The Maturational Processes and the Facilitating Environment,* pp. 29–36. New York: International Universities Press, 1965.

———— (1960a). Ego distortion in terms of true and false self. In *The Maturational Processes and the Facilitating Environment,* pp. 140–152. New York: International Universities Press, 1965.

———— (1960b). The theory of the parent–infant relationship. In *The Maturational Process and the Facilitating Environment,* pp. 37–55. New York: International Universities Press, 1965.

———— (1961). The varieties of psychotherapy. In *Home Is Where We Start From: Essays by a Psychoanalyst,* ed. C. Winnicott, R. Shepherd, and M. Davis, pp. 101–111. New York: Norton, 1986.

———— (1962a). Ego integration in child development. In *The Maturational Processes and the Facilitating Environment,* pp. 56–63. New York: International Universities Press, 1965.

———— (1963). Communicating and not communicating leading to a study of certain opposites. In *The Maturational Processes and the Facilitating Environment,* pp. 179–192. New York: International Universities Press, 1965.

———— (1965). *The Maturational Processes and the Facilitating Environment.* New York: International Universities Press.

———— (1967b). The concept of a healthy individual. In *Home Is Where We Start From: Essays by a Psychoanalyst,* ed. C. Winnicott, R. Shepherd, and M. Davis, pp. 21–38. New York: Norton, 1986.

———— (1970). Cure. In *Home Is Where We Start From: Essays by a Psychoanalyst,* ed. C. Winnicott, R. Shepherd, and M. Davis, pp. 112–120. New York: Norton, 1986.

———— (1971). *Playing and Reality.* New York: Basic Books.

Index

ABOUT THE AUTHOR

Charles C. McCormack, MSW, holds masters degrees from Loyola College of Baltimore in psychology and the University of Maryland in social work. He is a licensed certified social worker and a Board Certified Diplomate. Over the past twenty-six years, he has worked in a variety of outpatient settings including drug treatment, partial hospitalization, and physical and sexual abuse treatment programs. In 1982, he began working in long-term inpatient treatment and from 1988 to 1992 was the Senior Social Worker of Long-Term Inpatient Services at Sheppard and Enoch Pratt Hospital. In 1989, his paper "The Borderline/Schizoid Marriage: The Holding Environment as an Essential Treatment Construct" was published in the *Journal of Marital and Family Therapy*. Mr. McCormack has presented numerous papers and workshops in the United States and Canada on the treatment of "difficult to treat" individuals, couples, and families. He is on the teaching and supervisory faculty of Sheppard-Pratt Hospital and is a guest faculty member of the Washington School of Psychiatry's Psychoanalytic Object Relations Family and Couples Therapy Training Program. In 1994, Mr. McCormack was named Clinician of the Year by the Maryland Society of Clinical Social Workers. He currently supervises and maintains a private practice in Baltimore.